EUROPEAN IMMIGRANTS IN THE AMERICAN WEST

Historians of the Frontier and American West
Richard W. Etulain, Series Editor

EUROPEAN IMMIGRANTS IN THE AMERICAN WEST

Community Histories

Edited by
FREDERICK C. LUEBKE

Published in cooperation with the University of New Mexico Center for the American West

University of New Mexico Press
Albuquerque

Introduction © 1998 by the University of New Mexico Press
All rights reserved.
First edition

Library of Congress
Cataloging in Publication Data
European immigrants in the American West: community histories /
edited by Frederick C. Luebke.—1st ed.
p. cm.—(Historians of the frontier and American West)
"Published in cooperation with the University of New Mexico Center
for the American West."
Includes bibliographical references and index.
ISBN 0-8263-1991-2 (cl)   ISBN 0-8263-1992-0 (pbk)
1. European Americans—West (U.S.)—History—19th century.
2. Immigrants—West (U.S.)—History—19th century.
3. West (U.S.)—Emigration and immigration—History—19th century.
I. Luebke, Frederick C., 1927–
II. University of New Mexico. Center for the American West.
III. Series.
F596.3.E95E87   1998
978'.004034—dc21   98-24613
CIP

CONTENTS

INTRODUCTION vii
Frederick C. Luebke

1. Southwestern Indians, Spanish Missions 1
Henry Warner Bowden

2. Prairie Bound: Migration Patterns to a Swedish Settlement on the Dakota Frontier 15
Robert C. Ostergren

3. Fleeing Babylon: The English Mormon Migration to Alpine, Utah 33
Dean L. May

4. Irish Miners: From the Emerald Isle to Copper Butte 49
David M. Emmons

5. Italians in San Francisco: Patterns of Settlement 65
Dino Cinel

6. The Origins of an Ethnic Middle Class: The Jews of Portland in the Nineteenth Century 75
William Toll

7. Safe and Steady Work: The Irish and the Hazards of Butte 91
David M. Emmons

8. Childhood Memories of South Slavic Immigrants in Red Lodge and Bearcreek, Montana, 1904–1943 109
Anna Zellick

vi   Contents

9. Italians in San Francisco:
   The Second Generation   123
   Dino Cinel

10. Ethnicity, Religion, and Gender:
    The Women of Block, Kansas, 1868–1940   129
    Carol K. Coburn

11. Land, Labor, and Community in Nueces: Czech Farmers and
    Mexican Laborers in South Texas, 1880–1930   147
    Josef J. Barton

12. Steinbach and Jansen: A Tale of
    Two Mennonite Towns, 1880–1900   161
    Royden K. Loewen

    SELECT BIBLIOGRAPHY   179

    INDEX   187

    CONTRIBUTORS   195

    PERMISSIONS   197

INTRODUCTION

European immigrants are the forgotten people of the American West. Their stories are not told in the many books, paintings, and movies that have created the mythic West. Immigrants did not easily fit the image of the West as the bastion of unfettered individualism and self-reliance—a region peopled by the free, brave, and pure—battling against the urbanized, industrialized, and economically dominant East.[1]

Nor do European immigrants populate the pages of frontier history.[2] Ever since Frederick Jackson Turner opened the field a hundred years ago, general histories of the American frontier have tended to ignore them. Grounded on the Turnerian notion that the frontier environment overpowered ethnocultural behaviors and attitudes, such histories assumed that common frontier experiences created the so-called American character. Presumably, the environment worked equally on all frontier people regardless of origin; people of all cultures had to adapt to physiographic realities if they were to survive. Failing to fit the established interpretive model, European immigrants again were overlooked.[3]

They have fared no better in the histories of the American West. For example, Robert V. Hine simply dismisses European immigrants as unimportant for his interpretation in *The American West* (1984).[4] Rodman Paul's *The Far West and the Great Plains in Transition, 1859–1900* (1988) devotes two chapters to racial and ethnic diversity, but he summarizes the role of European immigrants in about seven pages.[5] One searches fruitlessly in these and other broad studies of the West for adequate descriptions of ethnic-group settlement or for recognition of the sometimes astounding proportions of European-born persons in certain communities. Equally scarce are analyses that illuminate internal social

viii   Introduction

structures or the intricate economic and political relationships of ethnic groups with each other or with so-called dominant elements in western society.

Curiously, even historians of immigration have also tended to overlook Europeans who settled in the West. In the 1920s, when general histories of American immigration first began to appear, scholars looked first to the cities, where immigrant populations were numerous and obvious, or to eastern rural areas. Although there were notable exceptions, most immigration historians preferred to study places where immigrants, their leaders, and plentiful historical sources were concentrated.[6] Moreover, many early historians of immigration tended to shoehorn their subject into Turnerian boots. Seeing America as a frontier of Europe, they concentrated not on the persistence of culture but on the many ways immigrants contributed to American civilization and on the speed with which they accommodated their behavior to American norms.[7] They viewed America as a great "melting pot" in which ethnic distinctiveness disappeared.

Labor historians have traditionally viewed the West from a different mountain. Unlike frontier historians, they saw plenty of European immigrants in western mines, forests, factories, and transportation systems. Appalled by the exploitation they observed, some surveyed the West through a Marxist lens. Preoccupied with the class struggle against capitalist oppressors, they acknowledged the persistence of ethnic culture in America but lamented its perseverance as an obstacle to economic justice. Diversity of language, religion, and custom, when combined with lingering ethnic animosities, seemed to hinder the formation of class consciousness, which was the Marxist prerequisite for successful protest against capitalist exploitation.

Nor do European immigrant groups fare well in the works of the "new western historians," even though ethnic societies fit comfortably in the analytical paradigms they have developed. Arguably the best known of these works, all published within the past decade, is Patricia Nelson Limerick's *The Legacy of Conquest: The Unbroken Past of the American West* (1987). A vigorous attack on Turnerian emphasis on *process*, Limerick's study substitutes *place*—the West as the meeting ground where culturally diverse peoples competed and often clashed to survive in the often unyielding western environment. Limerick tells a story of conquest—the conquest of a vast land by competing interests to exploit natural resources. In this version of western history, racial minorities—Indians, Mexicans, Asians, and blacks—are repeatedly victimized. Curiously, however, she says nothing about European immigrant groups—Irish or Southern Slav miners, Scandinavian loggers, Italian truck farmers, Basque shepherds, Jewish peddlers, or German farmers—or about how they were discriminated against.[8]

Frederick C. Luebke ix

TABLE 1

Distribution of Foreign-Born Persons in Western States and Territories by Number and Percentage of Total Population, 1860–1900

State or Territory	1860 N	1860 %	1870 N	1870 %	1880 N	1880 %	1890 N	1890 %	1900 N	1900 %
GREAT PLAINS										
North Dakota	1,774	36.7	4,815	34.0	51,795	38.3	81,461	42.7	113,091	35.4
South Dakota							91,055	26.1	88,508	22.0
Nebraska	6,351	22.0	30,748	25.0	97,414	21.5	202,542	19.1	177,347	16.6
Kansas	12,691	11.8	48,392	13.3	110,086	11.1	147,838	10.4	126,685	8.6
Oklahoma Terr.	—	—	—	—	—	—	2,740	3.5	15,680	3.9
Indian Terr.	—	—	—	—	—	—	13	0.0	4,858	1.2
Texas	43,422	7.2	62,411	7.6	114,616	7.2	152,956	6.8	179,357	5.9
ROCKY MOUNTAIN										
Montana	—	—	7,979	38.7	11,521	29.4	43,096	30.2	67,067	27.6
Wyoming	—	—	3,513	38.5	5,850	28.1	14,913	23.8	17,415	18.8
Colorado	2,666	7.8	6,599	16.6	39,790	20.5	83,990	20.3	91,155	16.9
New Mexico	6,723	7.2	5,620	6.1	8,051	6.7	11,259	7.0	13,625	7.0
INTERMONTANE										
Idaho	—	—	7,885	52.6	9,974	30.6	17,456	19.7	24,604	15.2
Utah	12,754	31.7	30,702	35.4	43,994	30.6	53,064	25.2	53,777	19.4
Nevada	2,064	30.1	18,801	44.2	25,653	41.2	14,706	31.1	10,093	23.8
Arizona	—	—	5,809	60.1	16,049	39.7	18,795	21.3	24,233	19.7
PACIFIC COAST										
Washington	3,144	27.1	5,024	21.0	15,803	21.0	90,005	25.2	111,364	21.5
Oregon	5,123	9.8	11,600	12.8	30,503	17.5	57.317	18.0	65,748	15.9
California	146,528	38.6	209,831	37.5	292,874	33.9	366,309	30.2	367,240	24.7
United States	4,138,697	13.2	5,567,229	14.4	6,679,943	13.3	9,249,560	14.7	10,341,276	13.6

SOURCE: *Reports of the Immigration Commission*, Sen. Doc. No. 765, 61st Cong., 3d sess., 41 vols. (Washington, DC: GPO, 1911), 3:444–47. Here, the data for foreign-born persons include non-Europeans, notably Chinese and Mexicans.

Similarly, the editors of the *Oxford History of the American West*, a brilliant epitome of the "new western history," chose not to include an essay that focuses on European immigrants.[9] One can only speculate why. There certainly is no shortage of published material on this subject.[10] Did the editors presume that European-immigrant stories were indistinguishable from those of other white Americans, or perhaps that they, unlike blacks, Indians, Hispanics, or Chinese, had in fact realized the promise of American life?[11]

And yet, as Table 1 reveals, huge numbers of European immigrants were

x   Introduction

TABLE 2

Number and Percentage of Total Population of Foreign-Born White Persons Plus
Native-Born White Persons of Foreign Parentage (First- and Second-Generation
Immigrants) by Country of Origin in the States and Territories of the American
West in 1900

Country of Origin	Contiguous United States (76,303,387)		North Dakota (319,146)		South Dakota (401,570)		Nebraska (1,066,300)		Kansas (1,470,495)	
	N	%	N	%	N	%	N	%	N	%
Austria	433,686	0.57	2,014	0.6	1,692	0.4	8,085	0.8	6,329	0.4
Bohemia (Czechs)	356,654	0.47	3,654	1.1	6,361	1.6	38,471	3.6	7,788	0.5
Canada (English)	1,298,349	1.70	31,086	9.7	13,058	3.3	19,304	1.8	18,939	1.3
Canada (French)	809,484	1.06	6,512	2.0	3,516	0.9	3,003	0.3	5,547	0.4
Denmark	307,303	0.40	7,139	2.2	10,450	2.6	26,418	2.5	6,687	0.5
England	2,136,814	2.80	7,710	2.4	12,402	3.1	33,586	3.1	45,633	3.1
France	264,544	0.35	582	0.2	835	0.2	2,897	0.2	5,813	0.4
Germany	7,816,562	10.24	32,393	10.1	55,860	13.9	191,928	18.0	131,563	8.9
Hungary	216,266	0.28	1,797	0.6	881	0.2	882	0.1	935	0.1
Ireland	4,965,537	6.51	11,552	3.6	16,017	4.0	45,535	4.3	48,525	3.3
Italy	731,226	0.96	731	0.2	566	0.1	1,278	0.1	1,543	0.1
Norway	785,116	1.03	71,998	22.6	51,191	12.7	7,228	0.7	3,726	0.3
Poland	687,450	0.90	2,112	0.7	1,146	0.3	7,328	0.7	1,478	0.1
Russia	634,391	0.83	23,909	7.5	25,689	6.4	14,537	1.4	25,048	1.7
Scotland	619,932	0.81	5,664	1.8	3,943	1.0	9,818	0.9	14,186	1.0
Sweden	1,081,516	1.42	14,598	4.6	17,163	4.3	54,301	5.1	35,219	2.4
Switzerland	254,594	0.33	845	0.3	1,638	0.4	5,852	0.5	9,204	0.6
Wales	246,167	0.32	452	0.1	1,889	0.5	3,098	0.3	5,748	0.4
Other	821,716	1.08	2,942	0.9	7,065	1.8	5,073	0.5	6,050	0.5
TOTAL	24,467,307	32.06	226,690	71.3	231,362	57.6	478,622	44.9	379,961	25.8

SOURCE: U.S. Bureau of the Census, *Census Reports*, vol. 1, *Twelfth Census of the United States, 1900*, pt. 1
(Washington, DC: GPO, 1901), cxcvi–cvcvii; for division into first and second generations, see *Report of the
Immigration Commission*, Sen. Doc. No. 756, 61st Cong., 3d sess., 41 vols. (Washington, DC: GPO, 1911),
3:512–21.

present in the nineteenth-century West. In 1900, when the proportion of all
foreign-born persons in the national population was 13.6 percent, the West
(not including the Great Plains states) registered 20.7, a regional percentage
second only to New England, which recorded 25.8. North Dakota, with 35.4
percent, had the highest proportion of all the states in the country, an average
well above Rhode Island with 31.4 percent. A decade earlier in 1890, the West
registered even higher rates.

Frederick C. Luebke   xi

TABLE 2 (*Continued*)

Country of Origin	Oklahoma Terr. (398,331)		Indian Territory (392,060)		Texas (3,048,710)		Montana (243,329)		Idaho (161,772)	
	N	%	N	%	N	%	N	%	N	%
Austria	1,032	0.1	356	0.1	15,114	0.5	5,240	2.2	463	0.3
Bohemia (Czechs)	2,698	0.7	50	—	22,713	0.7	362	0.2	158	0.1
Canada (English)	3,600	0.9	819	0.2	5,446	0.2	13,444	5.5	4,601	2.8
Canada (French)	702	0.2	173	—	1,004	—	5,725	2.4	846	0.5
Denmark	582	0.1	71	—	2,361	0.1	1,871	0.8	4,704	2.9
England	5,540	1.4	2,586	0.7	23,722	0.8	17,117	7.0	7,290	7.9
France	1,048	0.3	568	0.1	6,304	0.2	1,104	0.5	532	0.3
Germany	18,117	4.5	3,446	0.9	157,214	5.2	18,482	7.6	8,579	5.3
Hungary	280	0.1	40	—	979	—	449	0.2	61	—
Ireland	5,534	1.4	2,233	0.6	25,373	0.8	27,591	11.3	5,643	3.5
Italy	74	—	734	0.2	7,086	0.2	2,742	1.1	910	0.6
Norway	350	0.1	98	—	3,405	0.1	5,679	2.3	2,766	1.7
Poland	298	0.1	357	0.1	8,148	0.3	372	0.2	81	—
Russia	5,536	1.4	398	0.1	4,948	0.1	606	0.3	218	0.1
Scotland	1,596	0.4	1,008	0.3	6,839	0.2	6,023	2.5	3,044	1.9
Sweden	1,290	0.3	215	0.1	9,297	0.3	8,212	3.4	5,522	3.4
Switzerland	1,108	0.3	187	—	3,776	0.1	1,385	0.6	2,017	1.3
Wales	439	0.1	392	0.1	871	—	2,077	0.9	2,703	1.7
Other	744	0.2	410	0.1	146,643	4.8	4,533	1.9	1,120	0.7
TOTAL	50,568	12.7	14,141	3.6	450,343	14.8	123,014	50.6	51,258	31.7

When the data are expanded to include both the immigrants and their American-born children (the first- and second-generation immigrants), the proportions of European immigrants in the western states are even more startling. Table 2 records the distribution of foreign-born whites and their American-born children by country of origin in 1900. Again, North Dakota's immigrant percentage, an astounding 71.3 percent, ranked the highest in the country. South Dakota, Nebraska, Montana, Wyoming, Colorado, Utah, Nevada, Washington, and California all exceeded the national average of 32.1 percent in 1900.

Published in 1911, the data in Table 2 are abstracted from the reports of the Immigration Commission, a temporary agency created by Congress to study immigration, then perceived as a "problem," which in 1907 had reached the highest level in American history. The Immigration Commission, also known as the Dillingham Commission, based much of its work on the decennial

xii   Introduction

TABLE 2 (*Continued*)

Country of Origin	Wyoming (92,531) N	%	Colorado (539,700) N	%	New Mexico (195,310) N	%	Arizona (122,931) N	%	Utah (276,749) N	%
Austria	1,321	1.4	8,521	1.6	460	0.2	389	0.3	335	0.1
Bohemia (Czechs)	97	0.1	688	0.1	31	—	30	—	9	—
Canada (English)	2,061	2.2	14,465	2.7	1,206	0.6	1,868	1.5	2,873	1.0
Canada (French)	385	0.4	2,300	0.4	270	0.4	264	0.2	505	0.2
Denmark	1,815	2.0	3,846	0.7	129	0.1	538	0.4	24,751	8.9
England	7,290	7.9	33,139	6.1	2,319	1.2	4,250	3.5	66,207	23.9
France	426	0.5	2,857	0.5	594	0.3	512	0.4	509	0.2
Germany	6,064	6.6	41,919	7.8	3,888	2.0	3,573	2.9	5,830	2.1
Hungary	398	0.4	909	0.2	52	—	48	—	40	—
Ireland	6,028	6.5	33,233	6.1	2,474	1.3	3,630	3.0	4,977	1.8
Italy	973	1.0	10,171	1.9	934	0.5	954	0.8	1,485	0.5
Norway	727	0.8	2,095	0.4	109	0.1	228	0.2	4,554	1.7
Poland	137	0.2	1,073	0.2	100	0.1	33	—	94	—
Russia	134	0.2	4,734	0.9	141	0.1	142	0.1	171	0.1
Scotland	3,184	3.4	10,649	2.0	1,077	0.6	1,133	0.9	10,313	3.7
Sweden	3,155	3.4	18,861	3.5	446	0.2	605	0.5	14,578	5.3
Switzerland	401	0.4	2,851	0.5	234	0.1	368	0.3	3,349	1.2
Wales	937	1.0	4,778	0.9	244	0.1	405	0.3	6,570	2.4
Other	2,254	2.4	3,973	0.7	14,969	7.7	27,769	21.8	2,906	1.1
TOTAL	37,787	40.8	201,062	37.3	29,677	15.2	45,739	37.2	150,056	54.2

reports of the Census Bureau, especially those of 1900. Useful to historians, they provide a slice across American history at the end of the frontier era, a convenient point of reference in the march of time.

But the data in Table 2 must be used with caution. First, the numbers should never be regarded as precise or exact. Indeed, in the nineteenth and early twentieth centuries, immigrants were usually under-recorded; then even more than now census-takers missed people. Secondly, the old census categories are not the ones most social scientists identify today. Table 2 claims to record the numbers of white persons, but the Census Bureau did not adequately define the term *white.* The presumption is that whites were people of European origin, not of African or Asian or American Indian extraction. Yet it is clear that many persons in the "other" (presumably white) category were Mexicans, most of whom American society did not consider white.

Thus, while immigrants from Mexico were ignored, immigrants from Can-

Frederick C. Luebke   xiii

TABLE 2 (*Continued*)

Country of Origin	Nevada (42,335)		Washington (518,103)		Oregon (413,536)		California (1,485,053)	
	N	%	N	%	N	%	N	%
Austria	137	0.3	3,845	0.7	1,586	0.4	8,355	0.6
Bohemia (Czechs)	9	—	824	1.2	478	0.1	922	0.1
Canada (English)	1,384	3.3	27,545	5.3	11,675	2.8	44,841	3.0
Canada (French)	486	1.2	3,862	0.8	2,169	0.5	5,392	0.4
Denmark	746	1.8	6,564	1.3	3,319	0.8	16,416	1.1
England	3,084	7.3	25,519	4.9	16,394	4.0	84,690	5.7
France	460	1.1	2,354	0.5	1,905	0.5	22,983	1.6
Germany	3,055	7.2	43,555	8.4	36,547	8.8	154,809	10.4
Hungary	7	—	342	0.1	260	0.1	1,087	0.1
Ireland	4,019	10.0	23,548	4.6	14,058	3.4	152,006	10.2
Italy	1,893	4.5	2,997	0.6	1,536	0.4	41,632	2.8
Norway	95	0.2	18,814	3.6	5,566	1.4	8,522	0.6
Poland	33	0.1	931	0.2	583	0.1	2,450	0.2
Russia	49	0.1	3,830	0.7	3,136	0.8	5,376	0.4
Scotland	866	2.1	10,013	1.9	6,542	1.6	25,225	1.7
Sweden	435	1.0	21,361	4.1	8,270	2.0	23,728	1.6
Switzerland	542	1.3	3,527	0.7	5,472	1.3	19,742	1.3
Wales	345	0.8	3,600	0.7	1,098	0.3	5,020	0.3
Other	912	2.2	8,077	1.6	6,324	1.5	73,893	5.0
TOTAL	18,557	43.8	211,108	40.8	126,918	30.7	697,089	46.9

ada were carefully separated into "French" and "English" categories. But this distinction sometimes confused the status of immigrants and their Canadian-born children, chiefly Irish and German, who had lived in Canada for a time before moving on to the United States.

Problems of census categories do not end there. In Europe, national boundaries often ignored ethnic concentrations. For example, counting Germans was always problematic, especially in the American West, where most "Russians" were in fact Germans in language and culture. Similarly, most Swiss were German-speakers, as were many of the French (the provinces of Alsace and Lorraine, made part of the German Empire in 1871, were leading sources of emigration from France to America before that time).

The researchers employed by the Immigration Commission tried to compensate for such ethnocultural complexities as best they could. For example, even though Poland did not exist as a nation-state in 1900, they lumped Polish

xiv   Introduction

immigrants from Germany, Austria, and Russia into a separate group. But there were few Poles in the West; they usually settled in large eastern cities such as Chicago, Milwaukee, Buffalo, and New York.

One of the most challenging of census problems was the ethnic jumble known as the Austro-Hungarian Empire. In this case, the bureaucrats separated Bohemians (Czechs) from Austrians, but as a category, *Austrians* included the dominant German speakers plus such Slavic peoples as Slovaks, Slovenians, and Croats. Similarly, in the American West "Hungarians" usually were Germans from Burgenland or Transylvania, not Hungarians in language and culture.

In all of this confusion Jews were lost completely. They simply do not appear in the census of population, which is based on country of origin. Nevertheless, they constituted an important ethnoreligious group in the history of the West. Almost all the Jews emigrated from Germany, Russia, and Austria. Although they were generally united by religion and language, they retained important distinctions based on origin that often went unnoticed by non-Jews.

Finally, one might observe that the Census Bureau, true to the concerns and prejudices of the day, added refinement to their data by segregating British immigrants into divisions of England, Scotland, and Wales.

Despite these limitations, the data gathered by the Census Bureau and the Immigration Commission provide a convenient foundation for inquiry into the history of European immigrants in the American West. The large pattern emerges easily: in 1900, when foreign-born persons constituted 13.6 percent of the population of the United States, their numbers surpassed the national average throughout the West except in Kansas, Oklahoma, Texas, and New Mexico.

Table 1 shows that in the Great Plains tier of agricultural states (excluding present-day Oklahoma because of its former role as a territory reserved for American Indians), the proportion of the foreign-born in 1900 increased steadily from south to north: Kansas (8.6) exceeded the percentage in Texas (5.9); Nebraska (16.6) doubled Kansas; South Dakota (22.0) outstripped Nebraska; and North Dakota (35.4) easily topped them all. In the eight Rocky Mountain states and territories, where immigrants flocked to the mines, Montana registered the highest immigrant population at 27.6 percent; only New Mexico, with its large native Spanish-speaking population, fell below the national average. The Pacific Coast states, rich in mines, farms, and forests, easily capped the national average: California's 24.7 percent was exceeded in the West only by Montana's 27.6 and North Dakota's 34.5.

Table 2 provides a closer look at the numbers and distribution of European immigrants in the American West. In this case the American-born children are added to the presumably white immigrants in 1900 and the totals are broken down on the state level to the countries of origin. Germans from Germany, easily the largest immigrant group in the United States at that time, exceeded the national percentage (10.24) only in the northern Great Plains states, with Nebraska registering the highest proportion in the West (18.0). Still, they were the most numerous European immigrant group in all western states and territories except North Dakota, Utah, Arizona, and Nevada, even when the Germans from Russia and other countries are not included.

The second most numerous European immigrant group nationally in 1900, including both first and second generations, was the Irish at 6.5 percent. They surpassed that figure in four western states—Montana (11.3), California (10.2), Nevada (10.0), and Wyoming (6.5). They were concentrated especially in mining counties, although they were by no means limited to employment in that industry.

At the turn of the century, the English (2.8 percent) were the third most numerous group of European immigrants in the United States. In the West they surpassed the national norm everywhere except in New Mexico (1.2), Oklahoma (1.4), Indian Territory (0.7), and Texas (0.8). There were significant concentrations of English—about 7 or 8 percent—in Montana, Idaho, Wyoming, and Nevada. But the English presence in Utah (23.9) was phenomenal; when augmented by Scots and Welsh to form the British, the total expands to 39 percent—a huge slice of the population pie in Utah. It was eloquent testimony to the success of Mormon missionary work in Great Britain.

Mormon missionaries were also active in the Scandinavian countries, as the Utah data for 1900 also suggest. Danes constituted 8.9 percent of the population in Utah, by far their highest proportion in any western state. Swedes followed with 5.3 percent. Norwegian immigrants were much less numerous at 1.7 percent. When the three groups are lumped to form the Scandinavians, their proportion in Utah spirals to 15.9 percent. Although one may not assume that all British and Scandinavian immigrants in Utah—about 55 percent of the total population—were members of the Mormon church, the great majority were.

Elsewhere in the West, Scandinavians were most numerous in North Dakota (29.4), South Dakota (19.6), Washington (9.0), Nebraska (8.3), and Idaho (8.0). Norwegians, most of them farmers recruited by railroad immigration agents, registered their highest percentage in North Dakota (22.6). Similarly, South Dakota's population was 12.7 percent Norwegian in 1900.

The data in Table 2 permit dozens of other observations about the large patterns of European immigration to the West in the nineteenth century. But our purpose here is only to outline the large picture and, by implication, to suggest the possibilities for intensive research. The articles that follow are

xvi   Introduction

examples of insightful work that historians have done during the past few years to discover the role of European immigrants and their children in western history.

In order to lend coherence to this book I have narrowed my selections to studies that explore ethnic history in particular communities. Rather than selecting essays that treat immigration history broadly (for example, the history of Greeks in the American West, or agriculture among various immigrant groups in California, or the political behavior of immigrants in the late nineteenth century), I have chosen articles that delve deeply into the historical intersection of ethnicity and place. Such studies best illustrate recent scholarship in this field and demonstrate the kinds of sources historians use to develop or advance new concepts and methods in the pursuit of ethnic history.

In principle, I have selected articles that, to some degree, reveal the interaction of cultures and environments through the use of comparative methodologies. Ideally, comparisons should be made not only within an appropriate time sequence (which is the essence of historical analysis), but also between one immigrant group in a given place and (1) other ethnocultural groups, native- or foreign-born, who lived in the same or comparable physical environments, or (2) members of the same ethnic groups who lived in different environments. For example, one might compare, as has the cultural geographer D. Aidan McQuillan, the agriculture practiced in central Kansas over a period of fifty years by Swedish Lutherans, German-speaking Mennonites from southern Russia, and French-Canadian Catholics, thereby blending variables of time, place, and culture.[12] Similarly, one might compare, as has Robert C. Ostergren, the settlement histories of Swedish immigrants in the forested environment of east-central Minnesota with other Swedes in the grassland of southeastern South Dakota.[13] In my selection of articles, I have sought to maintain a balance, or at least to offer a sampling, of articles treating several major ethnic groups, various occupations, and different religious communities, all drawn from representative states and physical environments or regions in the American West.

The book is divided into three main sections. Chapters 1–5 offer several settlement histories in both rural and urban environments; chapters 6–10 focus on the development and maintenance of ethnic communities, rural and urban; and chapters 11 and 12 offer studies in comparative ethnic history. Most selections in chapters 1–10 treat history as change over time; the comparative histories in chapters 11 and 12 tend to be oriented spatially rather than temporally.

All of the articles represent recent developments in the concepts and methods of historical research. I have favored articles leavened by interdisciplinary thought and informed, as the case may be, by anthropology, geography, religion, and education. But it is not possible to include representative essays in all related fields, infused with vitality though they may be. Thus, studies treating ethnic literature, music, art, and architecture, as well as language studies and ethnic politics, are absent from this volume, though treated elsewhere in similar publications.[14] All selections treat ethnic history, but their authors are not all historians by training or profession: two are geographers, one is in religious studies, another in education; and one contributor is a gifted amateur historian.

All selections are based on books or articles published within the last twenty years. Some appear as originally published, others have been extensively revised and shortened. In several cases, for the sake of brevity, the notes have been dropped. Readers who wish to pursue sources in those instances should consult the original publications.

Finally, I wish to acknowledge my indebtedness to other scholars who have participated in the production of this book. It is first of all the product of the imagination, enthusiasm, and drive of Richard Etulain, the director of the Center for the American West at the University of New Mexico, who, as editor of the American West series, encouraged me to undertake this project. But I am especially indebted to David Emmons, Royden Loewen, Dean May, and William Toll for their willingness to interrupt their busy schedules and professional commitments to revise and condense their work for publication here.

In preparing this volume, I have been motivated strongly by the desire to illuminate the role of European immigrants in the history of the American West. But this book is no panegyric of immigrant accomplishment; I leave the recitation of heroic deeds by the ethnic fathers to the filiopietists. Instead, I hope that the examples of historical research presented here will stimulate students, both graduate and undergraduate, to pursue ethnic community histories, to conceptualize historical problems appropriately, and to employ sources and methods available at the local level. I hope especially that this book will help to dispel the notion that European immigrants had no significant role in the history of the American West.

FREDERICK C. LUEBKE

NOTES

1. For an elaboration of these ideas see David M. Emmons, "Social Myth and Social Reality," *Montana: The Magazine of Western History* 39 (Autumn 1989): 2–8.

2. I have explored the relationship of frontier historiography to European immigrants in my essay, "Turnerism, Social History, and the Historiography of European Ethnic Groups in the United States," in Frederick C. Luebke, *Germans in the New World: Essays in the*

xviii   Introduction

History of Immigration (Urbana: University of Illinois Press, 1990), 138–56. That essay is partially based on another, "Ethnic Minority Groups in the American West," in *Historians and the American West*, ed. Michael P. Malone (Lincoln: University of Nebraska Press, 1983), 387–413.

3. The preeminent text written from the Turnerian point of view is by Ray Allen Billington and its later revision by Martin Ridge: *Westward Expansion: A History of the American Frontier*, 5th ed. (New York: Macmillan, 1982). In this edition, Ridge occasionally incorporates factual materials on immigrant groups, but the Turnerian framework remains unaltered. Most other texts ignore immigrant groups entirely. Richard Bartlett, in his *New Country: A Social History of the American Frontier, 1776–1890* (New York: Oxford University Press, 1974), acknowledges the extensive presence of immigrants on the frontier but, astonishingly, asserts that *none* of the European immigrant groups "caused major changes in the basic characteristics that were 'American' in 1776" (p. 117). Perhaps Bartlett would have modified his bland and untested generalization if he could have read, for example, David Hackett Fischer's brilliant analysis of the culture of English immigrants from the Scottish borderland country in the American South and, by extension, into the American West. See *Albion's Seed: Four British Folkways in America* (New York: Oxford University Press, 1989), 605–782.

4. Robert V. Hine, *The American West: An Interpretive History*, 2nd ed. (Boston: Little, Brown, 1984). Hine merely asserts that European immigrants represented "only cultural differences" that "were not generally conceived as alien to the dominant society" (p. 237). The point advanced by the essays in the present volume is that it is precisely the cultural differences between European groups and "the dominant society" (assuming that there really was or is such a thing) that explain much of the history of the American West.

5. Rodman Paul's book, *The Far West and the Great Plains in Transition, 1859–1900* (New York: Harper and Row, 1988), represents a striking improvement, though it is conceived in traditional Turnerian terms.

6. An outstanding example is by John Bodnar, *The Transplanted: A History of Immigrants in Urban America* (Bloomington: Indiana University Press, 1985). Bodnar makes no effort to extend his analysis to rural or small town America.

7. The last synthesis of American immigration history to be fully conceptualized in Turnerian terms was Maldwyn A. Jones, *American Immigration* (Chicago: University of Chicago Press, 1960).

8. Patricia Nelson Limerick, *The Legacy of Conquest: The Unbroken Past of the American West* (New York: W.W. Norton, 1987). Richard White's more comprehensive survey of the American West, *"It's Your Misfortune and None of My Own"* (Norman: University of Oklahoma Press, 1991), includes many incidental references to Irish, Italians, Germans, Jews, and Swedes. But European immigrant groups do not occupy a central place in the book's conceptual schema, unlike Indians, Mexicans, Japanese, Chinese, and African Americans. Whereas Limerick is explicitly anti-Turnerian, White is non-Turnerian.

9. Clyde A. Milner II, Carol A. O'Connor, and Martha Sandweiss, eds., *The Oxford History of the American West* (New York: Oxford University Press, 1994).

10. See the hundreds of books, articles, and unpublished dissertations listed in Florence

R.J. Goulesque, *Europeans in the American West since 1800: A Bibliography* (Albuquerque: Center for the American West at the University of New Mexico, 1995).

11. For an extended review that shares this criticism, see David M. Emmons, "A Trip through Western Time and Western Space," *Montana: The Magazine of Western History* 45 (Spring 1995): 64–68.

12. D. Aidan McQuillan, *Prevailing over Time: Ethnic Adjustment on the Kansas Prairies, 1875–1925* (Lincoln: University of Nebraska Press, 1990).

13. Robert C. Ostergren, *A Community Transplanted: The Trans-Atlantic Experience of a Swedish Immigrant Settlement in the Upper Middle West, 1835–1915* (Madison: University of Wisconsin Press, 1988), especially pp. 185–89 and 207–9. Much less systematic is my comparison of German settlement patterns in the United States and in Brazil, 1830–1930. See *Germans in the New World*, 93–109.

14. For a collection of articles treating ethnic literature in the West, see Virginia Faulkner and Frederick C. Luebke, eds., *Vision and Refuge: Essays on the Literature of the Great Plains* (Lincoln: University of Nebraska Press, 1982). For examples of language studies, see Paul Schach, ed., *Languages in Conflict: Linguistic Acculturation on the Great Plains* (Lincoln: University of Nebraska Press, 1980).

CHAPTER ONE

SOUTHWESTERN INDIANS, SPANISH MISSIONS

HENRY WARNER BOWDEN

All people migrating to a new land must interact with inhabitants who precede them. Throughout world history such encounters have often been bloody, inevitably so if the migrants come as conquerors. When the Spanish conquistadores invaded the upper Rio Grande Valley in 1598, they did not come as immigrants. Their mind-set was different. They had no intention of adapting to Pueblo culture; they did not respect it; they made no effort to understand it. Immigrants recognize that some adaptations to established modes of belief and behavior are essential to survival; colonists do not.

The purpose of this article is to study the conflict between the seventeenth-century Spanish colonizers and the indigenous Pueblo Indian people, which climaxed in the Pueblo Revolt of 1680. The author, Henry Warner Bowden, draws on anthropological ideas as he analyzes the interactive behavior of these two societies in terms of their respective cultures. Although religion is central to his interpretation, Bowden is not concerned with questions of right and wrong, nor does he load guilt on one contending culture group or the other. Instead, he explains human behavior in terms of competing world views—contrasting belief systems that guided decisions and actions—and he describes both short- and long-term accommodations made by the Pueblos.

In the interest of brevity, all notes have been omitted in the excerpt that follows. Readers who wish to refer to sources should consult the original publication: Henry Warner Bowden, American Indians and Christian Missions: Studies in Cultural Conflict *(1981), pp. 40–58.*

2   Chapter One

THE FRANCISCAN MISSIONS

By mid-1521 Hernando Cortez had captured the Mexican capital of Tenoch-
titlán, murdered its ruler, Montezuma II, and stamped out the last pocket of
resistance at Otumba. Cortez thus added new territory to the Spanish realm;
what is more important, he fired imperialistic ambitions: exploiting new land
for riches and exploiting new peoples for religion. After 1521 the Spanish
conquistadores farmed out in all directions, usually followed by Franciscan
missionaries, as dedicated to their own type of conquest as their secular counterparts were to theirs.

Mineral wealth and heavy population led the Spaniards to concentrate in
the southern regions for fifteen years, but then, suddenly, in 1536, certain
officials heard of fabulous cities in the uncharted north when two survivors of
an ill-fated expedition to Florida arrived in Mexico after eight years of adven-
tures. A young notary public named Cabeza de Vaca and a black Moor known
as Estevanico told of shipwreck, enslavement, and wandering in the Sierra
Madres, but no part of their narrative fired the imagination as much as their
hints about the Seven Cities of Cibola. This chimerical image had already
persisted for years in Spanish legend despite a lack of substantiating evidence.
When the bedraggled travelers spoke of Indian stories of advanced cultures to
the north, visions of rich prizes danced again in aristocratic minds. Cortez and
Pizarro had acquired immense fortunes through daring acts, and every young
hidalgo felt that other plums were waiting to be plucked. Many of them
clamored for permission to enter the unexplored territory, but Cabeza de Vaca's
tales needed verification. In 1539 the authorities sent Estevanico and Marcos de
Niza, a Franciscan, adept in native languages, to map the area and determine
whether the fabled riches actually existed. A small company made its way to the
Zuni pueblo of Hawikuh, where the Moor was killed and Brother Marcos beat
a hasty retreat. Back in Mexico City, his fanciful reports confirmed preconceived beliefs in wealthy civilizations ripe for the taking. The stage was set for
northern exploration, with most Europeans bent on personal aggrandizement
and a few on the salvation of souls.

In early 1540 Francisco Vásquez de Coronado launched the first expedition in
search of fabled Quivira. Five months later he pushed into western New Mexico
and commandeered the town of Hawikuh, using it as a base for further explora-
tions. He searched for a year and a half, reconnoitering territory from central
Kansas and the Texas panhandle to the Grand Canyon, but found no gold or
native culture advanced enough to satisfy Spanish expectations. A Franciscan,
Juan de Padilla, who was part of the company, remained in Kansas to establish a
mission when the soldiers retraced their steps, to winter again in New Mexico.

Later reports disclose that he was killed only a short time thereafter. Coronado returned to Mexico in 1542 in disgrace, his health shattered and his fortune wasted. But despite his failure, new expeditions set out to prove that the northland would reward diligent seekers. In 1581 Agustín Rodríguez led a small band of missionaries north of the Rio Grande; two years later Antonio de Espejo mounted a relief party to locate and rescue them. Neither contingent accomplished much except to reaffirm the Franciscan policy of not allowing evangelists to precede Spanish troops. In 1521 Gaspar de Sosa received swift punishment for organizing an illegal *entrada*, while one led by Francisco Bonilla and Juan de Humana (1594) fell victim to murder and leaderless collapse.

The failure of these desultory excursions led to more systematic efforts. Juan de Oñate was appointed to head a substantial colonizing force, and early in 1598 he led a party of four hundred, including ten Franciscans, eight friars, and two lay brothers, up the Rio Grande Valley. By May the entire procession of men, cattle, horses, and wagonloads of furniture, seeds, iron tools, and leather goods rumbled through El Paso, the last Spanish outpost. Two months later they arrived in the heart of Pueblo country and appropriated a native village as temporary headquarters. The intruders had no misgivings about their right to dominate local affairs or to enforce a new life-style on the natives. As conquerors, they justified themselves by claiming the right of discovery and by offering the benefits that accrued to Christian belief and political vassalage. They also threatened severe retaliation against anyone refusing to cooperate with the new scheme of things.

Oñate summoned the chiefs of neighboring villages to a council, where he explained his twofold mission. He promised that if they submitted to Philip II, the most powerful monarch in the world, Spanish arms would protect them from all enemies. More important than political reorganization, Oñate also raised the crucial issue of native souls. He warned the Pueblo leaders that, unless they accepted baptism and instruction in Christian doctrine, they would suffer not only immediate physical punishment but eternal torment later on. After listening to these new ideas, and undoubtedly recognizing the technological superiority enjoyed by the intruders, the Pueblo leaders expressed a willingness to adopt both the Spanish king and a new deity. Whether or not they understood every implication of Oñate's message, it seemed prudent to acquiesce in the new situation and await further developments. It may be that the Indians accepted the Spanish ultimatum because they perceived that refusal seemed to entail both earthly disadvantages and future damnation!

Thus the Pueblos, who had been conditioned to conformity since childhood, accepted the new social forces that had entered their culture like the point of a wedge. In the ensuing years they faced all the institutions of Spanish

4   Chapter One

occupation: those redefining land-ownership and distribution, those establishing missionary assignments and ecclesiastical tribunals, and those demanding
native tribute paid in labor and material goods. Modest adjustments to early
change went peacefully enough, but the Pueblos did not know that the Spaniards planned to use these initial accommodations as the means of transform-
ing native life into their own model of civilization, including its religion.

Oñate proved to be a bad governor. For a decade he chased rainbows of
imagined wealth, searching for precious metals, dabbling in textiles and hides,
even hunting Apaches and Navajos to sell as slaves in Mexico. Ranches and
farms languished under his indifferent supervision, and the colonists began to
talk of abandoning the entire venture. Priests and people agreed that New
Mexico was an unprofitable land that did not deserve to be part of the Spanish
Empire. But, just as they had needed royal permission to enter the territory, so
they could not leave without specific authorization. In 1608, influential colonists therefore petitioned the Council of the Indies for permission to withdraw
from their distant and altogether barren outpost of civilization. Supporting
reasons included the prohibitive cost of bringing fresh supplies from Mexico.
Few civil servants or soldiers volunteered for duty there when the hope of easy
riches died. The missionaries had not mastered native languages, and so the
harvest of souls fell short of expectations. The situation discouraged both
religious and secular leaders, and almost everyone trapped there wished to
write off New Mexico as a bad investment.

Officials in the royal chain of command took such arguments seriously and
were inclined to terminate the colony. But in a curious reversal, never fully
explained, the missionary fathers suddenly opposed the departure. They in-
flated the number of converts and maintained that it would be unconscionable
to abandon so many at a critical stage of religious progress. Rather than allow
the Indians to lapse again into barbarism, the Franciscans urged that their
spiritual condition and the salvation of future generations were compelling
reasons for staying. Royal opinion tacked to sail with the clerical wind. The
king decided not to give up the region but rather to support it himself in order
to sustain missions in his empire. In late 1609 he replaced Oñate and provided
annual funding for sixty-six friars. Missionary rolls over the next seven decades
never approached that maximum, but royal expenditures for evangelization
amounted to a considerable sum, possibly a million pesos. Although a drain on
the royal treasury, the colony survived, largely because of the missions, and it
stood as a rare example of religious motivations overruling the quest for riches
and power.

The Franciscans interpreted the king's decision as an affirmation of their
central role in provincial affairs. Governors usually held office for no more than

three years, but each found time to resent the friars' presumption that secular government existed primarily to serve religious interests. Thus, instead of cooperating to transform the Pueblo way of life, the Franciscans and the magistrates squabbled over who was entitled to guide the Indians' destiny. Unseemly disputes over ecclesiastical immunity and clerical interference in secular matters vitiated missionary efforts. This bickering caused many Pueblos to lose what little respect they had initially had for Spanish authority.

Such were the conditions under which the missionaries tried to work against the Pueblos' religious proclivities and convert them to Christianity. Their difficulties with the Spanish civil officials hampered their work in many ways, but their own internal policies also kept progress to a minimum. For one thing, there never seemed to be enough missionaries for the job. When the king rescued their work in 1609, their numbers had dwindled to three. The new governor brought nine new ones with him, together with military reinforcements and fresh supplies. Others came three years later, so that in 1616 there were eleven flourishing missions staffed by twenty friars. By 1622 the number of Franciscans had risen to twenty-four, centered around a monastery built at Santa Fe. Three years later Alonso de Benavides brought twenty-seven friars in his new capacity as *custodio* to plan mission strategy. The crown ordered another thirty north in 1629, but, with deaths and transfers, that raised the net total to approximately forty-six. During the next five decades there were no more than forty Franciscans, and often fewer than thirty, scattered among the pueblos. The official quota of sixty-six was never filled, and, when disaster struck the mission stations in 1680, only half of the allotted number were preaching Christianity along the Rio Grande.

In 1610 the friars established a permanent base at Santo Domingo, near the Rio Grande, and divided the territory into seven administrative districts that covered 87,000 square miles. In their initial contacts with native peoples they enjoyed the advantage of offering a package of new materials and ideas. They brought domestic animals, an array of food plants, metal tools, and weaponry, all of which seemed connected with the religious concepts they advocated. Early missionary work was thus clothed in an aura of promising innovation, and perhaps because of this many Pueblos accepted such new rituals as baptism and the Mass. But instead of improving on these good beginnings, most of the later friars settled for an unpretentious round of daily Mass, vespers, and an occasional baptism, marriage, or burial. Rarely did they bother to learn the native languages or to translate the liturgy into local tongues. A few Indians memorized Spanish prayers phonetically, but instruction in reading or writing Spanish was not a regular part of the missionary program. Furthermore, the missionaries did not stay in one pueblo for long. They followed a policy of

6   Chapter One

constant resettlement that moved them from one language group to another and then, after an average of ten years' service, back to Mexico. Impermanence and superficiality thus characterized the manner in which the Spanish friars confronted the native Americans.

Still, the records indicate a surprising number of positive native responses. Enthusiastic missionaries listed a total of 7,000 converts in 1608, and they claimed 10,000 more baptized followers by 1620. Five years later, reports of Indian Christians in twenty-eight different pueblos went as high as 34,000; some irresponsible estimates numbered them at half a million. But instead of increasing further, the number of converts decreased in the aggregate when overall population declined along with the number of inhabited villages. The estimated seventy pueblos of Coronado's day fell to about thirty-five by 1650 because conflicts with Spanish soldiers were added to the familiar problems of drought, disease, and raids by marauding Apaches. Spanish domination started dangerous trends in Pueblo life, and routine missionary practices did nothing to counteract the downward tendency.

Compatible elements between Spanish and Pueblo ceremonial styles could have encouraged missionaries to appreciate fundamental aspects of native life. Both traditions emphasized the importance of priestly leadership, and, whether buildings were called churches or *kivas*, each religion stressed a special place for ritual activity. Additional parallels can be seen in the use of altars, special ornamentation, ritual chants, sacred utensils, and a religious calendar that regulated community life. Crucifixes and rosaries bore some resemblance to prayer sticks as aids to private devotion. The use of holy water could be likened to the "clouds" of yucca suds and consecrated water that native priests used for bringing rain. Incense in churches resembled ceremonial tobacco smoke. Catholic saints who had once been human beings blended easily with departed Indian heroes elevated to the status of powerful spirits. The sacrament of baptism found a parallel in the Indians' ritual bathing, especially in connection with initiations into the voluntary societies, which involved head-washing and name-giving ceremonies. Even on the darker side of life, the Catholic clergy were as likely to envision demons as were their native charges, for Spaniards accepted witchcraft with a certainty that matched that of the Pueblos, who looked for sorcery behind illnesses and social deviance.

The world-views were similar too, for both stressed divinely ordered reality. Both groups believed that the world had been made by power beyond human control, and they agreed that nature and human life conformed to laws determined by godly fiat. Each religion in its own way emphasized divine power as that which gave meaning and purpose to human identity and conduct. Definitions of good and evil followed logically from that supernatural norm. The full range of injunctions about personal morality and social ethics in both religions derived from perceptions of life made dependable and reasonable through divine decree.

Both Spaniards and Pueblos thought that compliance with holy power brought practical benefits. One group might revere a solitary god in three persons while the other obeyed innumerable *kachinas*, but each side was convinced that blessings flowed from a proper relationship with supernatural authority. The missionaries assured native listeners that venerating the Cross would protect them from traditional enemies, drought, and toothaches. The Pueblo priests reminded their fellow townsmen that correct performance of *kiva* rituals and *plaza* dances ensured favorable climatic conditions and produced bountiful harvests. Both religions saw a direct connection between divine will and personal fate coupled with national destiny. Conversely, each interpreted disease, drought, famine, and other catastrophes as punishment from demons or angry gods unwilling to overlook human failings. Between these positive and negative poles it would be difficult to say whether love of duty or fear of retribution predominated in the daily actions of either people.

Despite these compatibilities, the Pueblos' world-view and their conceptions of personal identity and moral obligation differed at important points from those preached by the friars. They referred to no exalted god who created matter *ex nihilo*, and the underworld, rather than a heaven beyond the sky, was the focus of their life. They thought all things came from the earth's navel instead of a transcendent source; gods, people, animals, and plants had emerged through the underworld's roof to dwell on this world's surface. Christian references to Hell or Purgatory in nether regions thus fell on uncomprehending ears, for the Pueblos could not accept the upper cosmos as humanity's ultimate destination.

Differing ideas about the nature of divine power added to the problems. The Spaniards were monotheistic in spite of the fact that they spoke of God as three separate persons. This view contravened the Pueblos' belief that a great number of divine beings were required to make the world's components work smoothly. The friars emphasized belief in one God, depicted with primarily male characteristics. The Pueblos viewed such male figures as Jesus and Santiago (patron saint of Spain) as similar to the twin war gods, Masewi and Oyoyewi, and they likened the Virgin Mary to the venerable female deity Iatiku. But the friars, glossing over these superficial resemblances, stressed the unitary character of Christianity's solitary deity, who ruled a cosmos that turned the Pueblo orientation upside down.

The Pueblo Indians gave the earth a respected status of its own; they therefore could not share the Europeans' belief that the natural world was simply an

8   Chapter One

economic resource. Instead of using natural objects for secular purposes, the Pueblos had a more profound regard for their sacred constitution. What really mattered to them was locating human life at the center of reality, with sacred space radiating in concentric circles throughout nature. Everything, from the points on the compass to the changing seasons, was bounded and controllable by reference to that center. Because of this orientation, the world was an orderly environment that circumscribed the harmony of all good things. The Pueblos affirmed mundane existence and husbanded their lives, along with nature, as cooperative parts of a sanctified ecosystem. For them it was a complete, satisfying world, and people could live in it safely and well, knowing that they fulfilled holy purposes by respecting its established ways.

Another point at which the two cultures contrasted sharply had to do with personal identity. Just as their worlds were different, the Europeans and Pueblos regarded the people in them differently too. Spanish assumptions granted individuals freedom of choice and opportunities to distinguish themselves from others. Personal merit was a virtue to be prized and cultivated, whether accomplished through valor or charity, by prowess or austerity. The Pueblos, however, always defined personal identity in reference to the community, not at its expense. They submerged the self as any Spaniard would have defined it and emphasized collective values instead of individual repute. They shunned personal distinctions and discouraged competitive innovation because they found the true self in group action. Anyone setting himself apart from others was more likely to be ridiculed than honored, and, if his separatism continued, he might be executed as a witch.

Christian doctrines of salvation, and church practice as well, pointed up the contrast with Pueblo ideas about personal identity. From its beginnings Christianity had generally thought of its adherents as a distinct people, a faithful remnant saved from destruction by a merciful God. But the church's salvation of separate individuals usually included some degree of voluntary belief and personal morality, a combination of faith and works in which individual responsibility helped secure the final result. There were no such thoughts in Pueblo life. Everyone there belonged to the group, and each person was sanguine of returning to life in the underworld through *shipapu* regardless of his personal merits or demerits. The only qualification placed on this cultural universalism was the idea that less-virtuous tribesmen would have a more difficult time in reaching the place of original emergence. There was no ultimate life of pleasure for the good and punishment for the wicked. The Pueblos had no conceptions of atonement, vicarious suffering, or redemption because none of these conceptions was necessary to their beliefs.

Christians came to Indians preaching a doctrine that required a psychological sense of separation from the aboriginal group. They saw the church as an institution composed of believers gathered in anticipation of rescue from earthly existence. This doctrine divided the Pueblo community because not all Pueblos would be saved, only the baptized. Only Indians or Spaniards gathered into the communion of saints were received at Mass. Church membership thus cut through families, clans, and voluntary societies, and Christianity's major threat to Pueblo life stemmed from its disruptive capacity to offer salvation only to individuals.

Differing ideas of moral obligation constituted a third area of conflict. The friars thought that their ethical guidelines derived from biblical and theological tradition, sources that transcended historical conditioning. The Pueblos derived their sense of duty from the local community and its pragmatic needs. The friars defined good and bad actions from an ecclesiastical perspective, basing standards on what they viewed ideally as a divine institution that did not coincide with any particular cultural unit. The Pueblos based ethical judgments on standards that complemented their social fabric, and, because the *kachinas* had established them, they did not see any reason to look elsewhere. The friars thought that sanctions against improper conduct would occur in the afterlife in addition to temporal punishment. The Pueblos considered it proper that sanctions, such as ridicule from the *koshare* or death for witches, belonged to this life alone, with no reward or punishment reserved for the future.

As the friars tried to convert the Pueblos, and the latter continued to follow their own view of right conduct, these fundamental differences became readily apparent. The Pueblos had aligned ethics with a divinely appointed natural order and had organized morality in terms of ritual obligations. Their central duty was to participate in ceremonies that perpetuated a well-ordered life for the pueblo and met its physical needs. For them, sin was failure to sustain elements that gave meaning and orientation to life in the pueblo. But the friars stressed attendance at Mass, monogamy, with no divorce, and obedience to royal magistrates. The Pueblos did not understand why such activities might be significant. Furthermore, they saw no need for the Crucifixion story and the accompanying appeals for repentance and reconciliation with a God propitiated by Christ's sacrifice. They could not comprehend why the death of one individual, long ago, could affect their own sacred obligations, designed to provide adequate food, continuing health, village harmony, and military defense. The Spanish message of sin, divine redemption, and sacramental aids to salvation fell on stony ground in the Southwest.

In trying to secure converts, the friars highlighted the elements that separated the two religious systems. By the late 1400s Christian wars against the Moslems had forged a strong alliance between the Catholic religion and Cas-

10   Chapter One

tilian customs. As Spanish arms advanced the cause of king and orthodoxy in
the New World, it became increasingly easy to disdain all who differed from
Spanish norms, and the missionaries pursued their evangelical program with
iconoclastic zeal, convinced that all native beliefs were superstitions and that
native behavior was depraved. As spiritual *conquistadores*, they regarded all
Indians as barbarians, lacking any civilized notion of law, morality, or proper
worship. Instead of beginning with compatible parallels and drawing the Pueblos through shared ideas to a specifically Christian perspective, they rejected
Pueblo religion as utterly misguided. From the outset they sought to eradicate
every vestige of Indian conduct and to fill the vacuum with Catholic doctrine
and practice. After 1609 royal support added repressive power to the arrogance
born of religious certitude. At times they promised rewards to Pueblos who
accepted the true faith, but condemnation was their dominant message. When
Pueblo loyalties persisted in the face of repeated denunciations, the friars used
force to destroy the base of local resistance.

Convinced that Pueblo rituals were totally wrong, the friars seized *kivas* and
confiscated as much ritual paraphernalia as they could find. They burned the
sacred masks, dance costumes, altar effigies, and prayer sticks. They tried to
seal off the sacred chambers and to prevent the voluntary societies from meeting in them. They forbade dances, whether conducted secretly or in the public
plaza. In sum, the central features of local institutions, plus essential duties
required in priestly observance, were the targets of all the destructive wrath the
missionaries could bring to bear on them.

The fact that it was necessary to raid the *kivas* over and over again shows that
the Pueblos persisted in their traditional ceremonies. Their institutionalized
religion provided both a coherent rationale and a tenacious structure for resist-
ing the friars' onslaught. Interestingly enough, the Spanish civil servants did
not always cooperate with the Franciscan leadership. Many governors resented
clerical tyranny and showed their displeasure by allowing pre-Columbian
habits to flourish under their administrations. But the friars remained adamant
in their doctrinaire perspective. If pagans adhered to traditional ways, the
gentle sons of Saint Francis directed that they be whipped as an obstacle to
pacification in this life and to their own bliss in the next.

In keeping with such forceful procedures, the friars also dictated a specific
regimen to natives who accepted Christianity. They gave neophytes European
names and insisted that they speak Spanish. But, curiously, they seem never to
have made language instruction or even catechizing an integral part of missionary routine. The Pueblos had long been accustomed to monogamous
marriages, yet they frequently allowed divorce. The friars denounced these
easygoing ways as promiscuous and permitted divorce only in extreme circum-

stances. They required daily attendance at Mass for all baptized Indians and punished those who failed to comply. Pueblos accepting baptism may have done so for many reasons that did not exclude loyalty to traditional patterns. The Spaniards viewed religion as an exclusive loyalty, however, and berated their charges for retaining old folkways after conversion. Delinquent Pueblo Christians often felt the lash of disapproval from their spiritual supervisors, either because they could not assimilate to Spanish standards or they clung to aboriginal habits while adopting secondary customs to appease their masters.

Repressive tactics were bound to create ill feelings eventually, but the habitually self-effacing Pueblos rarely expressed their discontent. In most cases they rebelled as residents of isolated towns against local conditions; there was no general rebellion against Spanish oppression at first. Indians at Taos, for instance, killed two soldiers and the resident priest in 1639 and destroyed the church and friary before fleeing to escape reprisal. During the early 1640s several pueblos, including Jemez, demonstrated against the imprisonment and flogging of natives who had in secret carried on the ancient traditions; the Spanish governor hanged twenty-nine leaders and jailed many more. In 1650 various Tewas and Keresans from Cochiti plotted to rid themselves of Franciscan domination, but Spanish troops stopped the insurrection before it started; nine conspirators were hanged on that occasion, and others were sentenced to a decade of hard labor. For a time it seemed that openly violent acts of rebellion had ended, so church and state officials resumed the more familiar pattern of squabbling with each other instead of sharing administrative responsibilities. Then a unique combination of events brought the pressure of intercultural conflict to a breaking point.

For five years, 1667–72, there was an extended drought in New Mexico. When their crops failed, native farmers began to question Spanish assurances that their Trinitarian God would bless agricultural work. In 1671 a great pestilence carried off many inhabitants, whose resistance was weakened by the inadequate diet. It began to appear that the Christian deity was no better at preventing epidemics than providing good weather. By 1672 the Navajos and Apaches, whose hunting-gathering life-styles left them more desperate for food than the Rio Grande farmers, began raiding the pueblos. The king's promise to protect his vassals proved as ineffectual as the other advantages supposedly accruing to Spanish rule. Famine, disease, and attacks from marauders convinced most Pueblos that they had seriously erred in accepting elements of the intruders' religion alongside their own.

Many had been willing to accept Christianity insofar as it harmonized with their customary understanding of how religion served material and social ends. Others had adopted the externals of the new viewpoint as long as it did not

12   Chapter One

displace their traditional world-view and the activities integral to it. But when the new ethos and its bewildering world-view proved incapable of guaranteeing good harvests and peaceful villages, where was the advantage in accepting Spanish ways? Despite Franciscan determination to abolish ancient ceremonials, the Pueblos rejected the foreign life-style because they thought it had caused their present difficulties; they returned to the voluntary-society rituals with increased dedication because a revitalized tradition seemed the only practicable recourse in times of stress.

Just at the time the Pueblos were reaffirming their traditional practices, the Spanish clerics and magistrates ended their habitual antagonism against each other. Juan Francisco de Treviño became governor in the early 1670s and placed his office at the disposal of missionary policy. As more and more Pueblos rallied to their old faith, Treviño swore to destroy it once and for all. In 1675 he arrested forty-seven prominent Indians on the vague charge that they had bewitched a clergyman. One Pueblo committed suicide while in prison; the authorities hanged three others and freed the rest, after severe beatings, when the townspeople demonstrated forcibly for their release. Among the forty-three survivors was a Tewa religious leader named Popé, from the pueblo of San Juan. Using distant Taos as a secret headquarters, he persuaded leaders in other towns to form an unprecedented intertribal alliance to resist foreign oppression.

The united Pueblos struck in early August 1680. Using a pincer movement that divided the Spanish forces, they sent the enemy's southern contingent reeling downriver at once. Then they concentrated on Santa Fe, where survivors had rallied to make a stand. In a few days they crippled the garrison, and all the Spaniards fled south to El Paso for refuge. The Pueblo warriors were content to let them go, wishing them good riddance instead of death. Out of 2,500 Spanish inhabitants in the province, the Indians killed only 380; they simply expelled the rest from a land where they had never been welcome. But of thirty-three missionaries in the area, twenty-one fell victim to native retaliation. Angry warriors burned most churches and obliterated tangible symbols of clerical influence, such as records of baptisms, marriages, and burials, together with all the statuary and altars they could find. The basically anti-ecclesiastical character of this revolt indicates how much the Indians considered the priests to be the real cause of their suffering. Missions had been essential to the province's continuing existence, and so the missionaries bore the brunt of the Indians' attempts to eradicate all things Spanish. The revolt was the concerted act of a people determined to reject Christian civilization because it posed a direct threat to their integrated religion and culture. The worsening conditions in the 1670s had proved Christianity to be an unacceptable alternative to the traditional safeguards of Pueblo survival. By late 1680 it seemed as if the *kachinas* had smiled on native efforts to realign themselves completely with baseline culture.

For the next fifteen years, sporadic expeditions moved north from El Paso to pacify the old colonial district. Popé was unable to maintain the pragmatic union and disappeared from historical view because the Pueblos preferred local autonomy to his grand alliance. As a result, the Rio Grande Pueblos once again fell piecemeal to Spanish troops, now bent on revenge. By 1696, when the latter had extinguished the last sparks of revolt, they had caused many more native casualties than they themselves had suffered fifteen years earlier. The native population had been declining throughout the seventeenth century, dwindling to less than 20,000 after seventy years of Spanish influence. The fighting that took place during the rebellion and the reconquest lowered their numbers even further, and by 1700 no more than 14,000 survived in the ancient pueblos.

The Spaniards hoped that revised administrative procedures would cause fewer problems in future red–white interaction. Since many investigators blamed missionary tactics for earlier difficulties, one change they insisted on was never to allow the Franciscans the power they had once had. By 1700 it appeared that pacification was complete and that prewar economic and political habits could be resumed. But thoughts on that score failed to note a significant cultural change, especially on the basic level where religion motivated human life. Many Pueblos had emigrated west to find refuge among the Hopis. Those who stayed in their traditional homeland found another way to resist Spanish domination. They adjusted to the foreigners' control over secular matters wherever necessary but rarely allowed Christianity to penetrate the private sphere of their religious sensibilities. By a compromising technique, known as compartmentalization, the Pueblos cooperated outwardly with dominant social patterns while maintaining their ancient integrity. Precontact kinship systems, especially the clans, which gave them their primary sense of identity, remained intact and in force. Imposed political offices, such as *alcalde*, did not replace the traditional voluntary societies, which still embodied each pueblo's real government. The native languages remained vibrant too. The Pueblos mastered enough Spanish to function in the workaday world, but they used the ancient tongues at home, and especially in the *kivas*, to remind each other of the true ground of reality.

Partly because of previous mistakes, partly due to demographic changes, the Franciscans did not return in large numbers. They never achieved effective contact with the Indian leadership and in fact aided the compartmentalization process by evangelizing less aggressively. If the Pueblos adopted elements of Hispanic Christianity, it was only the externals of the European faith, to appease the missionaries and keep them at arm's length. This double standard of external

14   Chapter One

acquiescence and internal resistance assured Christianity only a peripheral status. The Pueblo religion survived because its tenacious network of voluntary societies withstood every attempt to exterminate them. These durable, highly sophisticated institutions offer an important suggestion about what factors help native culture systems endure in the face of white domination.

Later generations of Pueblos grew up in an environment in which one could be nominally Catholic and still be loyal to another tradition. Church attendance and Hispanic holidays had some place in village routine, but Catholic elements that contrasted with baseline religious values were politely ignored. Since 1700, the Pueblos have added an unobtrusive Christianity to traditional patterns without fundamentally altering their solid precontact core. Such compromises and the enabling compartmentalization process have relegated Hispanic influences to secondary importance. Christian agencies exist in the general sum of things, but they have not really changed the world-view and ethos that sustain Pueblo life.

Old ways persist today despite the missionary efforts of various Christian denominations that compete for native loyalty. Ancient beliefs and rituals have endured side by side with ideas yet to be resolved into a new synthesis. The Indians learn English, but it is a second language. Many now live in single-unit houses instead of the old village structure, but they stay close to the land. Automobiles, electricity, and other technological changes affect native habits, but the ceremonial substratum of traditional existence survives. The organizational strength of Pueblo culture, embodied in the priestly and sociopolitical institutions, has been the key to native endurance over the past four centuries. It will probably withstand threats to its integrity in future times as well.

CHAPTER TWO

PRAIRIE BOUND: MIGRATION PATTERNS TO A SWEDISH SETTLEMENT ON THE DAKOTA FRONTIER

ROBERT C. OSTERGREN

Two centuries after the Pueblos drove Spanish colonists out of the upper Rio Grande Valley, immigrants from Sweden swarmed to the American Midwest, especially Illinois and Minnesota. No one has studied this migration with greater care than Robert C. Ostergren, a cultural geographer at the University of Wisconsin–Madison.

One of the special strengths of Ostergren's research is the way he connects the migration of people from specific areas in Sweden to particular communities in the United States. In this case, he traces the movement of 206 settlers and their families from three Swedish regions, especially the province of Dalarna, to Dalesburg, a farming community on the eastern fringe of the Great Plains in present-day South Dakota, in the decade following the Civil War.

Ostergren's major source (a collection of individual biographies) permitted him to follow migration patterns, either directly to Dalesburg, or indirectly, through intermediate Swedish-immigrant communities in Illinois, Wisconsin, Minnesota, and Iowa. He also discovered that the precise locations where Swedish farmers chose to settle in rural Dalesburg were determined primarily by church membership—Lutheran, Baptist, and Mission Covenant—and that the community was socially organized around religious institutions.

This essay is a revision of an article that originally appeared in Frederick C. Luebke, ed., Ethnicity on the Great Plains (1980).

A topic that is frequently addressed in settlement studies is the process of frontier migration. The fact that new settlers on the frontier had to come from somewhere else naturally raises questions about the origins of these people, the

16   Chapter Two

timing of their migrations, the routes they followed, and the communication process that motivated them. Moreover, the widespread occurrence of culturally homogeneous immigrant communities, especially on the homestead frontiers of the American Middle West, gives rise to a curiosity about the significance of migratory experiences and associations in explaining immigrant settlement behavior. To a certain extent, the selection of a place to live and the choice of one's neighbors must have been a product of experiences with places and people along the way.[1]

The study of historic patterns of movement to the American frontier, however, is not easily accomplished. Detailed information about the travels and stopping places of large numbers of immigrant settlers does not generally exist. When people are on the move they tend to make a far fainter imprint on the historical record than when they put down roots. Consequently, it is often possible to make only generalized comments about the migration patterns of frontier populations. Available data, for the most part, are place oriented. We know when people arrived in a certain place and when they left that place, but lack the connecting evidence necessary to determine where they came from or where they were going to. Faced with such data problems, most studies of frontier migration have dealt with the frequency of migration rather than the pattern. These "turnover" studies have yielded a great deal of information about population mobility rates in a variety of places and time periods.[2] They tell us little, however, about the cumulative migration experience of individuals and groups.

On occasion material does surface that lends itself to the detailed study of migration patterns for a particular population. This type of material usually appears in the form of collected pioneer autobiographies or life histories. A seminal example of the use of material of this nature is an article by John Hudson that delimits frontier migration patterns to the state of North Dakota on the basis of pioneer autobiographies collected in the late 1930s.[3] Hudson uses a sample of one thousand autobiographies to test and flesh out various notions about migration and mobility in American life. His article deals with these questions on a very broad scale in that the sample population is widely scattered in both time and space. It reflects the entire North Dakota frontier experience from the 1870s to the 1910–20 period. The patterns revealed are interesting in a comparative sense and hint at what might be achieved in working on a smaller scale.

This paper focuses on the migration experience of the early population of a single frontier settlement. The population is a group of 206 immigrant Swedish settlers who made their way in the late 1860s and early 1870s to the same place in southeastern South Dakota—the Dalesburg settlement of Clay County. The tracing of their presettlement activities is made possible by the existence of an uncommonly rich data source. In the 1930s a local resident wrote, as a hobby, detailed histories of all the homesteaders in the settlement[4] What makes his collection of histories so rich is the remarkably consistent attention paid to the moves and domiciles of its subjects. The information allows a nearly complete reconstruction of the migration experience of each homesteader from the time he left the home parish in Sweden until his death, whether it was on the homestead in South Dakota or elsewhere. The aim of this paper is to describe the migration experience of the Dalesburg settlers and to relate that experience to the early settlement patterns and associations that occurred in the community.

THE DALESBURG SETTLEMENT

The destination of the 206 Swedish settlers and their families who are the subject of this study was an area of rolling prairie situated on the east side of the valley of the Vermillion River, a sluggish tributary of the Missouri River located in Clay County, Dakota Territory (Fig. 2.1). Clay County was opened for settlement around 1860, roughly about the time that the rapidly moving pre–Civil War frontier began to push up the major river valleys into Nebraska and Dakota territories. A combination of Indian troubles, the Civil War, drought, and grasshopper plague caused the advance of settlement to halt just short of the area, which meant that until the late 1860s the only sizable population in the county was located at the town site of Vermillion.

With the return of better times, the lure of free homestead land, and the construction of the Dakota Southern Railroad up from Sioux City, the area underwent a boom period. From 1868 to 1873 settlers flooded into the county, advanced up the Vermillion Valley, and spread out onto the prairies. The influx was dominated by settlers of Scandinavian origins who, like most immigrants, segregated themselves in the process of settling the region. Norwegians settled largely to the west of the Vermillion River, Swedes to the east of the river, and Danes formed a number of communities in various locations across the county. The Swedish settlement area became known as the Dalesburg settlement—the name given to the first post office in that part of the county. The name, which was originally spelled *Dahlsborg,* was a reflection of the fact that many of the original settlers hailed from the Swedish province of Dalarna.[5] At its greatest extent, the settlement stretched for about fifteen miles from north to south along the east side of the Vermillion River and extended eastward from the river for a distance of six to eight miles.

The map in Figure 2.2 shows the location of most of the early Swedish

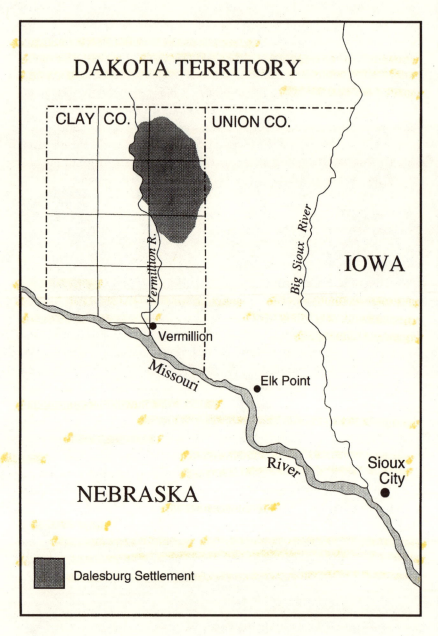

FIGURE 2.1.
Location of the Dalesburg Settlement in Clay County, South Dakota

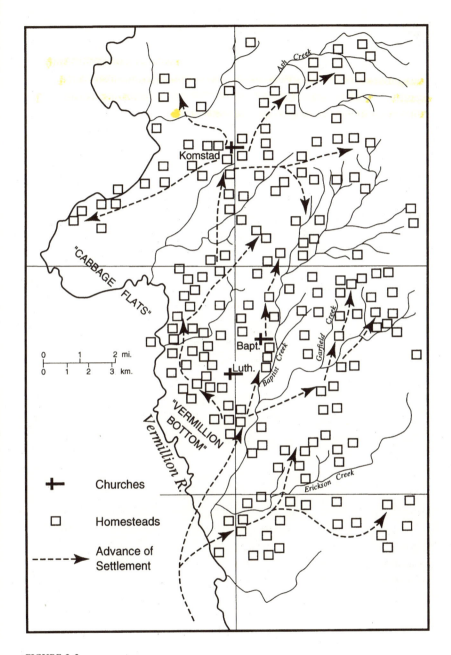

FIGURE 2.2.

Early Homesteads and the Advance of Settlement in the Dalesburg Settlement

20   Chapter Two

homesteads in the settlement. The arrows, which were drawn on the basis of
the dates when homesteads were claimed, show the general manner in which
settlement progressed across the community. The creeks that emptied into the
Vermillion clearly played an important role in determining the settlement
pattern. The advance of settlement tended to move up the creeks and the
homesteads tended to cluster near the creeks, which represented the only
convenient source of water and wood on the prairie. Two areas along the
Vermillion, labeled "Cabbage Flats" and "Vermillion Bottom" on the map,
were poorly drained and generally avoided in the settlement process.[6]

The settlement was organized socially around the religious institutions that
were founded within its boundaries. The first and largest of these was the
Dalesburg Lutheran Church, which was founded during the winter of 1871.
The Lutheran church could by no means command the allegiance of the entire
community, since a great deal of religious dissension apparently existed from
the beginning. The dissension resulted in the establishment later that year of a
rival organization, the Bloomingdale Baptist Church, just two miles away.[7]
Later on, a Mission Covenant church was organized in the northern part of the
settlement near the Komstad post office. All three churches functioned vig-
orously throughout the early history of the settlement, serving as focal points
for the social associations of the settlers.

ORIGINS IN SWEDEN

With few exceptions, the people who would eventually settle in Clay
County began leaving Sweden in the mid-1860s. Their departure was a part of
the ground swell of emigration that took place in Sweden as that decade drew
to a close. A series of bad harvests in Sweden, coupled with good times in
America, provided the impetus necessary for the mass migration. Most of the
Dalesburg migrants (75.6 percent) left during the period 1868–70, the three
peak years in the Swedish emigration curve for that period.

Of perhaps greater interest, in terms of differentiating the experience of the
migrants, is the exact location of their points of departure. The map in Figure
2.3 shows the distribution of parishes from which the Dalesburg people emigrated.[8] The "emigration field" covers nearly all of Sweden, but concentrations
of activity appear in certain areas. For purposes of analysis, it is useful to
regionalize the pattern. Three distinct regions, delimited on the map, serve to
group those emigrants that seem to have had a common cultural background.

The first of these culture groups is made up of those who emigrated from the
forested regions of Upper Dalarna and similar districts in northern Värmland.

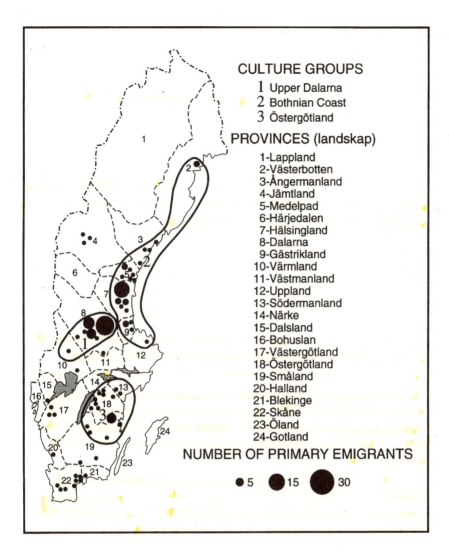

FIGURE 2.3.

Parish Origins in Sweden of the Dalesburg Settlers

This group, comprising sixty-eight primary emigrants and their dependents, will hereafter be referred to as the Upper Dalarna culture group. A second group, consisting of sixty-one primary emigrants and their dependents, emigrated from the coastal and lower river valley parishes of the Bothnian Coast. The third group hailed from the old historic province of Östergötland and

22   Chapter Two

adjacent districts in northern Småland (forty-three emigrations). The remaining thirty-three emigrations were from scattered locations, although it should be noted that there is a rather weak fourth group (ten emigrants) from the province of Skåne.

There is every indication that the emigrants left Sweden quickly. There are but one or two cases of children being born in Swedish coastal towns or cities, and in nearly all cases the records show that the emigrants arrived in America the same year that they left Sweden. Most proceeded to the larger Swedish ports and sailed first to England and then to America. The majority entered the United States through the port of New York. The major difference in their experience, up to that point, is that their cultural backgrounds differed, depending upon the part of Sweden they were from.

THE MOVEMENT TO CLAY COUNTY

Most scholars agree that the business of moving to the frontier was a serious undertaking that required planning and the acquisition of reliable information about one's destination. To be sure, the very first inhabitants of a newly opened area may have come there by happenstance, but the waves of settlers that filled the area in were the product of a complex communication system. Potential migrants were prompted to act by the receipt of information through both public and private channels. Many areas were widely advertised in newspapers and pamphlets or promoted by agents representing land and railroad companies. Even more reliable was the information that came through relatives and acquaintances.

For a substantial number of the Dalesburg migrants, the receipt of information about the Dakota frontier must have taken place in Sweden and must have played an important role in the decision to emigrate. The speed and directness with which many made the move is indicative of this. Eighty-one of the emigrants (39.3 percent) proceeded directly from a U.S. port of entry to Clay County. They made no intervening stops, which suggests that they knew exactly where they were going. The remainder (125 migrants) moved indirectly to Clay County, stopping at least once along the way for a period of a month or more. It is uncertain whether those who moved indirectly had information about their ultimate destination, but we can assume that many did because information about the Dakota frontier was widespread in Sweden at the time.[9]

The fact that some moved directly to Clay County while others did not is an intriguing one. What could explain this difference in behavior? The time of arrival of direct and indirect migrants in Clay County follows no particular pattern. Therefore, the explanation is not that the early migrations were indirect and that the later migrants, who possessed better information, were able to move more directly. Nor do variables such as age or marital status have any bearing on the way in which people moved to Clay County. The proportion of direct migrants to indirect migrants remains fairly constant over time. Furthermore, single migrants were just as apt to move directly as were married heads of households burdened by dependents. There was some difference in age. The average age of the direct migrants tended to be somewhat greater than that of the indirect migrants (34.5 years vs. 29.8 years), but the difference is not large enough to explain the divergence in behavior.

There is much to suggest that the explanation lies in the channels of personal information flow that individuals may have been following. It is reasonable to assume that if an immigrant was in contact with a relative or friend that had preceded him to America, his or her first action would be to go to that person. The immigrant could then proceed westward, with the encouragement and advice of trusted friends who knew what lay ahead. Moreover, the rigors of the journey could be lessened by following in the path of others who had left the settlement for points west in earlier years.[10]

If one considers the emigration history of the culture regions from which the Dalesburg people emigrated, it becomes clear that the probability of having such contacts was greater for some than it was for others. Emigration, for instance, began relatively late in the forested upland parishes of Dalarna and northern Värmland. The Dalesburg people who left the Upper Dalarna area in the late 1860s were among the first to leave the region. The opportunity for them to go to established settlements where they might have contacts was not great. Most immigrant Dalacarlian communities were located in places that were settled about the same time as Dalesburg or later. The Bothnian Coast, on the other hand, is a region that experienced earlier migration. One might expect emigrants from there to have had a greater opportunity to make intervening stops. The Östergötland region experienced the earliest emigration. Its later emigrants probably faced the greatest prospect of proceeding to the American frontier by way of a place where they knew someone.

In fact, the migrations followed exactly that pattern. The proportion of indirect migration was very low for those that emigrated from Upper Dalarna (38.2 percent) and considerably higher for those who emigrated from the Bothnian Coast (70.5 percent) and Östergötland (76.7 percent). Table 2.1 and the map in Figure 2.4 show the distribution of initial stops for the 125 migrants that proceeded indirectly to Clay County. Certain places figured prominently in the migration process for certain groups. Of special importance to the Bothnian Coast group is Allamakee County, Iowa, an important 1850s settle-

24   Chapter Two

TABLE 2.1

Indirect Migrations to Clay County, South Dakota
(Heads of Households)

Initial Stops	Total Population No.	%	Upper Dalarna No.	%	Bothnian Gulf No.	%	Östergöt-land No.	%	Others No.	%
Allamakee Co., Iowa	22	17.6	—	—	18	41.9	3	9.1	1	4.3
Andover, Illinois	16	12.8	5	19.3	—	—	10	30.4	1	4.3
Chicago, Illinois	15	12.0	2	7.7	—	—	5	15.2	8	34.7
Sioux City, Iowa	13	10.4	5	19.3	4	9.3	1	3.0	3	13.4
Moline, Illinois	10	8.0	—	—	5	11.7	5	15.2	—	—
Council Bluffs, Iowa	10	8.0	—	—	9	20.9	—	—	—	—
Galesburg, Illinois	6	4.8	4	15.4	1	2.3	1	3.0	—	—
Keokuk, Iowa	4	3.2	—	—	—	—	4	12.1	—	—
Omaha, Nebraska	4	3.2	—	—	1	2.3	1	3.0	2	8.7
Stockholm, Wisconsin	3	2.4	—	—	—	—	1	3.0	2	8.7
Dakota City, Nebraska	3	2.4	2	7.7	—	—	—	—	1	4.3
Rio, Wisconsin	3	2.4	3	11.5	—	—	—	—	—	—
Isanti Co., Minnesota	2	1.6	2	7.7	—	—	—	—	—	—
Madrid, Iowa	2	1.6	—	—	2	4.7	—	—	—	—
Le Seuer, Minnesota	2	1.6	—	—	—	—	—	—	2	8.7
Boonesboro, Iowa	2	1.6	—	—	1	2.3	1	3.0	—	—
La Porte, Indiana	2	1.6	1	3.8	—	—	—	—	—	—
Kandiyohi Co., Minnesota	1	0.8	—	—	1	2.3	—	—	—	—
Wapello Co., Iowa	1	0.8	—	—	—	—	—	—	1	4.3
Oakland, Nebraska	1	0.8	—	—	1	2.3	—	—	—	—
San Francisco, California	1	0.8	—	—	—	—	—	—	1	4.3
Detroit, Michigan	1	0.8	1	3.8	—	—	—	—	—	—
Unknown	1	0.8	1	3.8	—	—	—	—	—	—
Totals	125	100.0	26	100.0	43	100.0	33	100.0	23	100.0

ment of Halsingland people. Keokuk, Iowa, was an important Östergötland
settlement, and the Galesburg–Andover–Moline district of western Illinois
embraced settlements from Östergötland and the Bothnian Coast area. The
cities of Chicago, Council Bluffs, Sioux City, and Omaha had Swedish populations of mixed origins and served as staging areas for frontier-bound immigrants. The Missouri River towns of Omaha–Council Bluffs and Sioux City
were especially important to Dakota-bound immigrants. About 10 percent of
the indirect migrants made second and third stops. In most cases these stops
took place in these gateway towns of the Missouri Valley.

One might expect the difference between culture groups in their potential

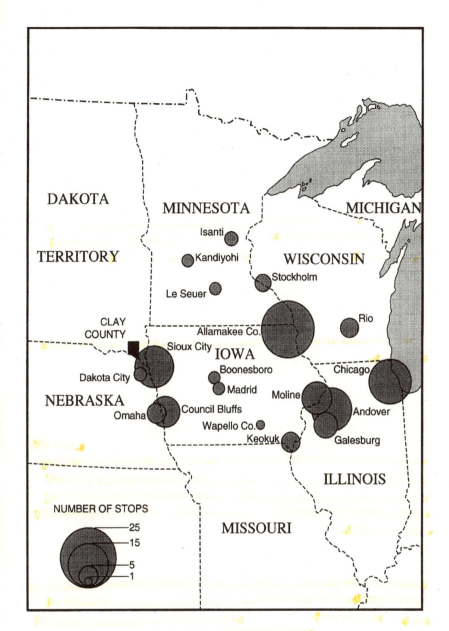

FIGURE 2.4.
Initial Stops of Indirect Migrants to the Dalesburg Settlement

26   Chapter Two

for stops on the way westward to have had the effect, in addition to varying their experience, of varying their time of arrival on the frontier. It was pointed out earlier that most of the Dalesburg migrants left Sweden at roughly the same time and proceeded directly to America. The overall effect of intervening stops, however, was to delay the arrival of the people from the Bothnian Coast and Östergötland more so than the people from Upper Dalarna. Nonetheless, it should be pointed out that there were also direct migrants in both the Bothnian Coast and Östergötland groups that arrived right alongside the earliest settlers from Dalarna. On the other hand, the Upper Dalarna lead was enhanced by the fact that the indirect migrations of the people from Dalarna were delayed for a shorter time on the average than those from the other groups. The average time from emigration to settlement for the indirect Dalarna migrant was 1.48 years. Migrants from the Bothnian Coast took an average of 1.9 years and those from Östergötland took 3.5 years.

SETTLING THE DALESBURG COMMUNITY

The collection point for settlers arriving in Clay County was the town of Vermillion, where the land office was located. It was customary for land seekers to leave dependents and possessions there while they went out to have a look at the land. Often this was done in small parties, since there were men who were in the business of guiding people out to survey the countryside.[11] In some cases, parties came up from Sioux City to find land and file claims. They would then return to Sioux City for their dependents and baggage.[12] These land-seeking parties were a key element in determining the spatial pattern of homesteading, for it was the timing of an immigrant's arrival in Vermillion, along with associations made with other migrants back in Sweden or along the way, that often determined the make-up of land-seeking parties and collective trips to the land office.

The map in Figure 2.5 suggests that culture-group associations played a remarkably important role in determining the settlement pattern. There was a clear tendency for those with common backgrounds to congregate along certain creek beds. People from Upper Dalarna colonized the areas along Erickson Creek, Garfield Creek, and the lower and central reaches of Baptist Creek. Immigrants from the Bothnian Coast area concentrated very heavily along the small unnamed creek that flows into the Vermillion River between Cabbage Flats and Vermillion Bottom. Others scattered northward along the Vermillion and some of its upriver tributaries. The Östergötland group occupied the area

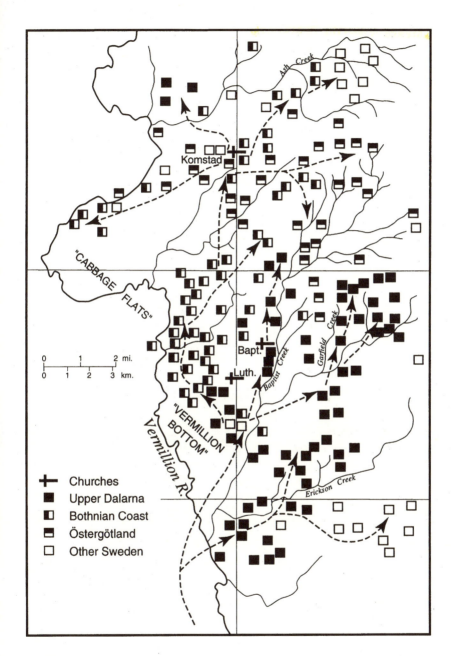

FIGURE 2.5.

Homesteads by Culture Group

28   Chapter Two

at the headwaters of Baptist Creek and along the unnamed creek directly to the west (near Komstad post office).

The importance of personal associations within the culture groups is evident if one inspects more closely the patterns outlined above. For instance, the Upper Dalarna people that settled along the lower reaches of Garfield Creek were all from the same place—the parish of Gagnef. Those that settled along Erickson Creek were largely from the parish of Svärdsjö, while residents of the neighborhood that emerged along Baptist Creek hailed largely from the parish of Rättvik.[13] Each of these groupings reflects associations that were made back in Sweden.

At another level, the Östergötland people who occupied the headwaters of Baptist Creek and the area around Komstad post office had, for the most part, the common experience of spending time near Andover in Henry County, Illinois. The large concentration of Bothnian Coast people located to the west of the Lutheran church came from widely scattered locations in Sweden, but had, in most cases, proceeded to Clay County by way of Allamakee County, Iowa. Most of the Bothnian Coast people settling to the northeast of Cabbage Flats had moved as a group to Clay County, stopping at Madrid and Council Bluffs, Iowa.[14] All of these are examples of associations made or strengthened by common experience in moving west toward the homestead frontier.

A remarkable thing about this clustering process is that not all the homesteads in each of the neighborhoods were taken simultaneously. There was usually a three- or four-year lag between the time that the first settler and the last settler of a neighborhood cluster filed their claims. During that period, the fringe of settlement would have advanced a considerable distance beyond. The formation of such distinct units was the product of conscious effort rather than the simple availability of land. A settler that was interested only in acquiring good land might well have chosen to settle elsewhere.

CONCLUSION

The degree to which these associations were perceived within the Dalesburg settlement and may have influenced the later life of the community is an important question. To investigate it is beyond the scope of this paper, but a possible line of inquiry would be a study of the religious structure of the community. A quick survey of the membership rolls of the Dalesburg churches suggests that church membership cut across neighborhood lines and may have been independent of the kind of cultural or experiential associations discussed here. A look at the internal organization of one of the churches, however, is

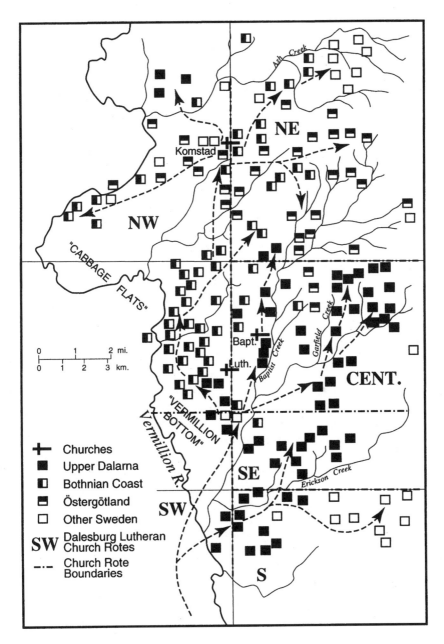

FIGURE 2.6.
Homesteads by Culture Group and the Dalesburg Lutheran Church Rotes

30   Chapter Two

more revealing. The Dalesburg Lutheran Church divided its membership into administrative districts called *rotes*. Although the boundaries of the rotes shifted somewhat during the history of the church, the map in Figure 2.6 gives a fairly good approximation.[15] It is quite apparent that the districts correspond reasonably well with many of the neighborhood settlement clusters identified above. One may conclude that there was an official acknowledgment here of a community social organization that was older than the community itself.

The settlement pattern and, quite likely, even the social organization of the Dalesburg community was the product of associations made or strengthened by common experience in making the journey from Europe to the homestead frontier. People who had known one another before the emigration began or who came to know one another at stopping points along the way grouped themselves into clusters or neighborhoods when they took their land. Axes of communication and migration that connected home districts with intermediate settlements in the Middle West and eventually Dalesburg itself were instrumental in guiding the entire process and promoting the spatial concentration of homogeneous groups that is so often associated with ethnicity on the agricultural frontiers of the Great Plains.

NOTES

1. There is a growing literature on ethnic settlement in American Middle West that emphasizes patterns of spatial segregation among cultural groups and the processes of chain migration that helped to produce these patterns. Some recent examples are Jon Gjerde, *From Peasants to Farmers: The Migration from Balestrand, Norway, to the Upper Middle West* (Cambridge: Cambridge University Press, 1985); Robert C. Ostergren, *A Community Transplanted: The Trans-Atlantic Experience of a Swedish Immigrant Settlement in the Upper Middle West, 1835–1915* (Madison: University of Wisconsin Press, 1988); D. Aidan McQuillan, *Prevailing Over Time: Ethnic Adjustment on the Kansas Prairies, 1875–1925* (Lincoln: University of Nebraska Press, 1990); and Anne Kelly Knowles, "Immigrant Trajectories through the Rural-Industrial Transition in Wales and the United States, 1795–1850," *Annals of the Association of American Geographers* 85 (June 1995): 246–66. For a treatment of segregation and migration flow among American culture groups, see John C. Hudson, "North American Origins of Middlewestern Frontier Populations," *Annals of the Association of American Geographers* 78 (September 1988): 395–413.

2. Knowledge about the comings and goings of people is normally extracted from place-oriented sources such as manuscript censuses, church registers, city directories, etc. The classic pioneering example of a study that dealt with population turnover in a frontier community is Merle Curti et al., *The Making of an American Community* (Stanford: Stanford University Press, 1959). See also John C. Hudson, "The Study of Western Frontier

Populations," in *The American West: New Perspectives, New Dimensions,* ed. Jerome O. Steffen (Norman: University of Oklahoma Press, 1979), 35–60.

3. John C. Hudson, "Migration to an American Frontier," *Annals of the Association of American Geographers* 66 (June 1976): 242–65.

4. August Peterson, *History of the Swedes Who Settled in Clay County, South Dakota and their Biographies* (Vermillion, SD: Swedish Pioneer and Historical Society of Clay County, South Dakota, 1947). The book actually contains 242 life histories, but the number used in this study was pared down to 206 by the elimination of multiple homesteads within the same family and a number of entries for which information was scant. The 206 individuals studied here are the heads of the families that homesteaded in the area.

5. Lloyd R. Moses, ed., *Clay County Place Names* (Vermillion, SD: Clay County Historical Society, 1976), 45.

6. Ibid., 34, 134–35.

7. Herbert S. Schell, *History of Clay County* (Vermillion, SD: Clay County Historical Society, 1976), 149.

8. The emigrations shown are those of primary emigrants. It was often common for other members of a family to emigrate later. These later emigrations are not shown, since they are viewed in this paper as a continuation of the first person's emigration.

9. Approximately one month is considered for the purpose of this paper to be a significant stop. Staying in one place for that length of time or longer implies that fairly permanent lodgings and perhaps employment had to be found. The type of employment sought during extended stops would be an interesting piece of information, but it is not uniformly available for this population.

Agents representing the railroads and immigration commissions of the plains states and territories were present in Sweden during the late 1860s and early 1870s. In addition, there were letters home from Swedes living in the Midwest, where information about the Dakota frontier was widespread. Examples of letters may be found in Bjorn Hallerdt, ed., *Emigration från Dalarna* (Falun: Falu Nya Boktryckeri AB, 1968).

10. An important feature of settlement in the Middle West was the strings of communities that were linked by bonds of kinship. When the population of a community grew beyond the capacity of the land to support it, surplus population commonly left the community in search of land, establishing daughter communities farther west.

11. Schell, *History of Clay County,* 111.

12. Homesteaders who had filed in Clay County often returned to Sioux City in order to find work, especially if they filed too late in the season to break ground and plant a crop.

13. These migrants represent an off-shoot of a much larger stream of migration from the Swedish parish of Rättvik to Minnesota's Isanti County. See Ostergren, *A Community Transplanted,* 159–89.

14. A relatively large group of emigrants from the parish of Gnarp in Hälsingland traveled together as far as Council Bluffs and then dispersed. These people were part of that group.

15. The map is based on information obtained from Pastor Robert G. Lundgren, Dalesburg Lutheran Church, South Dakota.

CHAPTER THREE

FLEEING BABYLON: THE ENGLISH MORMON MIGRATION TO ALPINE, UTAH

DEAN L. MAY

If religion was central to the social organization of Swedish immigrants in the Dakotas, it was the sine qua non *for Mormon immigrants to Utah. During the second half of the nineteenth century, converts to Mormonism from England and the Scandinavian countries swelled the population of Utah. In this essay, Dean May, a prominent historian of Mormonism and Utah, examines the origins of Mormon immigrants from England who settled in Alpine, an agricultural community in a mountain valley southeast of Salt Lake City. Unlike the people of most immigrant communities, few of the settlers knew each other before emigration, motivated as they were by their newfound faith to inhabit the Mormon Zion in the American West.*

In his Three Frontiers: Family, Land, and Society in the American West, 1850–1900 *(1994), from which this essay is drawn, May analyzes and compares three different agricultural frontier communities. In addition to the English Mormons in Alpine, he examines two non-immigrant rural societies: one consisting mostly of yeoman farmers from the American South, who brought traditional family-oriented culture to Sublimity, a settlement in the Willamette Valley of Oregon; and Middleton, located in the Boise Basin of Idaho, comprising farmers of diverse origin whose values were highly individualistic and acquisitive.*

May discovers that the English Mormons of Alpine were strikingly different in settlement patterns, agricultural practices, family and household structures, fertility, and voluntary associations. Although the physical environment of Alpine at the base of Wasatch Range conditioned much of the behavior of its inhabitants, communitarian values of Mormon ideology account for the sharpest distinctions.

34   Chapter Three

In 1847 some 30,000 Latter-Day Saints in the United States, England, and
Wales anxiously awaited the news that the leaders of their exodus from Illinois
had found a new place to settle. Their leader, Brigham Young, and a select
company arrived in the Salt Lake Valley in late July, followed by a substantial
migration of about 2,000 persons. After a month of reconnoitering, Young
returned east to "Winter Quarters," their temporary settlement near present
Omaha, Nebraska. He immediately dispatched a "General Epistle" to his
followers in which he urged all to gather to the newfound Zion in the Rockies.

> We found a beautiful valley of some twenty by thirty miles in extent, with
> a lofty range of mountains on the east. . . . The soil of the valley appeared
> good, but will require irrigation to promote vegetation. . . . The climate is
> warm, dry, and healthy; good salt abounds at the lake; warm, hot, and
> cold springs are common; mill sights [sic] excellent; but the valley is
> destitute of timber."[1]

By the time these Latter-Day Saints (commonly known as Mormons) began
their flight west, their missions in England, opened in 1837, had gathered
nearly 20,000 converts, of which a quarter had already emigrated to the United
States. They comprised a substantial number of those who responded to Brigham Young's message over the next few years. Most had occupied a singular
position in the rapidly industrializing English society, which may help to
explain the reasons for their migration to Utah. Though they settled throughout the territory, giving Utah a distinctively English cast, their experience can
perhaps best be understood by examining their role in one of the many villages
into which they gathered as they sought a livelihood in the spare Great Basin
environment.

The Mormon settlers rapidly took up available farmlands in the Salt Lake
Valley and began to spread beyond it. In July of 1850 eight men crossed south
into Utah Valley in search of farming opportunities. Though many of the best
lands were already claimed, they found a narrow alluvial fan nestled in a pocket
where the north-south–running Wasatch Mountains intersect a westering
spur, known as the Traverse Range. Mountain streams promised adequate
water and the soil was rich and dark. The men returned for their families, and
by the fall there were twenty-nine persons in the "Mountainville" settlement,
consisting of seven households, fourteen males and fifteen females. In 1855
Mountainville was incorporated under the more lofty name of Alpine City. By
that time, however, many of the founders, disappointed by the shortness of the
growing season, had left. The Wordsworths, Shermans, and Clydes, all Yankees, were gradually replaced by Strongs, Nashes, and Healeys, all British con-

Alpine, Utah
Birthplaces of Early Settlers

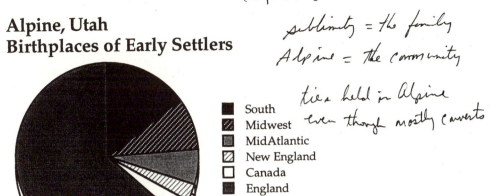

FIGURE 3.1.

Alpine, Utah, Birthplace of Early Settlers

verts to Mormonism who had left a country very different from the England that the first North American colonists had known.

By 1860 there were more English-born adults in Alpine than American. Twenty-one of the thirty-three adults in the town (64 percent) shared an English birth. Strolling down the streets of Alpine on a Christmas Day in the 1860s, you would likely have smelled puddings steaming in most houses and heard English accents in two of every three homes you might pass. There were four times as many adults in the town of English birth or recent background than from any other country or state in the United States—two English-born adults for every American-born. All of those who reported an occupation in 1860 told the census marshal they were farmers. In doing so, they were avowing an identity new to most, and one that effectively obscured their pre-Alpine lives.

Who were these English immigrants—farmers all? Charles Dickens, the eminent English writer, boarded an emigrant ship, the *Amazon*, chartered by English people bound for Utah as it prepared to embark from London on June 4, 1862. The emigrants, he observed,

> came from various parts of England in small parties that had never seen one another before. Yet they had not been a couple of hours on board, when they established their own police, made their own regulations, and

36   Chapter Three

set their own watches at all the hatchways. Before nine o'clock, the ship was as orderly and as quiet as a man-of-war.

Dickens noted the busy and determined scribbling of letters to post before sailing, the singing of the choir, the "universal cheerfulness," the abundance of children, and confided to the shipping agent his impression that "it would be difficult to find eight hundred people together anywhere else, and find so much beauty and so much strength and capacity for work among them." Though "there were many worn faces bearing traces of patient poverty and hard work, . . . there was a great steadiness of purpose and much undemonstrative self-respect among this class." The passengers, as near he could tell, represented "most familiar kinds of handicraft trades," including farmers and farm laborers, "but I doubt if they predominated."[2] Dickens's eye was quick. In a short visit he noted that this was a family migration of parties from several parts of England, hitherto unacquainted. He described them as literate, self-confident working people, unusually decorous and orderly.

Though none of the *Amazon* passengers, so far as I can determine, settled in Alpine, the English-born who did were much like those Dickens described. Family records show that sixteen of thirty-eight native English in Alpine left for the United States from the three counties of Lancashire (six), Staffordshire (five), and Derby (five).[3] Four were last in Devon before migration, and there were two each from Herefordshire, Northampton, Nottingham, Warwickshire, Wiltshire, Worcestershire, and the Channel Island of Jersey. One each was from Shropshire, Lincolnshire, and Gloucestershire.

The family records give us important information about this migration to Alpine. Most came as married couples, often with children. Twenty-two of the thirty-eight were married at the time they left England. But they did not come as broader kin or neighbor groups. No more than four lived in the same town prior to emigration: two couples from Pinxton, Derbyshire: George and Catherine Clark and John and Mary Healey. Our data show, as Dickens maintained, that they came from many towns and had little acquaintance before migration. Yet the great majority came from Lancashire and other counties close to the ports of Liverpool and Manchester in northwest England. This once rural, even rustic, region had become by the turn of the nineteenth century the first in the world to experience rapid industrialization and urbanization. The most dramatic part of that transformation, with all its attending dislocations, had taken place within the half century prior to the departure of the Alpine settlers. Though the process by which Lancashire and the surrounding districts became industrialized is complex, and the precise linkage between the dynamic forces is debated among economic historians, the main elements seem clear enough. Lancashire and portions of the adjoining counties had been sparsely populated before the sixteenth century, when settlers began to clear and plow lands that had never been cultivated. Because of this relatively late clearing, the open-field system and many other vestiges of feudalism were never fully operative in the region. There were few gentry, little influence from manorial overlords, and land-owning yeoman farmers were predominant. Gradually the local custom of partible inheritance divided land holdings into parcels too small to provide an adequate living, and by the second quarter of the sixteenth century many families began to convert their homes into small family spinning and weaving shops as a way to augment their income.

This dual farming and manufacturing economy characterized large portions of the region, with 50 to 88 percent of the adult males reporting textile occupations in several Lancashire localities during the last half of the eighteenth century. As the century wore on, cotton increasingly supplemented and then replaced linen and wool as the principal fiber. All of Britain imported just under 4 million pounds of cotton in 1772, nearly 42 million by 1800, and an astonishing 452 million by 1841.[4] By 1790 the Lancashire port of Liverpool had become the main British entrepôt for this trade. While the cotton trade grew, the domestic factory system was changing to a "putting out" system, where households did not operate as independent shops but were supplied fiber and machines by a merchant who paid a set price per piece of goods produced. This minimized risks but reduced the independence of the home textile producers, and often led to specialization and a fragmenting of the production process. By the 1820s spinning machines and the power loom began to eliminate home weaving, removing both spinning and weaving to factories strategically situated for use of water power, or increasingly within easy reach of coal to power the boilers of steam engines.

These changes transformed the accustomed world of the people of northwest England. They found it necessary to alter long-practiced modes of organizing production. The home was no longer a family work place where they could control the rhythms of their labor. Some moved to rapidly growing towns and cities or watched their old neighborhoods become crowded, losing the stabilizing complementarity of the farming/manufacturing economy. Increasingly they became subject to the severe seasonal and business-cycle fluctuations in income.[5] Many, angered and frustrated by what was happening, organized labor unions and cooperatives, struck out to smash machines, and in other ways attempted to stem or control the tide of change.[6]

The majority of those who became farmers in Alpine, Utah, grew up in the middle of all this. Before they left for America they had been among the first

38   Chapter Three

generation of industrial workers the world had known, and thus they became pioneers twice: first, helping to define new sets of relationships between workers and the factory production system with its wide-ranging effect on every aspect of their society, and second, trying to build a society from scratch in the arid American West. The appeal of Utah must have been remarkable. Persons born in England or Wales totaled 1.5 percent of the entire U.S. population in 1880, but in Utah their proportion was ten times as high at 15 percent.

It is difficult to tell, except in a few cases, from where precisely in the rapidly changing social system the future Alpine settlers were drawn. P.A.M. Taylor's sample of male emigrants bound for Utah offers some insights. Although Taylor's data do not tell us all we would like to know, they make it clear that emigrants to Utah were principally from the ranks of skilled and semi-skilled laborers, but they did not own their own workplaces. This was especially true of miners (15 percent), metal and engineering workers (10 percent), and textile workers (9 percent), with 55 percent of the whole group working in these and similar occupations. Another 32 percent were general laborers or domestics. At the top of the scale were a few (about 7 percent)—shopkeepers, professionals, and clerks—who probably owned some property and perhaps their own workplaces. A small minority (5 percent) were farmers.

Thus very few were agrarian rural people; the great majority were workers in the new industrial economy of England, owning little property, suffering a declining standard of living, and in any case reeling from social dislocation and unpredictability of income that attended industrialization.[7] For those persons who would convert to Mormonism and find their way to Alpine, all things were awash—their homes, families, and the purposes and products of their labor. The new direction they had chosen promised to stay the bewildering flux that their world had become.

In Alpine, as in nearly 500 other Mormon communities, these immigrants from industrial England found it necessary to abandon or relegate to marginality the trades they had mastered in their youth and learn how to farm in the unfamiliar and unyielding Utah environment. Though Mormon church leaders were desperate to found basic industries and made heroic efforts to do so, industrialization in Utah was slow in coming and progressed with fits and starts. Alpine may have had some advantages over the working-class districts of Liverpool or Preston, but it offered farmers only the meanest, hardscrabble living.

One of the best ways to discover what life was like for the English-born Alpiners is to compare their experience with that of other rural settlers in the West. Sublimity was a non-Mormon settlement in Oregon's fertile Willamette

Valley. The majority of its 592 inhabitants in 1860 were persons of southern origin or midwesterners with southern roots, and most of the gainfully employed were farmers. About 80 percent were people with roots in societies long dominated by an agricultural planter class jealous of its accustomed right to control the wealth, politics, religion, and social life of their region. For them, the extended family took precedence over the community values that were primary in Alpine. Middleton, Idaho, was another non-Mormon farming community. Founded in 1862, it was located twenty-two miles west of Boise, the state capital. There was no single group in Middleton that could by sheer numbers dominate and attach its own peculiar character to the place, as the English Mormons did in Alpine and southerners in Sublimity. Here individualistic values reigned.[8]

Contrasts between Alpine, Sublimity, and Middleton are especially evident in the size of farms. Most Alpine families lived in town rather than on their farmland, which usually lay outside the townsite in noncontiguous parcels. In 1860 the average size of these tracts was only 15 acres. A total of 323 acres was divided among the twenty-one Alpine taxpayers. Households in Alpine were about the same size as elsewhere in the West at that time, but the average farm was tiny by comparison. In Sublimity the average farm size was nearly 375 acres; in Middleton, 150.

Why were Alpine farms so small? In Utah, arable land had to be close enough to creeks and rivers for irrigation, level enough for water to flow evenly through ditch and furrow networks, and at an elevation not subject to early frosts. The quantity of land meeting these essential criteria was severely limited. But the austere character of the land is only part of the answer. Brigham Young had considered other options and rejected them.[9] The fact was that abundant land was not the first priority for the Mormons. What they sought above all was refuge—a place where they would be left alone to build a society according to their own lights. The principal qualities that the new home of the Mormons should have were isolation and remoteness.

Hoping to provide a sufficiency for all Latter-Day Saints who might wish to come to their new Zion in Utah, the Mormon leaders worked out their own land allotment system that began with the principle that one should have no more than one could till. In opening new settlements, they often distributed land by lot, in five- ten-, or fifteen-acre parcels, with fifteen to twenty acres deemed sufficient for a thrifty farm.[10] Not one of the Alpine taxpayers reported undeveloped lands that could open the possibility of future growth, a fact eloquent in its implications for the many children being born to Alpine couples.

Average farm production in Alpine in 1860 can be calculated from the county tax rolls. The median production of wheat was eighty bushels, fifteen

40   Chapter Three

each of corn and oats, and forty of potatoes. Alpine farmers had two milk cows (in the hope that at least one would be fresh at any time), two other cattle (beef or calves), two draught oxen, and two hogs. They produced thirty-five pounds of butter and put up two tons of hay with an average of $40 worth of equipment and no hired workers. The value of a typical farm, livestock, and equipment was $340. The milk cows were commonly kept on their town lots, where the women also tended a garden and a bevy of chickens.

It is no surprise that the Sublimity farmers outproduced those in Utah. Yet, on 25 times as much land, they realized only about twice as much production. Much of their land remained untilled, a consequence of a less commercial orientation derived from their southern yeoman past. They were wealthy, the average farm being valued at almost $1,500, but not highly productive. In Middleton the average farm was worth $2,000, and farmers efficiently tilled a much higher proportion of their land, raising staple crops for market, and producing some ten times as much as the farmers of Alpine.

Perhaps the pain of poverty in Alpine was mitigated by the centrality of religion. There the Mormon church was the motivating force behind politics and cooperative economic endeavors, as well as the center of social life. Alpiners could hardly imagine a viable faith except as expressed in the broader community. But in Sublimity, religious people found satisfying expression for their faith in very small kin and neighbor groups that did not favor a sense of community, and in Middleton, where religious practice was neither highly localized nor broadly communal, the faithful few found it difficult to sustain church life at all.

Obviously, the settlement and social pattern of Alpine favored organized religion. Formal organization took place within a year of the first settlement in Alpine, but not until a meeting house, the visible symbol of the community, was built. That structure was erected as a cooperative endeavor in less than a month. It was replaced in 1863 with a larger building, and this with a still larger one in 1872. In Sublimity, no group felt the need for such a structure until six years after the post office was organized, when the Mill Creek Church of God was built by some 15 or 20 of the 97 families in the area. Middleton's first congregation was not organized until a decade after settlement.

Leadership in Alpine was highly visible and centralized. There was an officially designated church leader from 1851 on, with one man serving as bishop (pastor) of the congregation for 37 years and as mayor for 27. The church, rather than being one of several competing voluntary associations, was central in the political, social, and economic life of the community and the dominant influence on a plethora of cooperative endeavors, such as stores, libraries, choirs, militias, and public works projects.

The census of religion in 1860 indicates that in Utah County (wherein Alpine was located) there were six churches, all Mormon, capable of accommodating 3,475, or 42 percent of the population of 8,248. The 1870 data show little growth in "sittings"—4,300 in 12 organizations—now capable of accommodating 35 percent of 12,203 inhabitants. The 1890 census (the first to show numbers of members) enumerates 19,547 church members, or 82 percent of the population (23,768). The comparable figures for Sublimity were 26 percent, 23 percent, and 26 percent.

In Utah County organized religion was much more intimately tied to the community, so that those who did not attend church or were not religious still reported themselves as members and thought of themselves as Mormons by virtue of their being citizens. It was very nearly a patriotic duty to be a Mormon. Thus, four-fifths of the population in Utah County were classified as church members in 1890. Because Mormons counted as members only persons older than eight years, and since in that prolific society 20 percent of the population fell into the eight-or-younger age group, the data suggest that virtually no one was unchurched. In Sublimity's Marion County, organized religion was successful in touching, in some sense, only a quarter of the population in 1890; in Middleton, only 16 percent.

These data raise interesting questions concerning the relationship of belief to behavior in Utah. Since building the Kingdom of God was equated with establishing a cooperative, prosperous, settled society in Utah, personal belief became less an index of commitment than public behavior. What the Mormons *thought* about religion, beyond a fundamental faith in Christ and in Joseph Smith and Brigham Young as his designated spokesmen on earth, was less an issue in the society than what Mormons *did* about it. The finer points of Mormon theology, then as now, are filled with much speculation and interpretation, and there is no creed or catechism to resolve differing views. Acquiring true religion, in the Mormon view, was rather like learning a skill. It was a process, not an event, a practicum more than a lecture course.

The Mormon settlement at Alpine was rather different from many, perhaps most, immigrant communities in the West, in that few immigrant families were related, or even knew each other before emigration. But they shared a common culture. At play in this case was a mixture of an English working-class culture and an adopted religious one that had incorporated many elements of the rural New England in which Mormonism had been founded. As we have

42   Chapter Three

seen, before most English Mormons had come to the West, their lives had been buffeted by a series of disruptions that all but severed the social networks they had known in their youth. Conversion to Mormonism was often instrumental in cutting family ties, but then it led to meeting a future spouse with similar experiences. Thus, the kin-based social networks that survived British industrialization were shattered by conversion to Mormonism, and new networks were forged that linked persons to the church and its hierarchy of leaders.

Such experiences are suggested by family names. In Alpine only one surname appears more than once; in Middleton only two, both families of southern origin. But in Sublimity there were twenty-seven families that shared a surname with at least one other, and some with two, three, or even four other families.

Clusters of kin, characteristic of Sublimity, were simply not present in Alpine. There the severing of family associations through industrialization, conversion to Mormonism, and migration to the American West had created a social world radically different from that of the Willamette countryside. For the English Mormons in Utah, old networks of association had been dissolved and new ones were being formed in the broader community. Middleton's settlers also came West as isolates, but they never did form a united community as in Alpine.

Even though there were no clusters of kin in Alpine, every individual in the population, with one possible exception, lived in a household as a part of a nuclear family or as a close relative to the resident family. All the homes had a married couple at the core, and there were children in all but that of one aging couple. Nine of the households consisted of parents (or one parent) and their children only. It should be remembered that at that time Mormons practiced polygamy, or plural marriage. Records show that at least one and perhaps five other heads of household in Alpine would eventually have more than one wife. But no one in the settlement lived alone, nor were there any all-male or all-female households. There were no boarders, lodgers, or hired hands.

Perhaps one reason for the more fixed character of Alpine households was that houses there were small, yet they contained on average nearly as many persons as did houses in Sublimity, where houses were larger. In 1860 the Alpine settlement consisted of twenty-three houses, mostly log, facing each other in a square and surrounded by a city wall, an arrangement advised by church leaders to protect the community in case of Indian unrest. On average these cabins housed 5.7 persons (median 6).

The typical Mormon home in Alpine was cramped and crowded, at least by modern standards, partly because of the high fertility of Mormon women. Although there were only sixty-nine men for every 100 women in Alpine, the ratio of children to adult women was 3.36. This compares to the much lower figure of 2.38 registered by the Sublimity population and 1.75 in Middleton. (The child/woman ratio commonly used by American historians is the number of children under ten years of age divided by the number of women aged 16 to 44.) This high birth rate is not attributable to the practice of polygamy, for there were few plural households in Alpine. The patriarchs there were not depleting unduly the pool of marriageable women. Moreover, there were six unmarried women in Alpine over the age of fifteen, four of them widows, but only one unmarried man.

High birth rates and large household sizes did not, however, cause the family to become the central unit of society, as in Sublimity. Instead, the center of existence for Alpine people was their community. When descendants of early settlers wrote their family histories, they took great pains to place them in the context of the town. Their family stories were nurtured in and took their meaning from connections to Alpine. Almost never do they speak, as Sublimity folk did, of family-owned fields and pastures as the matrix from which their race sprang. For them the center of the world was the village, its meeting house, and the neighborhood cemetery. These made up their physical world and set the bounds of their social world—all intertwined with extended family in memory and meaning. But people in Sublimity were family-centered, and they produced enough children to perpetuate themselves. Yet their end was family perpetuity, not countless progeny. In Middleton, where society was more individualistic, neither family nor community was central.

Among the Alpiners, the value placed on community grew from the belief, rooted in Mormon ideology, that a numerous progeny was a blessing beyond reckoning. Church leaders on every possible occasion lauded the rewards of parenthood and the joys of rearing children, their preachments imparting a strong pro-natalist bent to the society. The most solemn Mormon rituals, uniting men and women for eternity, promised a progeny to rival that of the ancient biblical patriarchs. The Alpine folk were taught and understood that they should have as many children as God would give them, and they responded with remarkable diligence and stamina. Yet, why all these children? What was the purpose of such a progeny? They saw the bearing of many children as in large measure their contribution to the building up of Zion—bringing as many spirits as possible into the ordered, harmonious world of Mormon belief and behavior, where they could assist in helping prepare the world for Christ's return.

What did all this mean for Alpine women? Men filled all positions of ultimate power in their society. Any man deemed worthy by the male church

44   Chapter Three

hierarchy could be ordained to the lay ministry, which gave him the responsibility of presiding in the home, as well as in most administrative offices of the church. Women could not. But the picture is not simply one of unalloyed male domination. Women, when married in the Mormon temple ceremony, were given powers of priesthood with their husbands. Many were ordained in a ritual that empowered them to anoint and bless others during childbirth, as well as to act as midwives.

A number of Alpine women occupied important (but never principal) positions in the church and in other community organizations. Yet Mormon theology taught that neither men nor women could achieve ultimate celestial happiness unless they married (obviously a condition more limiting for women than for men, who had more opportunity to take the initiative in such matters). But the vision of a patriarch and matriarch presiding over a family into eternity was deeply cherished. Their offspring would be an enduring blessing of incalculable magnitude. Ultimate perfection required the cooperation of men and women in forming a family.

The sense that wives stood with their husbands at the head of a dynasty extending into the future was as strong among them as among women at Sublimity. Yet they presided with their husbands not so much over a physical domain, identified by particular houses and stretches of land, as over a progeny extending into a celestial future. They did not expect, as did the Sublimity parents, that their descendants could remain physically close to the family home in this life, but they had not the slightest doubt that they would all share a mansion in the next.

Though men clearly held the key administrative offices in this society, women may also have felt themselves more a part of that power structure because the men presiding over congregations and conducting meetings were husbands or close neighbors, not ministers from elsewhere. Any man of the village might be called to preside in the local church. In some respects, formal church organization represented in Alpine an extension of the family organization.

Alpine women occupied roles in the home and family economy similar to those of Sublimity, though very different from those of Middleton, where commercial farming diminished the role of women as producers. Yet they were much more inclined to undertake the tasks of organizing and administering voluntary associations outside the home. Nurturing was their principal responsibility, but the church buildings and organizations extended their nurturing work to the entire community. They headed and staffed church-related volunteer societies for children and young women. For example, the Relief Society, for adult women, was organized in 1868 to direct relief and welfare efforts of the community. That year they raised funds to purchase a loom "to broaden manufacturing of the young people" through donations, in the cash-poor economy, of butter, wool, eggs, wheat, and honey. They also organized a women's choir and appointed a visiting committee to make regular visits to all families in the village needing assistance. Moreover, their work in the community often took them into more secular realms, such as theater groups and choral societies. Public space in Alpine was not exclusively male space; men and women mingled in the home and neighborhood, as in Sublimity, but also in most spheres of the broader society.

Alpine women, like Sublimity women, were the chief planners and administrators of household economies, and thus they consulted with the men when decisions were to be made about how much of what to plant and to market. Yet the fact that their husbands in a sense commuted to work in the fields outside of town made the domestic hearth, including garden and barnyard animals, more exclusively their domain. The women's production of vegetables, butter, and eggs from backyard gardens and pens accounted for much of the tiny marketable surplus their hardscrabble farmlands produced. Payments of tithes and contributions to community fund-raising efforts were often made in eggs and butter—principally the products of the women of Alpine. Women were also important producers in Sublimity, but less so in the more commercially oriented Middleton.

In Utah generally, though less in Alpine, where there were few polygamous families, the burden of managing the household was especially heavy for plural wives. Often economic survival required them to work as principal providers for their families. The frequent absences of the husbands led them to assume a degree of independence otherwise known in Sublimity only among widows. Yet, in these cases, their authority to act came principally from their relationships to their absent husbands. The number of polygamous men and men absent on missions (including, in the latter group, a good many from Alpine) probably made this responsibility more widespread and more frequently exercised in the Utah town than in Sublimity or Middleton.

In sum, Alpine exhibited a curious mix of the characteristics of protocapitalist rural life and modern urbanity. The men and women who headed families had a strong sense of continuity and eternal purpose in their lives that related to their role as parents. Their physical survival depended on what they could get a small, indifferent plot of land to yield, but that land had little meaning beyond its power to provide a meager livelihood. They pursued their lives in a shared social space that involved them in a rich variety of communal activities and expression, similar in nature but transcending in scale the narrow family/

46   Chapter Three

kin networks and rootedness in particular lands seen in Sublimity. Their rootedness seemed to make it possible for them build a critical mass of communal
attachment that seemed entirely absent among the individualistic farmers of
Middleton.

Alpine began with an agricultural economy of niggardly subsistence, and
over the early decades its citizens, although making some gains, still remained
far below the levels achieved in Sublimity and Middleton. During Alpine's first
decades, from 1860 through 1880, total farm land increased and farms became
larger. Nonetheless, the paucity of land and water, and the determination of
the people and their children to stay in the place, kept farms small and inevitably forced many out of farming. Whereas all of the heads of household had
been farmers in 1860, that number dropped to 66 percent in 1870 and to 63
percent in 1880, only slightly more than in Middleton. Still, farming remained
the base of the economy, and niches were opened to agriculturists as the Alpine
people built canals to water higher lands previously thought useless and
claimed grazing areas in the foothills.

All the land farmed in Alpine in 1860 had totaled but 324 acres. In 1867 the
principal streams and springs flowing into the area were formally claimed by
the city for community use, and over the next few years the town fathers
oversaw the building of a network of dams and canals for distributing the
water. Alpiners' expansion into areas previously thought marginal doubled
their agricultural land by 1870 to 649 acres. The next decade saw a five-fold
increase to 3,127 acres. Thus, though we might have expected that virtually all
the younger men coming of age would have been forced to leave the community or to seek occupations outside of farming, the opening of new lands
through extending irrigation ditches and the claiming of marginal foothill
tracts made farming or stock raising a possibility for many.

The settlers of Alpine were already part of the modern world when they
came to the West. They were converts to Mormonism, and were among the
first in the world to see the old order shattered by the mines and mills of
industrial Britain. Mormon missionaries taught of a haven in the West where
they could escape working-class poverty and dislocation, joining themselves to
a community of Latter-Day Saints. Their conversion and migration frag-
mented families and led them to form new ties to church leaders and ultimately to fellow citizens in the Utah villages where they settled. Neither land
nor family, in the broadest sense, were as important to them as community.
Usually not farmers before they came to the West, they did not invest land with
special meaning but saw it as a way to make a living. The small fields they
farmed outside the town yielded barely enough to survive on. Providing the

essentials for family survival became their first priority, but if they were lucky enough to realize a surplus, they would sell it for what they could get. Yet, in spite of relative poverty, their intense interaction with others in church-sponsored voluntary activities created a rich social life that helped form enduring bonds to the place.

During the three decades from 1870 to 1900, thirty-two percent of the Alpine people stayed attached to the town. In Sublimity and Middleton, where community networks were more limited, or hardly existed at all, fewer than five percent remained. If conversion to Mormonism and emigration from England severed traditional ties of family and kin, the new ties of community that Alpiners formed in Utah seem to have held them fast.

NOTES

1. December 23, 1847, "General Epistle from the Council of the Twelve Apostles to the Church of Jesus Christ of Latter Day Saints Abroad, Dispersed throughout the Earth." *Millennial Star* 6 (March 15, 1848): 81–88.

2. Charles Dickens, *Great Expectations* (New York: F.M. Lufton Publishing Co., 1889?). A set of journalistic essays titled *The Uncommercial Traveler* is bound in the same book on pages 449–706. The quotations are from pp. 631–43.

3. In this they varied somewhat from the general pattern of emigration from England to Utah, which is not surprising with so small a sample. See P.A.M. Taylor, *Expectations Westward: The Mormons and the Emigration of their British Converts in the Nineteenth Century* (Edinburgh: Oliver & Boyd, 1965), 248. Taylor reports that of 12,618 persons who emigrated between 1850 and 1862, the great majority were from Lancashire (2,250, or 18 percent), as was also true of Alpine (6, or 16 percent), but the other areas of great emigration were London (1,301), Yorkshire (1,203), and Warwickshire (1,178), of which only Warwickshire was represented in Alpine.

4. Peter Mathias, *The First Industrial Nation: An Economic History of Britain, 1700–1914* (New York: Scribner, 1969), 486.

5. John K. Walton, *Lancashire: A Social History, 1558–1939* (Manchester: Manchester University Press, 1987), 10–15, 62, 104, 109–10, 124.

6. See E.P. Thompson, *The Making of the English Working Class* (New York: Pantheon Books, 1964) for the development of a working-class mentality in England.

7. Peter H. Lindert and Jeffrey G. Williamson, "English Workers' Living Standards during the Industrial Revolution," *Economic History Review* 36 (February 1983): 4, 13. See also R.S. Neal's refutation in *Writing Marxist History: British Society, Economy, and Culture since 1700* (New York: Basil Blackwell, 1985).

8. The analyses that follow are based on data recorded in publications of the Census Bureau, census manuscripts (on microfilm), and a variety of local sources such as tax rolls. Readers who wish to pursue sources should consult *Three Frontiers: Family, Land, and Society in the American West, 1850–1900* (New York: Cambridge University Press, 1994).

48   Chapter Three

9. Sermon of Brigham Young, August 17, 1856, in *Journal of Discourses*, 26 vols. (London: S.W. Richards, 1857), 4:32.

10. For Mormon land distribution practices see Feramorz Y. Fox, "The Mormon Land System: A Study of the Settlement and Utilization of Land under the Mormon Church" (Ph.D. diss., Northwestern University, 1932).

CHAPTER FOUR

IRISH MINERS: FROM THE EMERALD ISLE TO COPPER BUTTE

DAVID M. EMMONS

Nearly four hundred miles directly north of the peaceful valley of Alpine lies the city of Butte, Montana, once the turbulent center of copper mining in the world and, as we are reminded by David Emmons, the most Irish city in the United States. One can hardly imagine two more different communities.

Like the other authors in this section, Emmons investigates the origins and social characteristics of European immigrants in a specific place. But he is especially attentive to questions of working-class formation, including wages, working conditions, and housing among the Butte Irish. He uses census manuscripts, city directories, family histories, folk songs, and other sources to trace patterns of chain migration, previous mining experience, and conduits of information about the mines, as well as family and friendship networks for jobs and housing. He also explores the relationship of the ethnic community to Marcus Daly, that immensely wealthy Irish immigrant who ran the show in Butte.

The physical environment is central to Emmons's history. Although he does not pursue this variable explicitly, it undergirds everything that happened there. When the rich copper veins eventually and inevitably played out, the city was exhausted, too—but that is another story.

The essay that follows is condensed from a chapter in Emmons's prizewinning book, The Butte Irish: Class and Ethnicity in an American Mining Town, 1875–1925 *(1989).*

Nowhere do all of the factors involved in the development of an Irish working class in the West converge as they do in the copper-mining center of Butte, Montana. Butte was the only one of the western mining camps that

50   Chapter Four

became an industrial city. In population, production, and size of work force it had no rivals among mining cities anywhere in the world. All of this is known and often recounted. Less well known is that Butte was one of the most overwhelmingly Irish cities in the United States. By 1900 there were approximately 12,000 immigrant and second-generation Irish in a total Silver Bow County (Butte) population of 47,365. Thus, 25 percent of the residents of Silver Bow County, 2,500 miles from the nearest eastern port, were either Irish-born or the children of Irish-born. For Butte City the numbers were 8,026 Irish in a total population of 30,470, or 26 percent. This is a higher percentage of Irish than in any other American city at the turn of the century.[1]

The men in this total were overwhelmingly miners. In 1894, in the Anaconda Mine alone, there were 1,250 Irish-born miners. Of 5,369 working-class Irishmen in 1900, both first and second generation, 3,589 (two of every three) worked in the deep mines. Approximately 1,200 more worked for the mining companies as hoisting engineers, carpenters, pumpmen, blacksmiths, or in any of a variety of other trades. This increased the percentage of Irish who working in the mines to a remarkable 90 percent of the whole.[2]

It cannot be known with any certainty from where in Ireland the immigrants among these thousands came. In Butte, Irish county distinctions had no meaning to the non-Irish. They knew the Irish as "savages," "harps," "cannibals," "maneaters," or "flannelmouths."

Somewhat imprecise but still useful data on the Irish county of origin can be had by determining Butte's most common Irish surnames and tracing them to the county in which those names are most frequently encountered. This method assumes a close association between name and place, but in the case of Ireland this is a relatively safe assumption.[3]

According to city directories from six representative years (1886, 1892, 1897, 1902, 1908, and 1914), the six most common Irish surnames in Butte were Sullivan, Harrington, Murphy, Kelly, Shea, and O'Neill. With the exception of Kelly, which is ubiquitous in Ireland, the half-dozen are all closely associated with County Cork. When the list is expanded to include such contending surnames as Holland, Crowley, Lynch, and McCarthy, all more commonly encountered in Cork than any other county in Ireland and all in Butte's first fifteen Irish surnames, the dominance of Cork becomes even more obvious. Assuming even a measure of accuracy to the name–place association, County Cork in southwestern Ireland supplied a hugely disproportionate share of Butte's Irish population.[4]

A recently published genealogy gives a more complete picture of this Cork connection. Riobard O'Dwyer traced the family histories of over 6,000 men and women from one parish, Eyeries, in one township, Castletownbere, in the westernmost section of County Cork. Over 1,700 people from that tiny corner of Ireland emigrated to the United States between 1870 and 1915; of that total, 1,138 (707 men and 431 women) made their way to Butte. The predominance of Sullivan among Butte surnames—there were over 1,200 of them in 1908—is more easily understood when it is noted that members of seventy-seven different Sullivan (or O'Sullivan) families left Castletownbere for Butte. As late as 1917 Father Patrick Brosnan, a Butte priest from County Limerick, wrote back to his father that "Everyone here is from Castletownbere. . . ."[5]

Some of these West Corkmen were landless farm laborers whose reasons for emigrating were the same as those of others of that class wherever found in the West of Ireland in the nineteenth century. The pattern of eviction and emigration, as rhythmic as the seasons, was as much a part of West Cork's history as of County Mayo's or County Donegal's. What distinguishes West Cork from Mayo or, indeed, from the rest of Cork, and what explains the dominance of West Corkmen among the Irish of Butte, was the presence of the Puxley family's copper mines at Hungry Hill near Berehaven.

There is no history of those mines, although Daphne du Maurier based her novel *Hungry Hill,* with the Puxley-like Brodericks as the mine-owning family, on an authorized use of family records. The novel is an accurate-enough retelling of the story of these mines to serve present purposes. Local Irish and imported Cornish miners worked Hungry Hill from its establishment during the Napoleonic Wars until competition from Michigan and Montana mines forced it to suspend copper operations and begin the less-profitable and far less labor-extensive mining of tin in the late 1880s. Soon after the conversion to tin, the Puxleys sold the mines to absentee owners in London. The new owners plundered the mines, then closed them, throwing 1,700 men out of work. Some of the Berehaven miners emigrated before the transfer of ownership, but the closure speeded that emigration appreciably and, seeking similar work in the United States, the veterans of Hungry Hill made their way to the copper mines of Michigan's Upper Peninsula or to the even larger mines of Butte.[6]

The other great suppliers of Irish immigration to Butte were those same Michigan copper mines, the anthracite coal fields of Pennsylvania, and the gold and silver quartz mines of California, Nevada, Utah, and Colorado. There was an abundance of Irishmen in each—to the extent that two related myths should be put firmly to rest: first, that the Irish-American experience was exclusively Eastern and urban and, second, that the West was settled by Anglo-Saxon Protestants. The Irish were the most numerous immigrant group in the

52   Chapter Four

four coal-mining counties of Luzerne, Schuylkill, Carbon, and Columbia, Pennsylvania, between 1870 and 1890. They occupied the same position in the copper-mining counties of Houghton and Marquette, Michigan in 1870, and, among European immigrants, in the quartz-mining counties of Lake in Colorado, Storey and White Pine in Nevada, Placer, Sierra, El Dorado, Amador, Calaveras, and Mono in California. In none of the major mining regions of any of those states did the Irish ever rank lower than third among European immigrant groups. Obviously, there was a large pool of experienced Irish mine laborers from which Butte could draw its work force.[7]

Quantitative evidence indicates that most of Butte's Irish miners came from these regions. The timing of their departures and arrivals would indicate that they came because the mines in which they had been working had closed—often taking entire towns down with them. But even when other mines were operating, a considerable number of Irish laborers were always on the move. They were part of a naturally roving work force, a vagabond proletariat that required little in the way of conventionally defined push-and-pull factors to put on the road again. These roaming Irishmen brought to Butte news of events and conditions in the different camps, often speaking before the Irish organizations to which they also belonged. These clubs served as clearing-houses of employment and related information for a significant percentage of the transient Irish work force.[8]

In sum, the Irish-born among Butte's thousands of Irishmen were principally drawn from the idled copper mines of West Cork and from the landless farm laborers and small farmers of the West of Ireland. Many of them, as well as many of the second generation, had made intermediate stops in the industrial cities of the United States, and many more had had some experience in mining either in the coal fields of the U.S. or the hard-rock mines of Michigan and the American West. They moved for the same reasons that prompted the relocation of others of their class. The mines in which they had been working played out, putting them once again on the road. This explains the immigration out of the copper mines of West Cork, but it explains as well much of the migration from Virginia City, Nevada; or from Cripple Creek and Aspen, Colorado; Park City, Utah; Wood River, Idaho; and though they had not been exhausted, the mines of Houghton, Calumet, and Hancock, Michigan. No American industry had a stable work force in the 1880s and 1890s, but a case can be made that the Irishmen of the western mining regions constituted the most surpassingly mobile working class in America. In this sense, Butte built its labor force by being at the end of a sequential if totally unsystematic immigration.[9]

II

The Irish who migrated to Butte came to fill jobs in the copper mines, and it was in this capacity that they formed an immigrant working class. But before Butte's industrialization, the town had had a brief and unpromising placer gold-mining period and a longer and considerably more profitable experience as a silver-mining district. As such it was one of the stops for America's hard-rock men—many of them Irish. Irishmen named the town, the creek from which the county takes its name, and what became its largest mine—the Anaconda. Another Irishman began the first mining company; yet another opened the first saloon. By 1880 there were more than six hundred Irish in Butte City, more than nine hundred in Silver Bow County.[10]

These early arriving Irish would doubtless have attracted a few hundred more, but one of their number, the Irish-born Marcus Daly, clearly influenced the migration of a few thousand. Daly came to Butte in 1876. His career until then was not strikingly different from that of hundreds of other Irish immigrants. Born in Ballyjamesduff in County Cavan in 1841, Daly left Ireland for New York in 1856. After five years in New York, Daly joined his sister in San Francisco and then moved on to Virginia City, Nevada, where he worked in the silver mines of the Comstock. He was a skilled and hardworking miner and he advanced quickly to a supervisory position. Leaving the Comstock, he took a job in Salt Lake City with the Walker Brothers' mining company. In 1876 the Walkers sent him to the struggling silver camp of Butte to investigate the commercial potential of the Alice Mine. Daly was favorably impressed with the property and recommended its purchase. He joined $5,000 of his own money to the Walkers' $25,000 and went to Butte to manage the Walkers' new property. Daly made a great deal of money on the Alice and in 1880 used some of it to buy the Anaconda Mine, another silver producer, from an Irishman, Edward Hickey.[11]

Thus began one of the most remarkable careers in the history of American mining. The story of Butte and Marcus Daly has been told often. It is a good story, revealing much of the history of American mining and finance. Daly converted the Anaconda Mine from silver to copper, bought other mines, built a smelter and a city to support it in nearby Anaconda, Montana, and amassed an enormous fortune from the whole operation. But the point is not this one Irishman's visible and substantial wealth. At issue is his influence on the immigration of thousands of considerably more modest and anonymous Irishmen who helped him get it.

Until the early 1880s the Irish miners drifted into Butte as they had drifted in

54   Chapter Four

and out of other mining camps in the West. As Daly began to develop the Anaconda properties, however, the lure of Butte began to appear brighter because of Daly's presence, and the Irish movement into the city became noticeable. There are some who assign to Daly a very direct role in that Irish immigration. An early source, for example, states that Daly "imported Irish miners," indeed, that he "brought in shiploads of [them] to work his properties." A recent history adds that Daly "even encouraged immigration directly from Ireland itself." That last point exaggerates his role. There is no evidence that Daly actively recruited Irish miners, though such recruitment was not unknown in the Pennsylvania mines. No deals for reduced fares for incoming miners appear to have been struck between Daly and the railroads that served Butte; there is no indication that Daly took out advertisements in Irish newspapers—including those of West Cork—or sent agents into Ireland to blazon Butte's opportunities.[12]

Still, there can be no question that Daly was the single most important reason for the massive Irish immigration to Butte in the 1880s and 1890s. The Montana Writers' Project history of Butte says that thousands of Irish "followed . . . Daly to the town." Father Brosnan made clear why. As he explained in a letter to his father, "Marcus Daly was the man that made Butte an Irish town. . . . He did not care for any man but an Irishman and . . . did not give a job to anyone else." Brosnan overstated the case—but not by much. Irishmen were not used to working for other Irishmen, in the east or the west. Add to that the fact that Daly was also a conspicuous supporter of Irish and Catholic "causes," and the opportunity to work for the "boss Irishman" as Daly came to be known, was not one many Irishmen were likely to miss.[13]

III

But even the magic of Daly's Irishness would have been inadequate had the promised job not been a good one, had Butte not been accessible, had there not been satisfactory housing or a strong Irish presence. Moreover, for those Irish who knew nothing of Daly or Butte—and that was probably a good percentage of those outside the mountain West—Butte's advantages would have to be publicized. Fortunately, Daly had powerful allies in promoting Butte, and the city's job opportunities compared well with those available anywhere else in America.

Ironically, Butte's rapid industrialization created a problem for the early promoters eager to tell the story of the American West to prospective immigrants. The image of the West, including Montana, was of a pastoral and agricultural alternative to the less-lovely aspects of the East. Butte—the name fit the place, short, squat, and hard—did some considerable violence to the image. It was, by all accounts, one of America's ugliest cities. Father Brosnan wrote to his mother that "there is not a tree nor a shrub nor a blade of grass up here but all the wealth is underground." This in 1917, forty years after Daly had begun the industrial mining of copper. Gertrude Atherton, in one of her Butte novels, wrote of the "appalling surface barrenness of the place," "the sulphur and arsenic fumes of ore roasted in the open or belching from the smelters." It looked "like a gigantic ship wreck." Clyde Murphy, another Butte novelist, said it resembled "a black and yellow jungle of smelters, roasting ovens, cranes and stacks which breathed out yellow, acrid smoke." Its "recreational" pleasures were equally industrial. By 1905 Butte's red light district was reported to be the second largest in the United States, behind only New Orleans's infamous Corduroy Road. In appearance and population Butte was the antithesis of rural and Protestant America.[14]

This gave pause to even the most sanguine promoters of western settlement. Linus Brockett, for example, wrote in 1882 that Butte was inhabited by a "rougher class," and that "infidel clubs . . . gambling and drinking saloons and brothels, [were] very numerous. . . . The only remedy . . . [was] for moral, and especially Christian people to put down . . . Sabbath-breaking, gambling and drinking." "Christian people," for Brockett, did not include Catholics. He allowed that "the struggle [would] be severe at first" but that the prosperity of the community required that the stable element assert its control. Butte's "stabilization" was nearer completion by 1887 when William Thayer wrote his *Marvels of the New West.* Thayer called Butte "clean, enterprising," (it was certainly that), with "schools, churches, and law-abiding" citizens. Sundays, he went on, were spent in church. But there was a hint that these social amenities were more in the process of becoming than the present circumstance, and more than just a hint that they had not always been the case. "The Anglo-Saxon race finally asserts itself in the mining camp, to control its boisterous elements." Butte was witnessing, Thayer maintained, an application of "Herbert Spencer's theories of Anglo-Saxon superiority." It would soon be a proper place for civilized habitation.[15]

It is doubtful that many Irish were deterred by Brockett's faint praise or by Thayer's references to Anglo-Saxon superiority. Butte's attractions would never fit the image of a paradisiacal West, but earthly paradise was hardly on the Irish mind—particularly if filled with Anglo-Saxon Protestants. What Butte promised was a fair living. There was no disputing that, and no shortage of agents eager to relay the message. The Union Pacific Railroad, completed to Butte by spur line in 1881, spoke of its mines as the "best in the world." Production

56   Chapter Four

values had jumped from $1,200,000 in 1881 to more than $27,000,000 in 1890, providing "employment to more men, at better wages, than those of any other mining camp in the world." Since that wage was the standard for the entire western region—$3.50 per day for underground work—Butte's claim to better wages was based on its mine owners' ability to offer steady employment, not on their willingness to pay more for a day's work. By 1891 the average wage for the 4,800 men working in Butte's mines was $100 per month; by 1899 the Anaconda Company alone paid more wages than all the textile mills of Fall River and Lowell, Massachusetts combined, "more than Kansas pays those who reap its wheat or Louisiana those who pick its cotton." In fact, wages for all classes and trades were high enough that all "can, at least, very soon own a home."[16]

   State and local agencies made similar promises. The state's inspector of mines referred to high monthly wages, as did Montana's delegate to the National Mining Congress held in Helena in 1892. The Butte Chamber of Commerce repeated the claim in 1895. Again, the theme was stability. Butte, said the chamber, was a copper town, not a silver camp. Copper demanded a major capital investment and a stable work force. As a result, although the boom was barely begun, the bust would never come. And the evidence was convincing. By 1895 Butte produced more than one-quarter of the world's copper; its 6,400 miners took home $640,000 every month.[17]

   What made the chamber's promotion so impressive—and so unusual—was its accuracy. When Thomas Edison turned on the Pearl Street Station in 1882, he not only lit up the streets of New York City, he created Butte. Copper was the ideal medium for electricity, and Butte was underlaid with it. By 1887 two of Butte's mines placed first and third in the world in the production of copper; this while the district was still second nationally in silver production. Little wonder that by 1890 Montana led the nation in percentage of total male population employed; by 1900 it was first in the nation in per capita income, reflecting its first place in wages paid. An 1889 study of the nation's 250,000 railroad workers indicated that 155,000 of them made less than $300 per year; only 5,000 made the $1,000 per year that was the average wage among twice that many Butte miners. Nationwide in the 1880s, industrial workers made less than $600 per year, with an average working day of eleven hours.[18]

   Butte's miners made $3.50 for a nine-, later eight-, hour shift. That was double the daily wage of most industrial workers. More to the point, every day was a workday. The Butte Miners' Union, for example, adamantly opposed any Sunday mine closing because many of the men wanted the option of working six or seven shifts a week. They seem also to have had the option of working fifty to fifty-two weeks a year. The censuses of 1900 and 1910 asked each wage earner how many weeks or months he had been idle in the calendar year preceding the census. Eighteen ninety-nine and most of 1909 were relatively prosperous times in Butte, and the data indicate steady employment particularly for the younger men, and the older miners, many of them home owners, seem not to have been laid off but to have taken four to six weeks' vacation time. One Butte Irishman put the matter in a way all Irish could understand: "The average working man," said Dan Lynch, "could get as much in Ireland as in America, outside of Montana." The claim that by 1905 Butte's payroll was the highest per capita in the world—a claim repeated in 1917 by Father Brosnan—was probably true.[19]

And getting there was easy. Between 1881 and 1908, four transcontinental rail lines entered Butte, guaranteeing access from almost every direction and every port of entry. Fares from New York City to Butte remained almost unchanged from the mid-1880s until 1914. An individual traveling "immigrant colonist" class, paid $48.00 for through service to Butte; this was less than the fare charged individual immigrants and considerably less than that charged "regular domestic" traffic. From Chicago or the Twin Cities, the fare to Butte was about $25.00. Few Irish, particularly since they were all but assured of employment upon arrival, could have been priced out of Butte.[20]

The same point can be made regarding housing upon arrival. Marcus Daly had built the Florence Hotel—the Big Ship as it was known—expressly for newly arrived miners. Praised by its managers as "the zenith of service for working men in America," the Florence had a library, gymnasium, billiard room, lobby, reading room, bath rooms, and a "dry"—a change room to miners. It was built near the Anaconda Mine, and the ethnicity of its employees and its residents reflected the preferences of its owner. One of its managers, himself Irish-born, remembered that "all the help were Irish, mostly born in Ireland, many of them spoke Gaelic." Over six hundred men could live in the Big Ship. According to the Census Manuscripts, 202 of the 377 residents in 1900 were first- or second-generation Irish. Other Irish, particularly those from West Cork, stayed at the Mullen House; only slightly smaller than the Florence, it was run by Nonie O'Sullivan Harrington primarily for the miners from her native village in West County Cork. In 1900, 199 of its 276 boarders were Irishmen. Cost for room and board, at all of Butte's "working-class hotels," was about $35.00 per month.[21]

Everything was in place for a large Irish immigration. There were some Butte Irish who discouraged further immigration because it might deflate wages; others who viewed every immigrant as a lost patriot warrior in Ireland's ongoing struggles with Britain; a few who saw the addition of more poor and unsophisticated Irish as a hindrance to the further advance of those Irish who were neither. Generally, however, the story out of Butte was altogether encour-

58   Chapter Four

aging to further Irish immigration, promising preferential treatment for steady jobs at good wages. The population figures reflect how strong that tug was.[22]

Sooner or later a resident immigrant population was itself enough to insure the steady arrival of others of the same group. When that point was reached, and it appears to have been reached in Butte by 1895, letters to Ireland became more important than any other pull. By 1895 the Irish immigration into Butte had become self-sustaining—Irish following Irish. Hugh O'Daly (or Daly), for example, visited other western mining towns but settled on Butte because many of the other towns were insufficiently Irish and/or had no Catholic church. As with O'Daly, the process was initiated by personal correspondence. Butte's Irishness and its employment opportunities—they were rapidly becoming the same thing—had to have been recounted in thousands of letters.[23]

But they were not the only objective sources of information. The repatriation of a Butte Irishman, or the receipt of money from Butte for whatever cause, spoke as persuasively of the prosperity of the town and of the Irish share in that prosperity. There is, of course, irony in some of this. Among the rewards of living in Butte was the opportunity to leave it. O'Daly "had the one idea of returning to Ireland when [he] had a stake." And a miners' song concluded with a

Hurrah for Old Ireland, the land of good miners
The dear little isle I see in my dreams.
I'll go back to Old Ireland to the girl who waits for me;
To hell with your mines and your mining machines.[24]

To hell with them perhaps—but they made possible the exile's return. The *Butte Bystander* estimated that 40 percent of the Irish who came to Butte between 1880 and 1890 went back to Ireland within the decade. Only eight percent of the Germans returned; only 10 percent of the Scandinavians. In fact, the Irish rate rivaled that of the notoriously homesick Italians. The *Bystander's* estimate is considerably higher than the actual percentage of repatriates. O'Dwyer lists only 124 West Corkmen who returned from Butte of the 707 who emigrated, and even this 18 percent figure is greater than that assumed for the Irish nationally. Perhaps what the *Bystander* story reflected was the number of Irishmen who talked about going home.[25]

As important as the number returning was the relatively prosperous condition in which they returned. Almost all of them went back to Ireland with enough money to "settle down," this is, to buy a small farm, or to "return to the home place." John Murphy, to cite only one example, immigrated to Butte, worked the mines for about ten years, returned to his native Cahirkeem, bought two farms, married a local girl, and fathered twelve children. The lesson cannot have been lost on many—either in Butte or Cahirkeem. Neither can that implied by the many Butte Irishmen who returned only for visits. Hugh O'Daly, despite his professed intention to return permanently, instead made six tourist trips to Ireland.[26]

Those trips can only have impressed his countrymen with O'Daly's, as well as Butte's, solvency. Those who sent money made the same point, if not quite as directly. Much of that money was to fund Irish freedom from British rule, but Ireland's needs went beyond the expulsion of Britain. In the late 1870s, the *Irish World,* the leading Irish-American newspaper, was filled with stories of hunger and suffering in the old country. Any response from Butte had three effects: it took some of the edge off the hard times; it convinced a grateful Ireland that Butte's Irish were doing well; and it called attention to Butte as a possible immigrant destination.[27]

The effects were regularly felt. In 1890, John Brondel, Catholic bishop of Montana, returned from a trip to Ireland and reported crop failures throughout the western counties. He instructed the priests in the Montana diocese to take up collections at Mass and send the money to Archbishop Walsh in Dublin. Butte's Ancient Order of Hibernians (AOH) also responded to the economic distress in the West of Ireland in the late 1890s. It sent five hundred dollars in April of 1898; "an entertainment" by the Ladies' Auxiliary of the Hibernians raised $250.00 more "to relieve the suffering." There were also routine requests for aid in the construction or repair of Irish churches. Two hundred and fifty dollars, for example, was sent by the AOH to "Father McFadden for the Cathedral to St. Columbkill" in County Donegal.[28]

IV

Some of Butte's Irish returned to Ireland; more returned money. But the largest share of them brought as much of Ireland as they could to Butte. The Irish, according to one historian, had a "unique reputation for the efforts they made . . . to reunite their families." Here was another immigrant lure. When the men left Ireland, it was with the idea of returning to, or paying for the emigration of the families they had left behind. The Butte newspapers, for example, periodically posted notices warning of emigration restriction laws that could prevent "husbands and fathers already located (in Butte) from sending for their wives and children." There are no data indicating how many Irishmen did, in fact, send for their families. The census manuscripts, however, lists 159 married Irishmen whose wives were not with them in Butte in 1900, 106 in 1910. Wives and children were widely scattered. Con Lowney left a wife

60   Chapter Four

and two children in Hancock, Michigan. This was in 1896 and Lowney had been working in Butte's mines for four years. John McVeigh's situation was similar. Like Lowney, he was a miner and had been in Butte since 1892. His wife and four children, however, were still in Ireland.[29]

There was another element to McVeigh's residency in Butte that was a part of the general Irish immigration. He was preceded to Butte by a brother and a sister, and his own immigration was at their urging. There is no evidence where and with whom he lived in Butte, but the well-established pattern was for the most recent arrival to join those who had already established themselves. Only if the immigrants stayed with their host kin for any length of time could these arrangements be called extended or stem families. Otherwise, they were simply nuclear families helping out—and being helped by the presence, however temporary, of other wage earners. Extended families influenced both the rate of immigration and the destination of the immigrants, but so did nuclear families willing to serve as temporary hosts. On this point the census manuscripts, by listing all occupants and their relationship to the head of the household, tell an important story about the elasticity and durability of the Irish family network. In 1900, 389 Irish wage earners lived with in-laws, siblings, or uncles and/or aunts. In 1910 the figure was 392. It seems reasonable that the overwhelming majority of these migrants came not only to live with their relatives but in response to promises made in advance of their immigration.[30]

Irish emigration, marriage, and family habits insured a large and constant supply of these host kin. The pattern was for only one or two members of large nuclear families to stay in Ireland, marry, and have large families of their own. The siblings of these childbearing Irish either remained celibate or emigrated. One result was that the Irish children of any given generation had an abundance of aunts and uncles or older brothers and sisters, or both, from whom they received news of America and to whom they could go upon their own immigration. If the host kin had married after his or her own immigration, the number of candidates for assisted emigration and later support would have approximately doubled. The census records of 1900 and 1910 reveal literally thousands of examples of the workings of this family based chain migration.[31]

These kinds of family arrangements were commonplace, but there may have been as many who immigrated to Butte in response to friends or more distant relatives whose exact relationship was obscured by a different surname. Here the records of the Butte Irish associations provide useful data. Both the Ancient Order of Hibernians and the Robert Emmet Literary Association had rules requiring that potential new members be known for at least three years by the person proposing them for membership. There may have been some interested Butte Irishmen who had to wait the requisite three years before seeking membership, but there cannot have been many. The records are filled with references like "known for 22 years" or "knew him in the old country." It cannot be shown that knowing someone meant assisting in or even influencing that person's immigration to Butte, but the cumulative weight of the references to previous knowledge together with the tight weave of Irish society offer powerful circumstantial evidence that it did.[32]

V

These, then, were the pulls that brought thousands of Irish and Irish-Americans to the mines of Butte. Few of these thousands arrived as strangers. They were part of a group migration, even when members of the group emigrated at different times. One story had it that when "Pat" wrote to "Mike" he told him, "Don't stop in the United States; come right on out to Butte." Another told of Irish who arrived at the port of New York with signs that said simply "To Butte" pinned to their jackets. There must have been many in the rural areas of the West of Ireland who knew more about Butte than they did about Dublin, and emigration to it was always an option for them. They would probably have known, too, that leaving their homes for Butte would be less disruptive of established cultural patterns than a move across Ireland to Dublin would have been. Pushed out of Ireland, pulled into Butte, they took the path of their friends and kin, establishing, according to one twentieth-century source, a standard, well-travelled route: "Skibereen to Queenstown; Queenstown to Boston; Boston to Butte and the Mountain Con Mine" where Jim Brennan was the foreman and known to favor fellow Irish job applicants.[33]

But the pull was stronger and its sources more diverse than is implied by the Skibereen to Mountain Con story. There was more to the attraction than jobs. There was a palpable Irish presence in Butte, and that presence was known from Waterford through Cork to Donegal. David Brody has argued that "the movement of immigrants into American industry . . . was not random, but—rather—flowed through well-defined networks based on family and village ties." The road from Ireland to Butte provides as telling and persuasive an example of Brody's thesis as can be found anywhere in industrializing America.[34]

NOTES

1. Butte's story was most recently told in Michael Malone's *The Battle for Butte: Mining and Politics on the Northern Frontier* (Seattle: University of Washington Press, 1981), 3–56. Bureau of Census, *Twelfth Census, 1900,* part I, *Population* (Washington, DC: Government

62   Chapter Four

Printing Office, 1901) clxxvi–clxxix, 768, 798, 875; *Thirteenth Census, 1910* (Washington, DC: Government Printing Office, 1911), 592, 594.

2. Bureau of Census, *Manuscript Census. Population Schedules: 1900. Silver Bow County, Montana.* Microfilm copy. Anaconda Copper Mining Company (ACM), "General Office Records," Subject File 522, ACM Papers, Montana Historical Society (MHS). Montana, Bureau of Agriculture, Labor, and Industry, *First Biennial Report. 1913–14* (Helena: Independent Pub. Co., 1914), 206.

3. Wayland Hand, "The Folklore, Customs, and Traditions of the Butte Miner," *California Folklore Quarterly* 5 (1946): 177 n. 64; Hand et al., "Songs of the Butte Miners," *Western Folklore* 9 (1950), 10, 11, 23, 32. On name/place association see Edward McLysaght, *Irish Families: Their Names, Arms, and Origins* (New York: Crown Publishers, 1972), 16–17, 28–37.

4. George Crofutt, *Butte City Directory, 1886* (Butte City: Crofutt, 1886); R.L. Polk, *Butte City Directory, 1891–92, 1897, 1902, 1908, 1914* (St. Paul and Butte: R.L. Polk Pub. Co., 1888–1916). McLysaght, *Irish Families*, passim.

5. Riobard O'Dwyer, *Who Where My Ancestors? A Genealogy of Eyeries Parish. Castletownbere County Cork* (Astoria, IL: Stevens Pub. Co., 1976), passim. A hand count was made of those who went directly or indirectly to Butte. Polk, *City Directory, 1908.* Brosnan to his father, February 18, 1917, Brosnan Letters, copies in possession of Professor Kerby Miller, University of Missouri.

6. Daphne Du Maurier, *Hungry Hill* (1943; reprint, Cambridge: Robert Bentley, 1971), 337, 343, 361; O'Dwyer, *My Ancestors*, vi, vii.

7. Bureau of the Census, *Ninth Census, 1870*, 346–47, 359, 364, 369–70; *Tenth Census, 1880*, 491–92, 512, 520, 527; *Eleventh Census, 1890*, 615–16, 640, 653, 663–64.

8. The quantitative evidence can be found in the author's *The Butte Irish: Class and Ethnicity in an American Mining Town, 1875–1925* (Urbana and Chicago: University of Illinois Press, 1989), 16–17. See also Kerby Miller, *Emigrants and Exiles: Ireland and the Irish Emigration* (New York: Oxford University Press, 1985), 513. The two main Irish clubs in Butte were the Ancient Order of Hibernians and the Robert Emmet Literary Association. The *Minute Books* (hereafter MB) of each contain numerous references to speakers from other mining towns recently arrived in Butte. *Minute Books* in Irish Collection, microfilm copy, University of Montana Library; hereafter IC.

9. On the point of workers transiency see Malone, *Battle for Butte*, 5–8, 57, 58; Ronald C. Brown, *Hard-Rock Miners: The Intermountain West. 1860–1920* (College Station: Texas A & M Press, 1979), 3–7, 10, 161–66; Richard Lingenfelter, *The Hardrock Miners: A History of the Mining Labor Movement in the American West, 1863–1893* (Berkeley: University of California Press, 1974), 3–4; Mark Wyman, *Hardrock Epic: Western Miners and the Industrial Revolution. 1860–1910* (Berkeley: University of California Press, 1979), 58–59, 252–53.

10. Malone, *Battle for Butte*, 3–34. WPA, *Copper Camp: Stories of the World's Greatest Mining Town, Butte, Montana* (New York: Hastings House, 1943), 16–17. Bureau of Census, *Manuscript Census, 1870, 1880;* Bureau of Census, *Tenth Census, 1880, part I, Compendium*, 518.

11. For Daly see Malone, *Battle for Butte*, 6, 17–20. Hugh Daly, *Biography of Marcus*

Daly (Butte: the author, 1934); Isaac Marcosson, *Anaconda* (New York: Dodd, Mead, 1957), 42–45.

12. C.B. Glasscock, *The War of the Copper Kings: Builders of Butte and Wolves of Wall Street* (New York: Gosset and Dunlap, 1935), 74, 104; Malone, *Battle for Butte*, 64.

13. WPA, *Copper Camp*, 245; Brosnan to his father, February 18, 1917, Brosnan Letters. For Daly's Irishness, see Emmons, *Butte Irish*, 19–21, 191, 214.

14. For descriptions of Butte, see WPA, *Conner Camp*, 291; Malone, *Battle for Butte*, 57–64; Brosnan to mother, November 20, 1917, Brosnan Letters; Gertrude Atherton, *Perch of the Devil* (New York: A.L. Burt, 1914), 57; Clyde Murphy, *The Glittering Hill* (Cleveland: World Publishing Co., 1944), 12–13.

15. Linus Brockett, *Our Western Empire or, the West Beyond the Mississippi River* (Philadelphia: Bradley, Garretson & Co., 1882), 1003; William Thayer, *Marvels of the New West* (Norwich, CT: Henry Bill Co., 1888), 341–44, 521, 714.

16. Union Pacific Railroad, *Resources of Montana . . . 1890* (St. Louis: U.P.R.R. Co., 1891) 78–79; idem, *Resources of Montana, 1891* (St. Louis: U.P.R.R. Co., 1892), 47, 51, 54–55. P.A. O'Farrell, *Butte: Its Copper Mines and Copper Kings* (New York: J.A. Rogers, 1899), 8–9.

17. Montana, Mine Inspector, *Report . . . 1889* (Helena: State Publishing Co., 1890), 75; James McKnight, *The Mines of Montana, Prepared for the National Mining Congress* (Helena: C.K. Wells Co., 1892), 21–22; Montana World's Fair Committee, *Montana: Its Progress, Prosperity* . . . (St. Louis: Con. P. Curran Co., 1904), 69–76; Butte Chamber of Commerce, *Resources of Butte: Its Mines and Smelters* (Butte: Intermountain Printers, 1895), 7–10.

18. Marcosson, *Anaconda*, 5, 48–49; WPA, *Copper Camp*, 20; *Engineering and Mining Journal*, January 7, 1888; Malone, *Battle for Butte*, 52–54; E.S. Lee et al., *Population Redistribution and Economic Growth. U.S., 1870–1950, vol. I, Methodological Considerations and Reference Tables* (Philadelphia: American Philosophical Society, 1957), 587, 753; Bureau of the Census, *Twelfth Census, 1900, part 2, Manufactures*, 500, 504, 505; Clarence Long, *Wages and Earnings in the United States, 1860–1890* (Princeton: Princeton University Press, 1960), 121–66; Wyman, *Hardrock Epic*, 35–37; 67–68; Brown, *Hard-Rock Miners*, 102.

19. Con F. Kelley, in U.S., Industrial Commission, *Mining Conditions and Industrial Relations at Butte, Montana*. Senate Document 415. 64th Cong., 1st sess., *Final Report and Testimony*, vol. 4, 1915, 3712. Bureau of Census, *Manuscript Census, 1900* and *1910*. Dan Lynch from AOH, Division 3, MB, July 15, 1907, IC. WPA, *Copper Camp*, 291; Brosnan to father, n.d., 1917, Brosnan Letters.

20. Emory Johnson and Grover Huebner, *Railroad Traffic and Rates*, II ((New York: D. Appleton, 1918), 119, 120, 124; Great Northern Railway, "Harvest Excursions . . . 1888." Great Northern Co., Advertising and Publicity Dept., Magazine and Newspaper Advertisements, 1884–1970. Minnesota Historical Society, St. Paul. Microfilm copy.

21. Daly, *Biography of Marcus Daly*, 7–8; O'Dwyer, *My Ancestors*, 101; O'Daly, *Life*, [35g Bureau of Census, *Manuscript Census, 1900*; the *Butte Bystander* had a story on living and working conditions in which the average monthly cost of room and board was given as $31.35 (March 17, 1894).

64   Chapter Four

22. On immigrants as lost warriors, see Arnold Schrier, *Ireland and the Irish Emigration. 1850–1900* (Minneapolis: University of Minnesota Press, 1958), 59; RELA, MB, October 3, 1907; September 1, 1910. Robert E. Kennedy, *The Irish: Emigration. Marriage and Fertility* (Berkeley: University of California Press, 1973), 23.

23. O'Daly, *Life* [3, 6, 7, 11].

24. Ibid., [6]; Hand et al., "Songs," 32.

25. *Butte Bystander*, December 30, 1893; O'Dwyer, *My Ancestors*, passim; Caroline Golab, *Immigrant Destinations* (Philadelphia: Temple University Press, 1979), 58.

26. O'Dwyer, *My Ancestors*, passim. Murphy's repatriation is found on p. 256. O'Daly, *Life*, [5].

27. Almost any issue of the *Irish World* from 1878 forward contained at least one story of conditions in Ireland. There were some explicit requests for relief money. Local Butte papers also reported on hard times in Ireland. See, for example, the *Butte Bystander*, January 19, 1895, and September 11, 1897.

28. Brondel to the priests of the diocese, December 4, 1890, Brondel Papers, Diocese of Western Montana, Helena; AOH, Div. 1, MB, August 25, 1897; April 13, June 1, July 6, 1898, IC.

29. *Butte Bystander*, February 18, 1893. Bureau of the Census, *Manuscript Census, 1900* and *1910. Butte Bystander*, April 14, 1896.

30. Bureau of Census, *Manuscript Census, 1900* and *1910*; Kennedy, *The Irish*, 13.

31. Kennedy, *The Irish*, Bureau of Census, *Manuscript Census, 1900* and *1910*.

32. AOH, *Constitution, 1886*; AOH, *Ritual and Manual, 1901*; AOH, Membership Ledgers; AOH, Divs. 1 and 3, MB; RELA, MB, IC.

33. Hand, "Folklore," 177. WPA, *Copper Camp*, 173.

34. Brody, "Workers and Work in America: The New Labor History," in *Ordinary People and Everyday Life: Perspectives on the New Social History*, ed. James B. Gardner and George R. Adams (Nashville: American Association for State and Local History, 1983), 147–48.

CHAPTER FIVE

ITALIANS IN SAN FRANCISCO: PATTERNS OF SETTLEMENT

DINO CINEL

Ethnic settlements in great urban centers such as San Francisco reveal patterns considerably more complicated than those of rural communities like Dalesburg or even smaller cities like Butte. San Francisco is famous for its Chinese district, but among European ethnic groups, the city's Italians are best known. One of the reasons why so much is known about them is that they have been studied intensively by Dino Cinel, who is himself an Italian immigrant.

Because San Francisco was ethnically heterogeneous, Cinel emphasizes that the Italian districts were not ghettos—never exclusive—and therefore that statistical comparisons to other ethnic groups—Irish, Germans, French, Chinese, Mexicans, Greeks—are essential if their main enclaves in San Francisco (of which there were three) are to be understood.

Cinel attributes the pattern of residential dispersion among Italians to the availability and cost of housing. Because so many Italian immigrants intended to return to Europe, they were reluctant to spend much money for this purpose. Geography was also a part of it: because San Francisco is cramped on a peninsula, space is at a premium and rents are high.

Although origins in Italy are important in Cinel's larger analysis, they are not treated systematically in the excerpt reprinted here. Readers who seek further development of the author's interpretation, as well as references to sources, should consult Cinel's From Italy to San Francisco: The Immigrant Experience *(1982).*

66   Chapter Five

SETTLEMENTS, NOT GHETTOES

Italians in San Francisco established two major settlements and one minor. The first and by far the largest was in the North Beach–Telegraph Hill area. In the 1850's the hill was first an Irish settlement and later predominantly German. When the Germans and Irish moved out to Bernal Heights and the Mission district, Italians took over. Photographs of Telegraph Hill from the 1860's and 1870's show dense settlements on the western and southern slopes. Italians eventually spread to the adjacent North Beach area, between the hill and the bay. By the mid-1880's the blocks north of Broadway and east of Montgomery Street housed large numbers of Italians.

The other main Italian settlement was in the Mission district. The first pioneers were farmers who had originally settled in the area where City Hall now stands in the early 1850's. As the city expanded and the value of real estate rose, they moved south, most of them to the Mission, and the rest to Noe Valley, the Outer Mission, and Visitacion Valley. The third and smallest settlement was started in the 1870's when some Italians moved to the Old Potrero district. From there, the settlement expanded to Portola and Bayview. The Portola district was predominantly Irish in the 1850's and German in the following decade. When these two groups began to move out, Italians moved in and found housing similar to that of Telegraph Hill. With the mass immigration between the 1890's and 1924, the concentration of Italians in these areas became greater; but no new settlements were created.

Data derived from the federal censuses allow us to assess the geographical distribution of Italians in the city. In 1900 about 13,000 people lived in assembly district 45, bounded by Montgomery and Kearny streets and the bay: half were American-born and half foreign-born. There were fewer than 2,500 Italians in that district, or about 40 percent of the foreign-born in the district and 20 percent of the total Italian population living in San Francisco. Ten years later the same assembly district had 22,000 people, an increase of about 75 percent since 1900. Of that total, 18 percent were native-born-of-native-parents, 32 percent were native-born-of-foreign-parents, and nearly 50 percent were foreign-born. The 6,700 Italians were by far the largest foreign group in the district, making up about 30 percent of the total population and almost 60 percent of the immigrants. There were also 550 French, 450 Germans, almost 400 Irish, smaller groups of Austrians, English, and Norwegians, and 1,300 immigrants of other nationalities. In assembly districts 31, 32, and 33, the Mission district, Italians made up 5 percent of the total population and 15 percent of the total foreign-born. There were about 15,000 foreign-born in assembly district 33: about 20 percent Irish, 25 percent Germans, 18 percent Italians, and the rest from various other national groups.

In 1920, 10,000 Italians lived in assembly district 33, roughly the former 45th district; this was about 40 percent of all Italians in San Francisco. The district also had over 1,000 French, 1,500 Spanish, about 1,200 Mexicans, 900 Germans, and representatives of thirteen other nationalities. Some 25,000 native-born whites—that is, a larger group than the Italians and the other immigrants combined—lived in the same district, and also 7,000 Chinese. In assembly districts 21, 22, and 23—formerly 31, 32, and 33—the Italians made up only 20 percent of the foreign-born population, Irish and Germans being the two largest groups. As these figures indicate, from 1900 to 1920, in all districts where Italians lived, there were also sizable numbers of Americans and immigrants of other nationalities.

Naturalization records of the 1930's, moreover, indicate that, with the exception of the western section of the city, Italians lived in all districts in some measure. About 10 percent of the city's Italians lived in a rather small settlement in the Richmond district. Another 9 percent formed a little enclave in a few blocks of the Mission district, close to the Italian Church of the Immaculate Conception. About 15 percent lived in the southwestern section of the Outer Mission; and about 9 percent in the southeastern section of the Bayview district. Another 15 percent lived in a rather compact settlement in the Old Potrero district, north of Army Street and west of Pennsylvania Avenue.

The remaining 40 percent lived in North Beach, [the core of which was] bounded by Columbus, Chestnut, Montgomery, Greenwich, Sansome, Vallejo, Kearny, and Filbert streets. In it lived as many as 10 percent of the total number of Italians in the city, or about 2,700 people living in 32 blocks. [Altogether, the North Beach settlements consisted] of about 170 blocks contain[ing] slightly over 9,000 Italians, more than one-third of all the city's Italians. . . .

Many contemporaries noted the unusual dispersion of the Italians in San Francisco. In 1913 an Italian from San Francisco commented that "unlike most other Italian colonies in the United States, that of San Francisco does not show a high concentration in one area. Even North Beach, which is popularly known as the Latin Quarter, is hardly an Italian enclave." The same year, Consul Daneo reported that the Italians in San Francisco had not created the exclusively Italian settlements found in New York and Chicago. Simon Lubin, the president of the California Commission on Immigration and Housing, told Governor Hiram Johnson that this was a fortunate condition and should be maintained, since more Italians were expected with the opening of the Panama Canal.

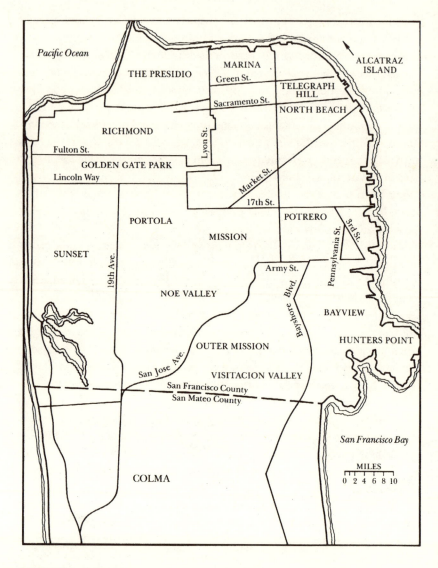

FIGURE 5.1.
Districts of Italian Settlement in San Francisco

The residential pattern of the Italians three to four decades after immigration may usefully be compared with the pattern of other immigrants, especially the Germans and Irish, who in numbers most closely resembled the Italians. The comparison is rather difficult to make; the United States census published residential statistics by ward and nationality only in 1910 and 1920, when many Germans and Irish had already been in San Francisco twenty to forty years. Most Italians were just arriving in those years, and thus were likely to be at the same stage as the Germans and Irish in the 1880's and 1890's. This time lag may be partially corrected by comparing the 1910 and 1920 data for Germans and Irish with the 1950 data for Italians.

In 1910 there were 24,000 Germans and 23,000 Irish in San Francisco. But in no single assembly district was there more than 15 percent of the total Irish population of the city or more than 10 percent of the Germans. We should keep in mind that at the time about 40 percent of all Italians lived in assembly district 35. Compared to the Italians, the Irish and Germans were more evenly distributed throughout the city's districts. Six districts each contained from 8 to 10 percent of the Germans and four others from 3 to 8 percent, with smaller groups elsewhere. As for the Irish, three districts each contained about 13 percent of the total Irish population, and six other districts from 5 to 7 percent each. The Russians, English, French, and other groups were as spread out as the Germans and Irish. A decade later, in no single assembly district was there more than 10 percent of the total Irish or German population of the city. At that time, 45 percent of the San Francisco Italians lived in district 33. Among San Francisco immigrant groups, only Mexicans and Greeks were as highly concentrated as the Italians.

By 1950 most Italians had been in San Francisco as long as the Germans and Irish had been in 1920. Of the 20,000 Italians living in San Francisco in 1950, almost 5,000, or 25 percent, lived in . . . North Beach. . . . Another 3,000, 15 percent, lived in the southern section of the Old Potrero district. And finally, about 2,700, over 13 percent, lived in the Mission.

These population distribution data show that in San Francisco, Italians lived in only a few districts, and that this pattern continued over the years. Immigrants of most other nationalities, especially Irish and Germans, were more evenly distributed in almost all of the city's districts. Moreover, to judge from what studies have shown about Italians in New York, Buffalo, Kansas City, Utica, and Omaha, the San Francisco Italians appear to have lived more intermingled with immigrants of other nationalities and with Americans than Italians in other cities.

Several factors explain the difference between Italians and other immigrants in San Francisco. Italians seem to have settled in some areas rather than others

70   Chapter Five

because of the availability and cost of housing. Virtually no Italian arrived in San Francisco able to make the down payment on a house. Italian sources, mostly the reports of mayors and prefetti, agree that most emigrants left with only what they needed for the trip, and no cash. As already noted, this was not only because they were poor, but also because they refused to sell their land and house before departing, even if they were owners. Newcomers to San Francisco, after spending the first few weeks with relatives or friends, rented a house or an apartment. But rent was high in San Francisco compared with Italy. The Italian Geographic Society reported in 1887 that it was 400 percent higher, and at the turn of the century it was reported to be 300 percent higher. In 1921 the Italian Welfare Agency noted that newcomers were appalled at the high rents and that their main concern was to find the least expensive apartment. Since most immigrants intended to save money and return to Italy as soon as possible, their goal was naturally to spend as little as possible for rent.

North Beach, the section with the lowest rents in town from the 1860's, was where most Italians headed. Carmelo Santoro, for instance, who arrived in 1912, spent a few weeks with relatives on Green Street and then rented a one-room apartment on the same street. As he put it: "I could save more by renting in North Beach than by renting in the Mission or Potrero districts." As late as 1940 the census found that rents in the North Beach tracts where many Italians lived were among the lowest in town. . . .

Rents were low in North Beach because the housing itself was poor. The Telegraph Hill–North Beach area had been developed haphazardly since the 1850's. After the earthquake of 1906 many San Franciscans hoped that the temporary quarters erected after the earthquake would be demolished and new houses built. One wrote: "We will build a new Greece under the skies of California." But new structures were instead built alongside the old. In 1911 Alice Griffith, the secretary of the San Francisco Housing Association, complained that the North Beach housing was so poor as to compare unfavorably with the worst areas of New York and Chicago. There was little new construction in North Beach after 1915; in 1950, of the almost 2,000 dwellings in tract A4, almost 1,600 had been built before 1915. As new immigrants arrived and settled in North Beach, the concentration of Italians there increased. A similar concentration, although on a smaller scale, occurred in the Outer Mission, where housing was poor and rents were traditionally low.

Apparently, almost the only buildings erected in North Beach after 1915 were speculative ventures promoted by Italian developers, most of whom were directors of the newly created Italian-American Bank. Since the demand for apartments was high and space was limited, developers came up with the idea of the Romeo Flats. These were miniature apartments, usually nine per structure, crammed into small lots where city ordinances allowed only two to four apartments. The San Francisco Housing Association denounced what it saw as the exploitation of newly arrived Italians by other Italians. Nothing, however, indicates that the denunciation stopped the developers. When Alice Griffith approached a number of Italians to have them testify in court against developers, she found no support. Most Italians were in San Francisco to save money, and as long as rent was lower in North Beach than elsewhere, immigrants were willing to put up with almost anything. After all, as an old Italian remarked in 1976, "What I got in North Beach was much better than what I had in Italy."

Italian immigrants did not go to North Beach or the Mission solely because of cheap housing. One reason they did not settle in other low-rent districts is suggested by the process of chain migration that brought many Italians to San Francisco. This process sharply limited the number of settlements Italians created in the city. The difference between Italians and other immigrants in the way they reached the city is striking. About 90 percent of the Italians came directly to San Francisco from the same city or village where they were born. This was true of only 30 percent of the Germans, 20 percent of the Russians, and 40 percent of the Irish. Moreover, 95 percent of the San Francisco Italians came there directly from Italy, and only 5 percent had lived somewhere else in the United States before settling in San Francisco. In contrast, 38 percent of the British, 20 percent of the Irish, 27 percent of the Russians, and 41 percent of the Scandinavians reached San Francisco after living in other parts of the United States or in other countries.

Non-Italians, then, were far more likely than Italians to have migrated, before reaching the United States, either within their own country or in other countries, and to have moved within the United States before reaching San Francisco. Italians, coming directly from their native place to San Francisco, were perhaps more likely than other immigrants to be following relatives or friends, and not arriving on their own. Non-Italians, because of migration prior to coming to San Francisco, may have had less need of the protection of compatriots in America.

That Italians went directly from their birthplace to San Francisco, in a process of chain migration, is an enduring theme in contemporary accounts. In 1868 Consul Cerruti noted that "almost all newcomers have someone who has sent for them and often advanced the money for the ticket." The point was repeated in 1887 in the survey of the Italian Geographic Society. And in 1903 *L'Italia* explained a sudden increase in immigration (which will be discussed later) by many letters that were sent from San Francisco to Italy, "not infrequently with money." When immigrants reached San Francisco they lived with

72   Chapter Five

relatives for a time; it was only natural that they settled in the same neighborhood when they took a place of their own.

Part of the explanation why Italians did not disperse throughout the city as
quickly as other immigrants is found in the way they came to San Francisco, as
well as in their goals in coming. Because Italian immigrants did not intend, at
least at first, to stay in America, most of them secured only temporary employment, usually seasonal, through well-established compatriots who mediated
between the new arrivals and American society. Under these circumstances,
Italians were under no compulsion to move out of their settlements. On the
contrary, as an 1887 consular report noted: "Most newcomers settle in North
Beach, where some blocks are inhabited almost entirely by Italians. Since most
immigrants intend to return, North Beach provides a home-away-from-home
during the exigencies of temporary emigration."

Discrimination against Italians undoubtedly had an impact on the creation
of segregated neighborhoods. A 1920 University of California master's thesis
gives a hint of popular attitudes: "The idea that Italian immigrants came from
an inferior race is not merely a matter of popular opinion; but one which has
received substantial corroboration from careful investigation." Discrimination
against Italian laborers reached its peak between 1900 and 1915. By 1900 the
city's unions claimed 40,000 members, an impressive organization, the sympathy of city authorities, and a good press. The unions felt threatened, however,
by the arrival of thousands of Italians, whom the Employers' Association could
and did use to break strikes and keep down wages. The Italians were denied
admission to the unions, and were the victims of a discrimination that some
likened to the persecution of the Chinese by the Workingmen's Party in the
1870's. It is likely that by the time most Italians experienced any discrimination
in America they had already made their choice of where to live. Thus discrimination probably played a larger role in the evolution of the Italian settlements
than in their original formation. That is, immigrants who became aware of
discrimination were less likely to move out of the settlement.

Finally, there are some indications that the way Italians regarded American
society became a conservative impulse that held the settlements together.
Many Italians disparaged the quality of life in American society and urged
resistance to assimilation. In 1902, for instance, the issue of Americanization
was debated among San Francisco Italians for several months. Surrounding
this debate was the larger concern of whether emigration to San Francisco
should be discouraged or not. One local newspaper, *L'Italia,* argued against
Americanization, the other, *La Voce del Popolo,* argued in favor. *L'Italia* maintained that American values were not suited to the Italian temperament, and

that Italians therefore had to preserve their traditions by living with other Italians. Of course, the refusal to mix with American society might have been an expression of resentment owing to a failure to achieve material success. But regardless of origin, such perceptions of America might have played an important role.

In the old country, life had been patterned by tradition and by the belief that the cycle of nature was sacred and untouchable. Change, on the other hand, seemed to be almost sacred in the New World. It was the key to personal advancement. Many immigrants, caught between the old and the new, perhaps sensed in the challenge of the new a kind of immoral seduction, and felt a moral obligation to preserve the old way of life. The close Italian settlements made this task easier. As Consul Francesco Lambertenghi reported: "Only in North Beach do Italians feel completely at home. On Sunday afternoons the Italians who live in other areas of town get together there: it is a way of recreating the security of the Italian village they have left behind."

The best explanation of why the Italian settlement in San Francisco was less concentrated than in other cities lies in the geographical location of the city. San Francisco, surrounded by water on three sides, simply had insufficient space for new immigrant groups. The proximity of different nationalities in San Francisco forced them to compromise with one another more readily than the groups in other cities, who interacted less. Moreover, the predominance of northern Italians that distinguished San Francisco from other cities probably made a difference. Americans loved to point out that northerners were especially adaptable to American society." As Edna Dessery put it: "Northerners are capable of great progress in the social organization of a modern society." Notwithstanding the discredited racial assumptions of her study, northerners were indeed likely to have had more exposure than southerners to the urban industrial world; this would have happened either in the province of Genoa or along the coast between Livorno and Pisa. Finally, internal migration was more common in the north of Italy than in the south, which might in part explain why northerners were more adventurous in moving out of their ethnic enclaves.

The process by which Italians reached San Francisco, the relatively high concentration of Italians in some areas of the city, and the stability of their settlements over a long period of time resulted in a preservation of old-world customs and a resistance to dispersion that were clearly stronger among Italians than among other immigrants. At the same time, San Francisco Italians were more exposed to the pressures of the host society, and thus subject to a faster pace of change, than Italians of other cities. A San Francisco Italian wrote in

74   Chapter Five

1913: "The dispersion of the Italians throughout the city is the major reason why this is a better colony than any other Italian colony in the United States. Dispersion brought about assimilation, modernization of the less desirable traits Italians brought from the Old World, and a healthy competition between immigrants of different nationalities."

CHAPTER SIX

THE ORIGINS OF AN ETHNIC MIDDLE CLASS: THE JEWS OF PORTLAND IN THE NINETEENTH CENTURY

WILLIAM TOLL

The following article shifts our attention from settlement patterns to the development of institutions designed to maintain and strengthen the ethnic community. This study of the Jews in Portland suggests that they had the advantages that accompany high socioeconomic status, compared to most other immigrant groups. Distinctive in religion and culture, the Jews of Portland, unlike the Italians of San Francisco, rarely thought of returning to Europe except for brief visits.

The author, William Toll, a specialist in the social history of Jews in America, first demonstrates the middle-class character of the Portland community. Merchants, manufacturers, and bankers often rose from humble origins to positions of leadership in both the ethnic community and the city, which suggests that success depended on good relations and frequent interaction with non-Jewish people in Portland and the surrounding region.

At the same time, the Jews in Portland, as in other cities, were a distinctive culture group, eager to sustain their special identity. This meant the creation of an effective network of voluntary organizations—cemetery associations, benevolence societies, synagogues, and lodges.

A particular strength of the article is the emphasis Toll places on the role of women in the formation of families and in efforts to develop and strengthen the Jewish community. This essay is a revision and condensation of two chapters in the author's book, The Making of an Ethnic Middle Class: Portland Jewry over Four Generations *(1982).*

Between 1855 and 1900, Jewish immigrants from various German states traveled thousands of miles across land and sea to the Pacific Northwest, where

76   Chapter Six

they created complex ethnic communities in cities such as Portland, Oregon. A steadily growing commercial city that exported timber, wheat, and meat, Portland also imported manufactured good for distribution throughout the region, and it needed people to provide a variety of mercantile and artisanal services. Jewish men were eager to satisfy the need, and at first they came as bachelors starting careers as merchants. Most women came a little later to become wives and mothers, and sought to create a communal life for their growing families. Jewish men and women worked together, and sometimes separately, to sustain their community and to forge links between it and the broader society. Through their voluntary associations—burial societies, synagogues, benevolent associations, lodges, and social clubs—they gave coherence to their lives.[1]

The evolution of an ethnic community in what was then a remote region of the United States can be studied within several contexts. Although most of Portland's Jews embraced the opportunities offered by the city, they also maintained links with their families of origin and with similar bourgeois enclaves in hundreds of other dynamic new centers of industrial capitalism in the United States.[2] They were on the extreme western edge of a movement from the insular villages of central Europe to the new centers of cosmopolitan exchange and industrial production. Moreover, Jews were also entering an American society whose norms for family relations and gender roles were changing rapidly. Young Jewish women maturing in late nineteenth-century Portland could easily compare their options with those of middle-class gentile women and participate in a quiet gender revolution.[3] The Jewish community that emerged by 1900 in Portland thus rested on an expanding business network, stable families, and an array of formal institutions that were fully integrated into the city's middle class.

PIONEER MERCHANTS AND ARTISANS

The first Jewish men to arrive in Portland, as in so many other American cities between 1830 and 1860, emigrated from the several German states, primarily Bavaria, Hesse, and Baden. Although Bavaria sent relatively few immigrants to the United States during those decades, many Jews left because of restrictions placed on them by town governments.[4] Most German states maintained order by granting autonomy for most economic and social policies to municipal authorities. Masters of local guilds exercised power by controlling town councils, which often restricted competition by limiting the rights of permanent domicile, suffrage, and even marriage.[5] Jews, Gypsies, and journeymen were considered to be interlopers and therefore were carefully regulated.

After 1830 economic competition combined with legal proscriptions to stimulate Jewish emigration. Most Jews settled in cities such as Munich and Frankfurt, but some of the more adventurous young men continued the trek to England or America.[6]

Jewish merchants were prominent among the earliest and most important founders of Portland. Bernard Goldsmith, an early mayor of the city, is an outstanding example. His experience typified the growing stream of young Jewish youths who left a peasant economy to find new opportunities in a broader, trading world. Goldsmith recalled in the 1880s that his father, a successful small-town merchant, paid for his passage to America and gave him several hundred dollars to begin a business in America. "The inducement to come over was this," he remembered, "I was the oldest of eight boys and I did not like things over there. In 1848 there was a general revolution and dissatisfaction . . . and I just made up my mind that I would come here, that was all."[7] Thus he emigrated, not to escape poverty, but because his chances seemed limited in Bavaria.

In Portland as in other western commercial centers in the 1850s, young peddlers made the town their base as they traded through a sparsely settled region that lacked sedentary merchants.[8] Like the farmers whom they served, the Jewish peddlers created a "chain of migration" through which contact was maintained with native villages in Europe. Continued emigration was thereby encouraged.[9] By 1860 a Jewish merchandising network of brothers and cousins stretched all along the Pacific slope.

Many of these young men were, in effect, serving a kind of retail apprenticeship in the rural areas. When they reached their mid-thirties, they would often decide to try their luck in Portland. There they established businesses, enlarged their families, and sustained lengthy mercantile careers. Among them were Aaron Meier and Sigmund Frank, who went on to establish what was to become the largest department store in the Pacific Northwest. Another was Julius Durkheimer, who served eastern Oregon in the late 1880s. When he opened new stores in Prairie City in 1887 and Canyon City in 1888, he summoned his three bachelor brothers from their clerking jobs in Portland to assist in the rural stores. By 1896, when Durkheimer and his family returned to Portland, he had accumulated enough capital to buy one-third partnership in the city's largest wholesale grocery firm. Meanwhile his brothers stayed in eastern Oregon for many more years.[10]

Although merchants like Durkheimer often served as the nuclei for the formation of ethnic enclaves, they inevitably endured the difficulties common to their occupation, including the over-extension of credit, the termination of partnerships, and bankruptcy. For example, in the early 1880s Ben Selling, a

78   Chapter Six

prominent Portland general merchant, also operated a store in Prineville with Gus Winckler, who managed operations. Winckler had extended more than $25,000 in credit and his reports to Selling were infrequent. In spring 1883, Selling cut off supplies and berated Winckler for failing to make collections. "In the Spring you say you will collect in the summer. In the summer you say in the Fall, in the Fall the Spring," Selling concluded. "Do you wonder that I am disappointed?" In August 1883, Selling sold his Prineville store at a slight profit to two Jewish merchants who operated a general store in Albany, Oregon. His partnership with Winckler was finally dissolved in a lawsuit.[11]

Artisans were also important in the formation of Jewish communities. Beginning as tailors or tinsmiths, they often built their traditional craft skills into manufacturing firms. The technology they used required only limited capitalization, and even though most such firms remained small, they could still become the foundation for successful industrial development.

Most Jewish manufacturing in Portland in the 1880s was short-lived. None of the firms that existed in 1870 was listed in the manuscript census of manufacturers in 1880. In that year the largest capital investment among the Portland Jewish manufacturers—$70,000—was made by Levi Hexter and Levi May, sheet metal and stove manufacturers. The firm with the largest annual payroll—$14,000—was Fishel and Roberts, clothing manufacturers. In business since 1871, they employed 21 men and five woman over the age of 16. By 1882, however, Charles Fishel had dissolved the partnership and left the city. Other firms were then organized to satisfy the demand for skilled tailors, but a Jewish clothing industry did not develop until the 1920s.

Portland Jews played only minor roles in banking, though several were listed in the 1890 city directory as capitalists who invested in real estate and lent money at interest. Among them was Philip Wasserman, who after a successful career in trade and many speculative ventures with his friend Bernard Goldsmith, helped organize the First National Bank of Portland. By 1870 he had sold out to the Corbett and Failing interests, who had far more capital. Benjamin I. Cohen, after a career in law, became president of the Portland Trust Company in the 1890s. Though he had a reputation as a "tight-fisted banker," he remained in the shadow of the leading gentile banks. Bernard Goldsmith invested—and lost—several hundred thousand dollars constructing locks to bypass the falls of the Willamette River at Oregon City in the early 1870s, and then became the regional agent of the German Loan Association of California. Goldsmith also speculated in mining claims and stock with gentile friends, along with other prominent members of the Jewish community, including Joseph Simon, who was elected to the United States Senate in 1898. But Sol Hirsch, a partner in the largest wholesale merchandising business in the Pacific

Northwest, voiced the mood of most Jewish investors when he confided to a gentile friend, "I am such a thorough coward in everything which looks like share speculation that I naturally move very slow."[12]

SOME DEMOGRAPHIC CHARACTERISTICS

Merchants, manufacturers, and bankers thus provided a stable base for a slowly growing but highly mobile Jewish community in Portland. The 1860 census manuscript data show that 120 Jews, almost half of whom were unmarried young men, lived in Portland. But of the 60 men for whom occupations are listed in the census of 1860, only 23 percent persisted to 1870. This rate is about average for young, unmarried men in other cities and towns that have been studied for such information.

New immigration boosted the Jewish population to 429 in 1870. Among the newcomers, for example, were the spouses of Bernard Goldsmith and Philip Wasserman. Both men had returned to Germany for wives and then started families in Portland. In 1870 Jews constituted 4.2 percent of the city's population, a proportion somewhat lower than the seven percent registered in San Francisco at that time. Furthermore, the social structure of the Portland community had changed dramatically: only ten percent were single males residing in rooming houses, compared to almost fifty percent in 1860. The rest were either married or residing with Jewish families.

During the 1870s, a decade of depression and diminished immigration, the Jewish community grew only by about 60 persons to 490, and the proportion of Jews in the city fell to about three percent. However, the number of Jewish women over sixteen years of age increased more than the number of men, which suggests that the community had come to consist mostly of stable families.

In the 1880s, as Jewish wholesaling operations expanded, many young men came to town to serve as clerks, as traveling agents for San Francisco businesses, or as tailors, express men, and carpenters for the town's growing middle class. Most of those who remained eventually married, and by 1900 the ratio of males to females among German Jews and their adult children was virtually even.

FAMILY AND THE EROSION OF PATRIARCHY

Jewish families, like businesses, mixed traditional contacts with patterns from the new American social environment. Scholars often characterize traditional Jewish families as patriarchal, which implies not only that property is passed from father to son, but that men make the major decisions linking the family to the outside world. Of course, there was substantial variation in family organization within the group of Jewish immigrant families. They displayed many differences in the timing of family formation, in family size and household structure, and in the institutions they created, some of which were highly susceptible to erosion. Although the term "patriarchy" helps us understand the initial organization of German Jewish families, women and their daughters in Portland seem to have shown considerable independence. Their ability to organize for mutual assistance and to create independent social lives for themselves was similar to that displayed by Jewish women in Germany's largest cities, but greater than in Oregon's rural areas.

The reinforcement of a patriarchal tradition can be seen most easily in family structure and emerging gender roles. Although men in Bavaria, for example, generally married women two to four years younger than themselves, almost two-thirds of Portland's German Jewish men in 1880 chose wives seven to ten years younger. Marrying markedly younger women suggests that men who expected to be financially secure before marriage found that migration had separated them from the cohort of women from which they would ordinarily have chosen wives. Younger women, in turn, could find men in Portland who could promise them a reasonable prospect of financial security, even though it meant living thousands of miles away from their mothers and sisters in Germany.[13]

Differences in age and experience reinforced the authority of the husband and implied that the wife would not be expected to exercise independent judgment in financial and most other matters. The demands of life on the urban frontier, however, required young women to assume communal responsibilities that the demographic profile of families fails to reveal.

Nevertheless, the pattern of youthful marriage to older men continued after the pioneering era. The abolition of marriage restrictions in conservative Bavaria in 1870, like the achievement of a fairly even sex ratio among German Jews in America, had only a limited effect on marriage patterns. In 1900 most women in Germany did not marry until their mid-twenties, when they selected men about three years older than themselves. At the same time in Portland, only 24 percent of American-born Jewish women under the age of forty had married when they were in their teens; but among German-born Jewish women over the age of forty, 40 percent had been teenaged brides. The majority in both groups, however, married men at least seven years older than themselves, which suggests that younger women continued to see the importance of selecting a spouse who could provide an established home. Moreover, they lived in a social setting in which men who sought wives still would be in their late twenties and early thirties.

The patriarchal family, however, faced dramatic erosion in Portland because American-born Jewish women by 1900 had substantially lower fertility rates than their German-born mothers. Studying the number of children born to 133 Jewish women in Portland reveals startling contrasts: among the German-born women who were 30 to 39 years of age, 33.3 percent had given birth to four or more children, compared to only 5.5 percent of the American-born. Among the women who were forty years of age or older, 45.7 percent of the German-born women had given birth to six or more children, compared to only 5.1 percent of the American-born. Thus the fertility rate of the American-born Jewish women of Portland was much closer to the rate for American women generally (which in 1900 was 3.5 live births per married white woman) than it was to German-born Jewish women. These data demonstrate that migration to an American city did not induce German-born women to limit family size. But their American-born daughters married several years later than had their mothers, and substituted human agency for nature's dictates in determining pregnancy and family size.[14]

The dramatic decrease in fertility among Jewish women in Portland has no precise explanation, although similar declines occurred in the late nineteenth-century in cities in Germany as well as in the United States.[15] Their behaviors probably stemmed from a pattern of social emulation: they adapted to the middle-class norms that they observed among their gentile acquaintances. Declining fertility rates, it seemed, were associated with increases in wealth and sophistication. Thus, the tendency to postpone marriage and the practice of birth control seem to suggest that the successful sons and daughters of the pioneers were emerging as a Jewish elite that paralleled the banking and commercial elite among the gentiles.

MALE SOCIAL ORGANIZATIONS

The first voluntary organizations founded by Portland's Jewish men illustrate how fragments of an ethnic tradition fostered social stability in America. Their first ethnic institution, founded sometime in the 1850s, was the Mt. Sinai Cemetery Association. This concern for ritual burial reflected, first, a desire to rejuvenate loyalties that extended beyond the immediate family, and second, high death rates from disease and accidents. Such a society organized to provide proper rituals for the burial of the dead could be formed easily because most of the men emigrated from villages in southern Germany where Jewish

82   Chapter Six

communities had no elaborate ritual traditions. The Jewish men of Portland simply joined together in a burial society to show respect for the faith of their ancestors.

The formation of synagogues was more complex. The first was Congregation Beth Israel, established in 1858. The founders, mostly in their early thirties, sought moral sanction for their passage into a new stage in the life cycle: they wished to remain in Portland and raise families. In 1862, when Beth Israel was only four years old, it absorbed the Mt. Sinai Cemetery Association and erected a building for $4,500, a substantial sum at that time. It also started a school, partly because Portland still lacked a public school system. Organized by a well-educated Bohemian Jew who made his living as a shoemaker, the school offered instruction in both the German and Hebrew languages.

Congregation Beth Israel was not troubled by disputes over religious doctrine, probably because no members had received higher education in Germany and therefore had no desire to argue over abstract questions. Instead, they vacillated over questions of ritual.[16] For example, in 1865, the congregation affiliated with the Board of Delegates of American Israelites, which was led by the well-known reformer Isaac Mayer Wise. But at the same time Beth Israel continued to follow traditional or orthodox ritual. Then, in 1872, it hired Rabbi Mayer May, a twenty-four-year-old Bavarian who sought to impose the ideas and practices of the German-Jewish reform movement. This led to seven contentious years marked by frequent disputes with board members who stoutly resisted changes in ritual. After a violent confrontation with an officer of the congregation, May was finally forced to resign as rabbi and to accept a cash settlement of $1,200.

Beth Israel then hired as its rabbi Jacob Bloch, a young biblical scholar who showed no desire for reform. The congregation retained its membership in the reformed association, now renamed as the Union of American Hebrew Congregations, but Sabbath services were poorly attended and membership failed to grow. Finally, in 1895, Beth Israel adopted the reformist *Union Prayer Book*, not in response to the leadership of Rabbi Bloch, but to that of young laymen in the congregation. Five years later they quietly forced Bloch into retirement even though he was only in his late fifties. They then turned enthusiastically to Stephen Wise, a dynamic young preacher from New York. Trained in the United States, Wise ably led the congregation into the twentieth century and effectively represented its young members to the liberal Protestant clergy who counseled Portland's business elite.

In 1868 Jews in Portland founded a second congregation, Ahavai Shalom. Its members were immigrants from Prussia and from western Poland, then a part of the Russian Empire. By 1870, almost 30 percent of Jewish males in Portland were of Prussian birth and by 1880 they equaled the number of Jews born in southern Germany. Uncomfortable among the southern Germans, they felt the need to form a separate congregation. The membership of Congregation Ahavai Shalom included many Polish Jews and its long-term rabbi and cantor were both from Poland. Neither the congregation nor its leaders showed any inclination toward Reform Judaism.

The organization of the First Hebrew Benevolent Association was another manifestation of the sense of collective responsibility felt by Portland's Jewish men, especially merchants and artisans. Its members were required to contribute one dollar each month to a fund that was used for both commercial loans and the relief of private and communal emergencies. Jews thus used their communally generated capital to initiate or expand their businesses. In other cities, Poles, Italians, and Serbs used funds collected in the same way to build homes, but not to start businesses. As immigrant peasants, they turned their desire for land into the ownership of real estate.

By 1884 the 103 members of the benevolent association had accumulated more than $17,000, most of which was lent at interest. Taking advantage of the lack of banks on the frontier, the association made its largest loans ($5000) to non-Jews who were willing to pay 10 percent interest for two or three years. Smaller amounts were loaned at slightly lower rates to association members to finance short-term partnerships. Accrued interest, supplemented by some incoming dues, was dispensed as charity to individual Jews in need. The association reimbursed physicians, nurses, and hospitals for the care of the indigent sick, and synagogues were paid to bury the dead. Other charities included paying the room and board expenses of individual applicants, as well as transportation costs of persons who sought work in other cities. By 1895 the association had negotiated more than $23,000 in active loans, most of which ranged from $25 to $100; terms were from one day to six months. Some loans were to non-members (often Jews of eastern European origin) at no interest. In this way the association provided male members of the community a foundation for economic independence that was shielded from public scrutiny. At the same time, it sought to save all but the most desperate persons from public asylums.

Fraternal lodges were yet another variety of voluntary association formed to provide mutual-benefit services and opportunities for social interaction. The most important were the local chapters of the Order of B'nai B'rith, which was a national organization founded in New York in 1843 by German-Jewish immigrants familiar with the rituals and philosophies of Masonry. B'nai B'rith lodges functioned like the several Masonic and related orders found in most expanding American cities in the mid-19th century. The lodge provided a

84   Chapter Six

meeting ground for young shopkeepers and clerks in search of both sociability and mutual-benefit insurance. Just as the Masons accepted white males of most religions (including Jews), so the B'nai B'rith lodges accepted Jews of all synagogues. Although the members of gentile fraternal lodges often consisted of the local mercantile and professional elite,[17] the B'nai B'rith, at least in its early stages, did not serve a socially selective function within the ethnic community. Because most young Jewish men were clerks, small merchants, or artisans, the lodges served to integrate young men socially rather than to create boundaries within the ethnic community.

The first B'nai B'rith lodge in Portland (Oregon Lodge 65) was founded in 1866, only nine years after the first one on the Pacific Coast had been organized in San Francisco. Its members came from Bavaria, Prussia, and Poland, which implies that differences in places of origin were not significant, as they were for the synagogues.

The age distribution of its members reveals contrasts with the national pattern. Nationally, most Jewish lodges were founded by men in their late twenties and early thirties. Such men were beginning small sedentary businesses, starting families, and seeking stable social connections and insurance services commensurate with their householder status. But for the twenty-seven members of the Portland lodge whose names are recorded in the 1880 federal manuscript census, the mean age was forty-two. With two exceptions (both recent inductees in their twenties), all were married; all but five owned their own businesses. One may presume that they expected to remain in Portland and wanted health and death benefits for their families. It appears that younger men may have been reluctant to join a lodge with so many middle-aged members, and then watch their premiums paid out in benefits to older men.

In 1879 a second B'nai B'rith lodge, North Pacific Lodge 314, was organized in Portland. According to the 1880 manuscript census, the mean age of its thirty members was thirty-two years, significantly lower than that registered for Lodge 65. Members in their twenties were mostly clerks, traveling agents, or skilled craftsmen (mostly tailors); those in their early thirties were retail merchants. Age was also a correlate of place of birth among these men. Compared to the members of Lodge 65, all of whom were European-born, about one-third of Lodge 314 members were American-born. Of the European-born members of Lodge 314, only one came from Bavaria and seven were born in Prussia. Both groups, presumably the products of different cultural influences, found common ground in Lodge 314. There they shared a common stage in the life cycle and found other men who occupied the same occupational niche in the Jewish mercantile network.

WOMEN'S ORGANIZATIONS

The Jewish women of Portland also created institutions to meet their needs as wives and mothers. In May 1874, about forty married women organized the First Hebrew Ladies Benevolent Society "to administer relief to the poor, the needy, the sick, and to prepare the dead for interment" among "ladies of the Jewish faith." They expected to care for one another as they had in the villages of central Europe. Because their husbands were often away on merchandising trips and their mothers and sisters were thousands of miles away in Europe, they came to rely on one another for many social services.

The Ladies Benevolent Society regularized the visitation of sick women and the care of their children by empowering the vice president to recruit members for these tasks. When members could not remain with sick women over night, the society raised funds to pay for nurses. They also paid doctors for home visits and hospitals for the treatment of female patients. The society also supported several destitute women whose husbands had died or deserted them, and provided travel funds for wives and children who wanted to rejoin husbands in distant cities. Some women also sought privately to enable poor families to fulfill ritual obligations in their homes.

At first the society was supervised by men, possibly because so many members were much younger than their husbands. For example, the original constitution specified that the president and secretary of the organization could be men, and they were authorized jointly to dispense charity without the consent of the all-female board of directors. Such was the case until 1879, when Cecilia Friedlander became secretary. She was then thirty-one years old, the mother of one child, and the wife of a jeweler whose safe could hold the society's treasury. In 1884, following the resignation of the male president, Emma Goldsmith (Bernard Goldsmith's forty-two-year-old wife) succeeded to the office. She was soon joined by her next-door neighbor and close friend, Sophia Wasserman, who assumed the office of treasurer. A woman of exceptional managerial skills, Goldsmith gave the society strong leadership.[18] Stressing the need for recruitment, she saw the society grow from 43 members in 1875 to 177 in 1893. It never again turned to men for its officers.

The society also helped women confront the most serious form of continual grief—the death of their children. Infant mortality rates were still high in the late nineteenth century. Requests for burial in the Beth Israel cemetery reveal that many more children than adults were interred. For example, from August 1872 to December 1873, nine of eleven requests were for the burial of children. Through the mid-1880s, children less than ten years of age accounted for nearly

86   Chapter Six

43 percent of the total, and infants under one almost 25 percent. By the early 1890s, however, the proportion of the deceased who were children under ten years of age declined to 18 percent. Later in the decade the rate fell to about 8 percent, a trend that reflected both better health care and smaller families.

By 1900 the leaders of the society had aged, and they were reluctant to alter their ideas about welfare. Earlier, in the 1880s, they had responded to the growth and changing character of the Jewish community by including a few women of eastern European origin, some of whom filed frequent requests for aid for poor Jewish families in need of food, clothing, and fuel. In 1903 the society expanded the scope of its charities slightly by donating $100 for the relief of victims of the Russian pogrom in Kishinev, the capital of Moldavia, and in 1906 they gave $500 to Jews hurt in the San Francisco earthquake. But these donations were part of a city-wide fund-raising effort led by the men of the B'nai B'rith, the First Hebrew Benevolent Association, and Temple Beth Israel. In 1903 Rabbi Stephen Wise prodded the society into joining the National Conference of Jewish Charities, but it refused to amend its constitution to allow donations to non-Jewish causes. Thus it appears that to most ladies of the Benevolent Society, philanthropy did not transcend the piecemeal charity typical of European villages, despite their long residence in the United States.

CLUBS FOR THE MERCANTILE ELITE

By 1891 Jewish men in Portland, mostly sons of the pioneer merchants, organized two new societies: a third B'nai B'rith lodge (No. 416) and a city club called Concordia. Both reflected the values of a comfortable social elite.

For seventy-seven members of Lodge 416, the mean age at induction was thirty-two during its first five years. Members in their twenties were clerks, bookkeepers, and traveling agents; more important, they were the sons of the established mercantile elite such as the Meier, Frank, and Fleischner families. Members in their thirties included physicians, attorneys, and the U.S. customs inspector of Portland. Tailors, peddlers, or expressmen were not included. It was the first Jewish lodge in Portland to have more than 10 percent of its members in the professions.

At first the members of Lodge 416 performed the traditional functions such as visiting the sick and accepting fraternal visits from officers of the older lodges. But membership and attendance at meetings lagged until the social chairman (who was the manager of Portland's exclusive Marquam Opera House) introduced entertainments or performances of various kinds into the meetings. For example, the lodge's meeting of October 1893 included vocal and instrumental solos by wives and female friends of members. By contemporary feminist standards, such operatic arias, romantic ballads, and piano and violin recitations may have symbolized the decorative character of bourgeois women in the Victorian era. But performances by women at male lodge meetings also reflected a far more egalitarian relationship between husbands and wives than could have been imagined by their parents twenty years earlier.

The organization of Portland's Concordia Club was a local manifestation of a national movement. In the late 19th century, Concordia Clubs were being formed throughout the United States by Jews of German descent in emulation of exclusive city clubs founded by white Protestant elites. In the "instant cities" of the West, Jews were in a unique position because their ambitions were readily acknowledged by gentiles who were themselves newcomers in pursuit of wealth and status. In Portland, distinguished non-Jewish families such as the Ladds, Corbetts, and Failings had arrived about the same time as the Fleischners, Goldsmiths, Hirsches, and Meiers. They appreciated how Jews had helped to build the city's commercial, financial, and cultural institutions. Although elite Protestant businessmen did not invite Jews to join their exclusive clubs, Jews rarely expressed displeasure with such treatment, partly because both groups interacted in Masonic lodges, Republican party affairs, and business contacts. Instead, wealthy Jews created sociability for themselves through their own clubs and lodges.

Portland's Concordia Club had been founded in 1879. Its evolution shows how a Jewish elite received recognition in the larger urban society. The Portland city directory for 1879 reveals that the officers of the Concordia Club were clerks, salesmen, and partners in small businesses. By 1887, when the club was legally incorporated, its officers were wealthy merchants—Ben Selling, Nathan Baum, and Edward Bernheim—plus the lawyer Julius Silverstone. Its exclusive character is suggested by an initial membership of one hundred Jews of German descent; new members were limited to the sons and male relatives of the original members. In 1888 the Concordia Club moved from rented quarters to its own hall in the heart of the business district, where its members plunged into a whirl of card parties, full dress balls, and galas. It was one of only four social clubs whose membership lists were printed in the city's first social register, *The Portland '400' Directory*, published in 1891.

Thus, by the mid-1890s, the founding, development, and decline of various ethnic voluntary associations in Portland illustrate the increasing complexity of an ethnic community as families were formed, as sons succeeded fathers, and as newcomers arrived to start new businesses. The absorption of the cemetery association, the growth of the synagogues, and the expansion of the lodges and clubs, as well as the decline of the Ladies Benevolent Society, reflected chang-

88   Chapter Six

ing demographic patterns and suggest that for Portland Jewry the key transition was its inner transformation into a modern middle class. Ideas held by the immigrant generation about family and welfare were obsolescent while such new institutions as B'nai B'rith Lodge 416 and the Concordia Club redefined what it meant to be Jewish in America.

NOTES

1. For full documentation of sources, see William Toll, *The Making of an Ethnic Middle Class: Portland Jewry over Four Generations* (Albany: State University of New York Press, 1982), chapter 1 and a small portion of chapter 2. Activities of the various voluntary organizations can be documented in the minute books of the respective organizations. Details about individuals usually come from the federal manuscript census and from city directories. Some key secondary sources, especially those published since 1982, in addition to oral histories and letter collections, are cited in the notes that follow.

2. See Lawrence Schofer, "Emancipation and Population Change," and Avraham Barkai, "The German Jews at the Start of Industrialization: Structural Change and Mobility, 1835–1860," in *Revolution and Evolution: 1848 in German-Jewish History,* ed. Werner Mosse (Tübingen, Germany: J.C.B. Mohr, 1981), 63–89 and 124–44.

3. Paula Hyman, *Gender and Assimilation in Modern Jewish History: The Roles and Representations of Women* (Seattle: University of Washington Press, 1995), 93–133; Linda Gordon Kuzmack, *Woman's Cause: The Jewish Women's Movement in England and the United States* (Columbus: Ohio State University Press, 1990); William Toll, "A Quiet Revolution: Jewish Women's Clubs and the Widening Female Sphere, 1870–1920," *American Jewish Archives* 41 (Spring/Summer 1989): 7–26.

4. Wolfgang Köllmann and Peter Marschalk, "German Emigration to the United States," *Perspectives in American History* 7 (1973): 526.

5. Mack Walker, *German Home Towns: Community, State, and General Estate, 1648–1871* (Ithaca, NY: Cornell University Press, 1971), 6, 18, 52, 76, 81, 87, 104, 140.

6. Mack Walker, *Germany and the Emigration, 1816–1885* (Cambridge, MA: Harvard University Press, 1964), 52, 158; Bill Williams, *The Making of Manchester Jewry, 1740–1875* (New York: Holmes and Meier, 1976), 5–6, 11, 25–31, 34, 62–64.

7. Bernard Goldsmith, "Interview," Portland, Oregon, November 29, 1889, p. 2, Hubert Howe Bancroft Papers, Bancroft Library, University of California, Berkeley, California.

8. Jonathan S. Mesinger, "Peddlers and Merchants: The Geography of Work in a Nineteenth Century Jewish Community," Discussion Paper Series, No. 38, Department of Geography, Syracuse University (October 1977), 7–10; Steven Hertzberg, *Strangers Within the Gate City: The Jews of Atlanta, 1845–1915* (Philadelphia: Jewish Publication Society, 1978), 18–19; Marc Lee Raphael, *Jews and Judaism in a Midwestern Community: Columbus, Ohio, 1840–1975* (Columbus: Ohio State University Press, 1979), 35–46.

9. An excellent description of chain migration may be found in Josef Barton, *Peasants and*

Strangers: Italians, Rumanians, and Slovaks in an American City, 1890–1950 (Cambridge, MA: Harvard University Press, 1975), 6, 22.

10. Sylvan Durkheimer, Interview, p. 10, March 3, 1975, Oral Histories Collection, Oregon Jewish Historical Society, Portland, Oregon.

11. Ben Selling to Gus Winckler, January 31, 1883; Selling to Dear Uncle, March 1883; Selling to Winckler, August 9 and September 1, 1883; Selling to Julius Prechet, May 22, 1886. Ben Selling Papers, Oregon Historical Society, Portland, Oregon.

12. Solomon Hirsch to Jonathan Bourne, Jr., August 18, 1895, and Joseph Simon to Bourne, October 22, 1889, Jonathan Bourne Papers, Oregon Collection, University of Oregon, Eugene, Oregon; Ben Selling to W.K. Tichenor, February 23, 1883, Selling Papers, OHS; Laddie Trachtenberg, Interview, December 11, 1973, p. 4, OJHS; "Judge Deady in Relation to B. Goldsmith," p. 4, Bancroft Papers.

13. William Toll, "Jewish Families and the Intergenerational Transition in the American Hinterland," *Journal of American Ethnic History* 12 (Winter 1993): 23–25.

14. The same decline occurred in central Europe. See Vicki Caron, *Between France and Germany: The Jews of Alsace–Lorraine, 1871–1918* (Stanford, CA: Stanford University Press, 1988), 159–62; Paula Hyman, "Jewish Fertility in Nineteenth-Century France," and Steven M. Lowenstein, "Voluntary and Involuntary Limitation of Fertility in Nineteenth-Century Bavarian Jewry," in *Modern Jewish Fertility*, ed. Paul Ritterband (Leiden, Netherlands: E.J. Brill, 1981), 82–84, 97–98.

15. John E. Knodel, *The Decline of Fertility in Germany, 1871–1939* (Princeton, NJ: Princeton University Press, 1974), 90, 97, 136–37.

16. The Jews of Portland were like their counterparts in other American cities of the time. In 1880 there were only five professionals in a Jewish population of about five hundred. See Leon Jick, *The Americanization of the Synagogue, 1820–1870* (Hanover, NH: Universities of New England Press, 1976), 39.

17. For Jews on Freemasonry, see Tony Fels, "The 'Non-Evangelical' Alliance: Freemasonry in Gilded Age San Francisco," in *Religion and Society in the American West: Historical Essays*, ed. Carl Guarneri and David Alvarez (Lanham, MD: University Press of America, 1987), 240–42; Don Doyle, *The Social Order of a Frontier Community: Jacksonville, Illinois, 1825–1870* (Urbana: University of Illinois Press, 1978), 179.

18. "Judge Deady," p. 2.

CHAPTER SEVEN

SAFE AND STEADY WORK: THE IRISH AND THE HAZARDS OF BUTTE

DAVID M. EMMONS

The comfortable middle-class Jewish merchants of Portland enjoyed lives that contrasted sharply with those of the Irish miners of Butte. Here we return to David Emmons's detailed study of a unique ethnic community to discover the hazards of underground copper mining and the ways the Irish coped with them. The Butte mines, Emmons informs us, were the most dangerous in the world, not merely because of frequent accidents and deaths in the mines, but also because of devastating diseases.

Emmons approaches his subject from the viewpoint of labor history. He shows that the Irish were numerous and powerful in the ranks of both labor and management. This meant that exclusionary policies could be followed that benefited both Irish workers and their Irish bosses, at the expense of miners of non-Irish ethnicity. Inevitably, the latter suffered even more cruelly than the Irish.

The instruments of exclusion were the Irish ethnic associations—the Ancient Order of Hibernians and the oddly named Robert Emmet Literary Association. Both functioned something like unions, but for Irish workers they were much more effective than the local miners' union. The ethnic associations were vital, not only in hiring, but also for placement in favored jobs, relief from extremely hazardous working conditions, and benefits for sickness and death.

Like the earlier contribution by Emmons, this article is a revised and greatly reduced version of a chapter in his book, The Butte Irish *(1989).*

Butte's Irish enclave was fully formed by 1900. It was a complex community consisting in almost equal parts of family, parish, ethnic associations, and occupation. Of the ethnic associations, the largest and most important were

92   Chapter Seven

the Ancient Order of Hibernians (AOH) and the Robert Emmet Literary Association (RELA). The core of this enclave was the stable underground miner, the worker who had somehow passed through the transient stage of his trade and had settled in. Butte was where he would make his living. Using five years as a reasonable standard of persistence, there were approximately two thousand of these stable, enclave Irishmen by the turn of the century. Steady jobs were both the source and the object of this Irish workers' world. It was steady work that created the enclave; it was the enclave that attempted to insure the steady work.[1]

Stable employment, however, often required those who had it to cooperate with those who provided it for the purpose of closing employment to the unskilled, the unorganized, the unsettled, or, if necessary, those not in the ethnic and social community. This power to exclude, "never mind how," gave a kind of aristocratic status to workers. If the exclusion was based on skill, the result was a natural aristocracy. If based on any other criterion—ethnicity or associational membership, for example—the resulting aristocracy had a contrived element about it. Natural labor aristocrats held their jobs because only they could do them; contrived aristocrats held theirs because only they could get them.[2]

Butte's Irish enclave contained both sorts of "aristocrats." In the early years, before about 1905 and the widespread use of power drills, hardrock mining had about it a kind of artisanal quality; it was skilled work and only a limited number of men could do it. These labor aristocrats—and many Irish were counted among them—were a valuable commodity because a scarce one. But power drills "deskilled" this aristocracy; the men retained their skills but the skills had lost their economic usefulness. Mechanization meant that anyone, almost anywhere in the world, strong enough to lift a power drill and desperate enough to go underground with it, could be a "miner." A scarce commodity had become a commonplace one. In Butte, as elsewhere in the mining West, getting and holding work was no longer a matter of practiced job skills—no real skill was required. It was now a matter of controlling the job market in the interests of an ethnic enclave and that meant that the power to exclude had to be based on contrived (i.e., ethnic) rather than natural (i.e., occupational) considerations.[3]

But the aristocracy was never as occupationally secure as this reference to the power to exclude might suggest. Whatever the nature and source of their aristocratic status, Butte's Irish miners encountered various obstacles to getting and keeping their jobs. One was that mining gold and silver bearing ores was an inherently unstable enterprise; few workers can have entered it because it promised steady employment. Nor was there any reason—in its early silver years at least—to assume that Butte's history would be any different, or any longer, than that of other western mining camps, those ephemeral phantom towns that barely survived their settlement years, the victims of played-out mines and played-with markets.

Two developments saved Butte from suffering the fate of the "camps." (The word itself suggests making and breaking.) The first was the corporate decision to concentrate on copper rather than silver bearing rock. Companies mined copper for the long haul; it was an enterprise requiring thousands of men and millions of dollars. Markets for copper were more nearly depression proof than those for silver—or gold. The second was the corporate consolidation of most of Butte's properties under Anaconda and/or Amalgamated Copper Mining Company (ACM) control, ending years of litigation and corporate in-fighting and stabilizing job as well as resource markets.[4]

The decision to become a copper town rather than a silver camp came in the mid-1890s; the consolidation of copper operations under Amalgamated/Anaconda control came in 1899, 1906, and 1910. There were still fluctuations in the job market; still instances of corporate cupidity or caprice. In one sense, industrial jobs in America were always held on sufferance; the risk of being "out of work" had always to be taken into account, nowhere more so than in the West. Butte's economy, however, was less fragile than those of most Western (or Eastern) industrial towns, and infinitely less precarious than those of Western gold and silver camps. It gave the miners of Butte a fighting chance at steady work and they clung to it with dogged tenacity.[5]

None, however, held on with quite the same determination as the Irish. Victims of both an Irish land system so disordered as to appear chaotic and an American industrial system to which "No Irish Need Apply," they were among the world's most economically insecure people. For Butte's Irish miners, the power to exclude was not some kind of instrument of revenge, but rather the predictable response of a people themselves too often excluded. When Cornelius Kelley, at the time general manager of all ACM properties in Butte and Anaconda, said that "when a man obtains a job underground it is a very steady position if he takes care of it," he was speaking generally. But Kelley was an Irishman and an associational one at that and the Irish miners of Butte assumed his remarks had particular applicability to them.[6]

They may be forgiven this assumption. It was not based on naiveté, nor did it indicate class collaborationism, a betrayal of working-class "solidarity." On another occasion, Kelley spoke of the "community of interests" between the Anaconda Company and the Butte Miners' Union. But the Union was run by Irishmen and it remains uncertain whether Kelley was talking about Irishmen cooperating across class lines or capitalists and workers cooperating across

94   Chapter Seven

ethnic. The Irish assumed the former. And why not? From 1876 to 1956, the Anaconda Company was run by four "involved" Irishmen: Marcus Daly, William Scallon, John Ryan, and Con Kelley. By involved, I mean affiliated with the Irish nationalist organizations that gave substance and cohesion to the enclave.[7]

Slightly lower on the corporate ladder could be found other associational Irish, more than 150 hiring officers, shift bosses and foremen who quite literally owned the jobs that allowed the enclave to survive and flourish. As Catholic Bishop John Brondel said in 1888, "many of our richest mine owners . . . are Catholic. Our most skillful mining supts. and foremen are Catholic and Irishmen." Miners were saying the same thing when they referred to waste rock as "Protestant Ore." One of the largest and certainly one of the most influential Irish "clubs" in Butte was the Anaconda Copper Mining Company.[8]

The Irish miner enclave understood the benefits implied by Irish-run mines. How much easier "cooperation with the more powerful" would seem if the more powerful were or had been in the enclave. One member of the Ancient Order of Hibernians put it succinctly. "So many of our members," said David Ryan, "are in a position to give employment." That being the case, cooperation could be made to seem like fraternal good will. Certainly the scores of "job committees" sent over the years by the Hibernians and the Robert Emmets to visit ACM officers in "the employment interests" of their brothers operated on that assumption.[9]

And once again, with good cause. The minute books of both associations are filled with references to the job committees and to "progress" being made in finding jobs, or "the matter being handled," or "the bros. were assured that they would get employment." There were a "few grumblers," men who were not placed through the AOH, but John J. McCarthy, a mine foreman and former Union officer, had some hard advice for the likes of them: "let them join the 'Birds and Animals' organizations and see how many jobs they will secure for them." That was the point. The Eagles, Elks, and Moose did not enroll the hiring officers of the Anaconda mines. The Hibernians and the Emmets did. This may not have been as uncommon as the conventional interpretation, with its emphasis on native Protestant managers and immigrant Catholic workers, would have it. But neither can it have been a pattern routinely encountered.[10]

As for those hiring officers, their interests were also well served by this intra-ethnic cooperation. The AOH and the Emmets appealed to the most work-experienced, careful, and skilled members of the Irish labor force. Both associations had requirements that prospective members be well known to the men proposing them for membership; both had residency restrictions on eligibility for associational benefits; both had rules against overly rowdy behavior and public drunkenness; and both had initiation fees that exceeded a day's pay for an underground miner, as well as monthly dues and periodic fund drives. All of these served as partial checks against casual membership. Giving job preference to associational Irish made good business sense; it meant that ACM was getting the steadiest and most experienced of Butte's Irish.[11]

As for the unaffiliated Irish, those not members of the AOH or the Emmets, according to one Hibernian, they "were scabs, worse than scabs." Job preference was reserved for the committed—workers committed to Ireland and to Butte and the Anaconda Company. Lest any be too quick to charge collusion, however, let the point be made again: Marcus Daly and those Irishmen who followed him were offering Irish immigrants something few Irish had ever known—steady work at decent wages in an Irish-run industry. That these Irish might have been grateful and that their gratitude might find expression in loyalty to job and place does not figure to have escaped the attention of Anaconda's Irish "bosses."[12]

For non-Irish miners, these were meaningless distinctions. They knew only that the Anaconda Company did not distribute jobs fairly, that Irish-run mines and the availability of settled Irish miners excluded them. In 1889 a member of the Montana territorial legislature noted that it was "a matter of common report that the laborers of [the] Anaconda were almost exclusively Irish." "Clannishness," he went on, "was characteristic of the human race," but it was unfair that "of two men equally competent to fill a position, the Irishman invariably got it." The non-Irish were left to mine the "Protestant ore." Or as the Cornish miner was said to have lamented when he learned of the Anaconda takeover of the once Cornish-controlled Parrot Mine, "Good-bye, birdie, savage got thee; no more place for we."[13]

The virulently anti-Irish and anti-Catholic American Protective Association was less philosophical. In 1894, the APA charged that Anaconda mines were Irish because, like all "soulless corporations," it preferred "those they (sic) can control." The result was that "'NO MAN OF ENGLISH BIRTH NEED APPLY' was virtually posted on the doors of the Anaconda syndicate of mines." English miners, in fact, were "insulted and treated with contempt by the Irish bosses," while hundreds . . . come directly from that little island beyond the herring pond, men who know nothing about mining . . . and are given work at these mines immediately on their arrival." It would be impossible for the historian of Irish-American workers to invent a more apt variation on the theme.[14]

Clearly, the Irish exclusion of non-Irish (and unaffiliated Irish) was the long road to worker solidarity, conventionally defined. The Irish organizations in

96   Chapter Seven

Butte were dominated by workers and they functioned in the interests of those workers. In that sense, ethnic and social class allegiance coincided. The problem for those who sought (or for historians who still seek) evidence of worker unity was that in Butte worker solidarity had about it a fine and obvious ethnic bias.

II

The Irish enclave's efforts to stabilize the work force in the most uncertain of America's industrial trades is another example of working-class involvement in what was once thought a uniquely middle-class responsibility: the steadying of entire industrial communities. The fact that that community was restricted to the Irish component of the whole does not affect the central point. The Irish enclave required steady employment; the enclave tried to insure it. Within obvious limits, it succeeded. In fact, had Butte been a steel town, had it been almost anything other than what it was, the world built by its Irish workers might have been even more durable and stable than it proved to be. But Butte was a hard-rock mining town and to job insecurities must be added the occupational hazards of underground work.

These are related issues. If job insecurity demeaned workers, so did daily exposure to injury or death; if the constant influx of new men destabilized the work force, so did it also make the work more dangerous; if job insecurity threatened the families of established miners, so did miners' consumption; if all-Irish work crews were more congenial, so too were they safer—for the deceptively simple reason that Irishmen were more considerate of the safety of other Irishmen. In sum, it was not enough for the enclave to find work for its members. It had also to assume some of the risks that that work involved.

This may have been the single most important of the enclave's responsibilities. Butte's mines were arguably the most dangerous in the world. Statistics from the years 1899–1906 show 1.14 mine accident deaths per 1,000 men working in the United Kingdom; 1.07 in Germany; .75 in Belgium; and 2.02 in France. In the period 1909–11 India's mine fatality rate was 1.18; Russia's .98; the notoriously dangerous Transvaal's 4.29. In 1896 the death rate in Montana was 11.6 deaths per 1,000 miners employed; the next year it was 5.95; in 1898, 4.86. For the fourteen years from 1893 to 1906, the fatality rate was 4.72, more than five times the rate in Czarist Russia during this same period.[15]

The Anaconda Company kept more precise figures, particularly for the years 1910–13. During that four year period, 162 men died from accidents in ACM mines, another 5,233 suffered injuries requiring medical attention. Death came, in descending order of occurrence, from falling ground; falls, usually down a shaft; blasts, most often premature detonations of dynamite; being mangled by machines; hoisting accidents; and electrocutions. Among the accidents were 349 fractures, including twelve broken skulls and 129 broken legs; sixty-seven eye injuries resulting in twenty cases of blindness; forty-six amputations; and eighteen "scaldings."[16]

It was almost impossible to pick up a Butte newspaper between 1880 and 1930 and not find a notice of a death or serious injury. The descriptions were graphic: "Skull fractured and brains scattered around," "blown to bits," "scalded to death," "torn apart" were among them. Major disasters (more than four men killed in the same accident) occurred in 1889, 1893, 1895, 1896, 1898, 1904, 1905, 1906, 1909, 1911, 1912, 1915, 1916, 1917 (when 165 men died in a fire), 1918, and 1919. Little wonder that there were 434 Irish widows by 1910; that of 302 families at the almost entirely Irish parish of St. Lawrence O'Toole, 137 were headed by widows; or that by 1940 the "population" of Butte's cemeteries exceeded that of the town. Father Brosnan exaggerated only slightly when he wrote home from Butte that "poor men [were] killed every day in one or another mine." Countess Markievicz, in town to raise money for relief in Ireland, was not far wrong when she reported that "the hospitals are full of men suffering from work in the mines. . . . They told us few men live to be old in Butte, Montana."[17]

The countess's reference was not to mine accidents—they took only hundreds of lives—but to diseases, which took thousands. The most common and the most deadly of these was miners' consumption or silicosis. Often confused with tuberculosis, to which it could also give rise, miners' consumption was the result of breathing the dry silicate dust of the mines. It was the deadliest of the hazards of working in Butte's mines. Mortuary reports for fifteen months in 1906–7 show 106 fatal mine accidents, but the reports list 277 more miners who died of respiratory illness. Of these, the average age at time of death was 42.7 years. The youngest to succumb was twenty-two; seventy-five of those who died were under forty. Clearly, working in the dry, ill- or unventilated mines and breathing silica-laden dust was to risk early death. The risk, however, was routinely assumed. From 1916 to 1919 a U.S. Bureau of Mines study found that of 1,018 Butte miners interviewed, 432 (42.5 percent) had miners' consumption, another sixty-three had tuberculosis.[18]

Some of these hazards may have been unavoidable. Butte's mines were sunk to depths of 4,500 feet; the ore-bearing rock was friable and crumbled easily; ventilation, particularly before the use of electric fans, was difficult. But whether the problems were easily corrected or not, they resulted in nightmarish working conditions. The county Board of Health provided documentation in a 1912 report. Carbon dioxide levels in working shafts reached highs of 61.4 parts per 10,000, more than twenty times the carbon dioxide in "pure

98   Chapter Seven

country air," ten times that in the air of Butte. The temperature and humidity often reached tropical if not unearthly highs. At the 2,300-foot level of the Original Mine, the temperature was 93 degrees, the humidity 97 percent. One observer testified that men worked full ten-hour shifts in one of these "hot boxes" without ever urinating; they sweated out the gallons of water they drank.[19]

It must also be kept in mind that there were no seasonal fluctuations in temperature and humidity, which meant that in the winter men were hoisted, in five minutes' time, from 90 degree mine shafts into outside air that could reach a brittle 40 degrees below zero. Longtime Butte residents remember men emerging from the mines "covered with sweat," hitting the cold air and disappearing in balls of steam. Before the construction of change rooms, or dries, these men then walked home with their clothes frozen to them.[20]

Some occupational hazards resulted from worker neglect and/or company penury. As late as 1912, for example, of the ten mines investigated by the Health Department only two provided toilet cars and only one delivered drinking water in sealed metal containers. In the other mines, including four recognized as mostly Irish in work crews, the men urinated wherever they happened to be and "answered nature's call," in the delicate phrase of the commission, in waste drifts, covering the excrete with rock. Water was sent down in open wooden kegs, a most unhygienic practice given the tendency of miners to "spitting indiscriminately." Water arrived at the 2,100-foot level of the Mountain Consolidated, for example, with an "earthy" odor, a "decidedly yellowish-brown" color, and "considerable flocculent" sediment (flocculent: "little wooly balls or tufts"). Some of this may also have been owing to the presence on that same level of a horse barn described as "very bad, absolutely filthy . . . horse dying."[21]

These conditions provided a fertile breeding ground for a great variety of bacteria. Air samples turned up the presence of colon bacilli, albus, diplococcus pneumonia, streptococcus, staphylococcus, bacillus of putrefaction group, bacillus of Vincent's angina, anthrax, citreus actinomycoses, meningococcus, Fraenkle's pneumococcus, influenza, and typhoid bacillus. This last was particularly ominous, but the commission concluded that at least forty, and more likely as many as sixty, typhoid carriers were working in the mines, prompting the commission to report that typhoid was "by no means a rare disease in Butte."[22]

Health conditions scarcely improved when the men went off shift. In fact, the commissioners believed that "the conditions under which we found many of the miners living [were] more conducive to the introduction of disease germs into the system than are the conditions . . . in the mines." Specifically, they meant conditions in the miners' boardinghouses. Their descriptions were lurid. One house was described as "very unsanitary, many flies, no screens, dirty rooms never disinfected." In one small rooming house, six men lived in one sixteen-by-nine-foot room, allowing each man twenty-five square feet of living space, 228 cubic feet of breathing space. Each resident, in other words, had room for a cot and a footlocker. The place had no windows and the outside privy was "filthy." Of the larger boarding houses, one had seventy-five miners in thirty-five rooms; another put up ninety men in forty-eight rooms; a third had three hundred men in fewer than one hundred rooms. Air and water samples taken from these places turned up consistently high counts of infectious bacilli, particularly for tuberculosis, completing an unrelentingly grim picture of industrial working and living conditions.[23]

But the commission, for reasons that are not clear, extended its investigation to include three unidentified working-class saloons, one of them on North Main in the middle of the Irish enclave. The bacteriological examinations of the air in all three proved "negative"; carbon dioxide counts ranged from 6.2 to 7.4 parts per 10,000; temperature and humidity rates were 62 degrees, 69 percent; 55 degrees, 82 percent; and 57 degrees, 56 percent. That miners might stop off at a saloon between work and "home" is more easily understood in light of the conditions detailed in the commission report. That some miners might, in fact, use home only for sleeping should occasion no wonder. With an average floor space in more than 1,400 residences of less than 40 square feet per person, sleep was about all they could to there.[24]

Also of interest was the commission's discovery of what the miners had always known: that there were enormous differences in working conditions within the same mine and from one mine to another. While the temperature at the 2,300 foot level of the Original Mine, for example, was 93 degrees, at the 2,100-foot level it was only 78. At the 2,000-foot level of the Neversweat the temperature was 58 (accounting for the mine's name); on the same level of the Anaconda Mine it was 54. Understandably, men sought work in the cooler mines or in the cooler drifts of the same mine, meaning they sought out those hiring officers who could provide them not just with regular work but with safe and tolerable working conditions.[25]

These were related considerations. The favored assignments went to the good miners, the steady men, or—and they were not always the same—the well-connected men, men of the same "national origins" as the hiring officers. It is worth pointing out that the Anaconda and the Neversweat, the two coolest mines on the Butte Hill, were known as Irish mines. Since, technically, shift bosses hired new crews every day, with preference given to those whom they

100   Chapter Seven

knew, a rough kind of seniority system evolved. Since the Irish were the first to Butte and the first to be hired (and re-hired), this seniority system had about it a clear ethnic bias.

The pattern that emerges is clear and understandable. As important as steady work, in fact an integral part of it, was work in cool, safe drifts with congenial mates and a friendly shift boss. It may not need saying, but a broken head or miners' consumption had the same effect on steady work as a mine shutdown. Certainly no one, particularly the inherently nervous Irish, could have missed the point of the sign posted on the North Butte Mine: "Don't Get Hurt. There are TEN MEN waiting for YOUR JOB."[26]

Here then was another place where "cooperation with the more powerful" might serve the interests of family and enclave. And the stable Irish miners knew it, playing on shared ethnicity in the interests of safe and steady work. As elsewhere in industrial America, persistence was rewarded with a chance to persist; it meant job seniority, and, even more significantly in a place like Butte, it meant a slim chance to beat the actuarial odds of a frighteningly hazardous workplace.

The key word is "slim." As previously cited mortality statistics would indicate, no underground miner in Butte, regardless of how "well placed," could dodge the hazards of his job. Fifty years was old by the standards of Butte miners—whether Irish or not. In fact, the longer a man worked underground, whether in cool drifts or hot, the longer his exposure to miners' consumption and the harder he pushed his luck in the deadly gamble with rockfall or dynamite blasts. The laws of probability knew no ethnic distinction; they were exclusively a function of time on the job. And the Irish had worked Butte's mines from the beginning.

The death of other miners, particularly when "untimely," caused a variety of responses. Ironically, pride was clearly one of them. Like combat soldiers, miners assumed uncommon risks; the miners knew that and so did the "civilian" population. American workers spoke often of their "manliness," of their willingness to take on tough and dangerous work. And they spoke as well of the respect that that willingness earned them. In this sense, Butte represented the industrial front lines.[27]

Ultimately, however, as with war, when death occurred with such numbing frequency, it produced feelings of fear, anger, frustration, fatalism, and despair. But, though seldom commented upon, these deaths must have given rise to even more complex feelings. In the first place, industrial death in Butte was an occupational and class phenomenon. Miners died earlier than non-miners; the poor earlier than the non-poor. This commonplace needs to be recalled, particularly when studying a town like Butte. Every work-related death reinforced the miner's understanding of the essential difference between his world and that of the middle class.

Second, for all the prestige that attached to the assumption of risk, there was something about the "con" and about the deaths and injuries in the mines that was ultimately and profoundly insulting. The accidents occurred so suddenly and so randomly. But the con, too, was a sentence of death, only the length of the sentence was indeterminate. Both deeply offended the workers' sense of their own dignity and it must be noted that, for all their pride in what they did, mining was not an occupation Butte's Irish sought for their sons. Wages were good, the work was honest and steady enough, and worthy of an Irishman. But men died underground and the statistics make the point clearly: immigrant fathers worked in the mines so their American-born sons would not have to.[28]

III

Butte's Irish lived with and died from these pervasive hazards. Where and when it could—and it did have some influence—the enclave made it possible for its members to avoid some of the more obvious insecurities and dangers. Still, most of the objective hazards had to be assumed. Some of their effects, however, could be blunted. Medical bills could be paid, mortgages retired, fatherless children cared for, wakes and burials arranged. These may have been the most important of a worker enclave's responsibilities anywhere. In a place like Butte, the enclave was preoccupied with them. They were inescapable. Thus, as elsewhere in this miners' world, the largely mythical individualism of the nineteenth century gave way to associational, even communal, effort—in this instance, to minimize the full effects of the occupational risks.

Once again, the Irish associations took the lead. Both the Hibernians and the Emmets had programs to provide aid to sick and injured members and, upon a member's death, to absorb funeral costs. The AOH was, if not more active in providing relief, at least more regular and systematic. All AOH members between the ages of sixteen and forty-five were eligible to receive sick benefits beginning the second week and extending for thirteen weeks, for any disabling illness or injury. The more overtly Irish nationalist RELA offered benefits only intermittently, as the political and revolutionary demands on its money permitted. There were, of course, restrictions on AOH eligibility. The recipient had to have been a member for a least six months, his dues and fees had to be fully paid up, and the illness or injury could not be chronic or owing to carelessness or intemperance. In addition, a weekly physician's certificate attesting to the legitimacy and lingering nature of the complaint was required,

102   Chapter Seven

and a "sick" or "visiting" committee called on the disabled brother to confirm his complaint and verify the physician's certificates. If all these conditions were met, and they were thousands of times, the disabled received sick benefits of $8.00 per week for up to thirteen weeks, or $104.00. Since the death or funeral benefit was $100.00 ($500.00 for those willing to pay an extra "premium"), this limit possessed a certain logic.[29]

Though less than half the average wage for a Butte miner ($3.50 to $4.50/ day for this period), these benefits, added to the $8.00 to $10.00 weekly benefits paid for up to ten weeks by the unions, were sufficient to cover most of the costs of all but extended layoffs. Since Montana did not have a workers' compensation law until 1915, these benefit payments were all that was available in most cases. Fortunately for the bookkeeping departments of both the unions and the AOH, most of the injuries and illnesses that extended beyond the ten- and thirteen-week limits seem to have proven fatal before the expiration of benefits. When extended custodial care was required, as occurred with blindings, the Hibernians and the Emmets sponsored raffles and dances to aid the stricken member.[30]

Needless to add, the demands on the AOH's sick and funeral benefit funds were unrelenting. In 1896 the AOH paid out sick benefits alone of $1,884.00; in 1899, sick benefits totaled $2,549.00; in 1903, $2,572.00; in 1911, $2,712.00. In one six-month period in 1898, sick and death benefits together amounted to $1,768.00. The total for the nineteen years for which records are complete between 1885 and 1911 was $30,496.00. There were years, 1904 and 1910 for example, when almost one in every five eligible AOH members drew sick benefits. A typical entry in the weekly minute books for 1904 listed thirteen members as either "sick," "injured," or "slowly improving." It must also be kept in mind that benefits did not begin until the second week of a disabling illness or injury. The AOH funeral benefit fund was kept as busy, averaging almost $400.00 per year for the nineteen record years between 1885 and 1911. The five-year experiment with $500.00 benefits between 1905 and 1909 increased the total appreciably, though not proportionately to the membership, suggesting that few miners could afford to pay for the increased benefits.[31]

Obviously, in an era of $3.50 per day wages, with dues set at $.50 per month, the sick and death benefit programs of the AOH required rigorous economies and stable membership totals. Benefits for all members were suspended in 1889 and again in 1915, the consequence of hard times and declining memberships. In 1899 and 1901 membership drives were mounted for the express purpose of replenishing badly depleted sick and death benefit funds; AOH "generosity," as one member put it, had led to "financial embarrassment." Seven years later, the order was "in good shape . . . except the Death Benefit fund is a little short

David M. Emmons   103

on account of the number of deaths during the last quarter." In 1910, the Hibernians sponsored a dance "to build up the treasury . . . which has suffered badly since the first of the year on account of the death of five of our brothers. We hope [Butte's Irish] will deal generously with us."[32]

Certainly they had dealt generously with their membership. Thirty thousand dollars in sick benefits over nineteen years adds up to almost three hundred thousand lost man-hours of work for which some money was received. No Irishman in Butte, however young and healthy, can have missed the lessons in this display of community support. When John O'Leary, a member of the RELA, spoke of "our people" and how he "hoped the brothers [would] do all they can to help each other out"; when Patrick Kelly of the AOH urged the "brothers to stay by each other and always support a brother in distress," they were believed. There were no self-congratulatory cries of individualism from this associational working class.[33]

There was one other form of associational relief, one in which the RELA seems to have been the more active of the two Irish societies. The Emmets sent members to sit with and nurse "afflicted brothers" during the night. These "nurses" were paid the standard Butte scale of $3.50 for an eight-hour "shift," the money coming out of the RELA sick fund. It appears that only the very sick or the severely injured were assigned nurses. Obviously, providing medical attention was less the object than combating fear and loneliness. Dying away from home was a frightening prospect and the comforting presence of an old friend from Butte—often, it would seem, a man originally from the same village in Ireland—extended the definition of home and quieted some of the terrors. These vigils took place in an injured or ill member's home or in the hospital; they lasted as long as a man needed help.[34]

When a member of either organization died, resolutions of condolence were passed, sent to the nearest relative—often in Ireland—and published in local and Irish newspapers. The AOH was kept so busy with this responsibility that it composed "blank suitable resolutions of condolence . . . to suit single and married members" to speed the process. The resolutions were predictable in content. Ed Gilmore was described as an "ardent and consistent supporter of Irish independence"; Peter Harrington had been an "active and esteemed member, Company A, Irish Volunteers"; with the death of Con Murphy, the AOH "lost a faithful member, the National League of Ireland an earnest worker, and Ireland a true, devoted and patriotic son." As for Anthony Shovlin, he had "met with the vicissitudes that are too often the lot of the Irish exile. . . . The dream of his life was to see Ireland a free and independent nation."[35]

The associations were also in charge of wakes and burials. Death might come violently and sooner even than workers had a right to expect, but they

104   Chapter Seven

would have no paupers' graves, no unattended wakes. In death, if not always in life, these working Irishmen would be accorded a proper respect, and no Protestant or bourgeois sensitivities figured to intrude. The wakes, particularly in the early years, were three-day and three-night affairs; bands played, the women keened, the men reminisced and grieved, celebrated and told lies—about the deceased and about themselves. It was said that more rock was broken at an Irish wake than could possibly have been loaded and taken from the mines. The wakes represented, in other words, the same mix of solemnity and hilarity as they had in Ireland. They were just as culturally determined and as culturally necessary in the new world of Butte as in the old world of West Cork or Donegal.[36]

IV

Thus did the community of Irish miners attempt to deal with the insecurities and hazards, both physical and psychological, of life in the world's greatest mining city. The English historian Eric Hobsbawm has written of the importance to manual workers of safeguarding against their "primary life risks . . . namely accidents, sickness and old age, loss of time, underemployment, periodic unemployment, and competition from a labor surplus." He could have been speaking of Butte and of its miner enclave. Led by its Irish associations, the enclave found steady employment for its members, then attempted to absorb and blunt some of the risks that employment entailed. In the process it freed public agencies—and to a lesser extent, the Miners' Union—from having to provide those services, and freed the Irish from having to attach themselves to non-Irish and non-Catholic organizations to get them. Ethnic loyalties, as a result, were enhanced rather than surrendered, even to the point that Irish and miner became mutually reinforcing roles.[37]

Nothing makes this community assumption of risk clearer, however unconscious the lesson, than a U.S. Navy recruiting notice that appeared in a Butte newspaper in May, 1916, almost two years after the outbreak of the Great War and less than a year before America's entrance into it. No one, in other words, could have assumed that this was recruitment into a guaranteed peacetime Navy. Even war, however, was made to seem preferable to life in Butte's mines.

Mining jobs, said the Navy, were uncertain; there were strikes, layoffs, and the omnipresent threat of illness—even a mild one meant lost wages and high medical costs. The Navy, by comparison, promised steady work, paychecks that came whether sick or well, and free medical and hospital care. A disabling illness or injury meant economic catastrophe for the miner—no job, no prospect of a job, no income. The disabled Navy man received a "generous pension." Accidental death in the mines, "stuffy, gloomy" places at best, left "your family with only what you've saved." The Navy's death benefits were six months' pay and full pension benefits to the survivors. In the mines, promotion was slow and uncertain and marked by favoritism. In the Navy it was sure and quick and "the best man wins." Old miners were not just scarce, they were unknown. Illness and age related debilities either killed them or meant that their jobs went "to younger men." Sailors, on the other hand, retired after only thirty years' service, service spent, moreover, in "fresh air, sun, sea, clean, healthful, athletic life," at three-fourths their pay at the time of retirement.[33]

This was a remarkable set of comparisons. But what marks it, other than an unintentional gallows humor, was how near the AOH and the RELA came to providing something like the same kind of security the Navy promised. The point is not that military service was a form of twentieth-century welfarism—though the emphasis on security indicated not just the Navy's but the government's assumption of new responsibilities. What the recruiting notice did was provide a kind of checklist against which the "welfarism" of Irish associationalism can be measured and tested. Given the hazards and uncertainties of Butte, the associations, in fact the entire Irish community, performed remarkably.

NOTES

1. Persistence figures are drawn from an analysis of 1900 and 1910 *Manuscript Census* data. For workers' worlds and enclaves see John Bodnar, *Workers' World: Kinship, Community, and Protest in an Industrial Society* (Baltimore: Johns Hopkins University Press, 1982), 1–2, 63–65, 177–79.

2. Bodnar, *Workers' World*, 65; Eric Hobsbawm, "The Aristocracy of Labour Reconsidered," in *Workers: Worlds of Labor* (New York: Pantheon, 1984). The "never mind how" citation is from p. 234.

3. On power drills, see Mark Wyman, *Hardrock Epic: Western Miners and The Industrial Revolution* (Berkeley: University of California Press, 1979), 12, 84, 88–90, 169; Ronald Brown, *Hard-Rock Miners: The Intermountain West. 1860–1920* (College Station: Texas A & M University Press, 1979), 53–56, 73–74; Richard Lingenfelter, *The Hardrock Miners: A History of the Mining Labor Movement in the American West* (Berkeley: University of California Press, 1974), 17–18.

4. On both see Malone, *The Battle for Butte: Mining and Politics on the Northern Frontier* (Seattle: University of Washington Press, 1981), 24–31, 131–211.

5. For consolidations see Malone, *Battle*, 131–211.

6. For Kelley's Irishness, see David M. Emmons, *The Butte Irish: Class and Ethnicity in an American Mining Town, 1875–1925* (Urbana: University of Illinois Press, 1989), 83, 107–8, 144. Kelley's statement is from U.S. Industrial Commission, *Mining Conditions and Indus-*

106   Chapter Seven

trial Relations at Butte, Senate Doc. 415. 64th Cong., 1st sess. *Final Report and Testimony*, 1911 and 1915, 3701; hereafter, Industrial Commission, *Mining Conditions at Butte*, 1911 or 1915.

7. Kelley's remark is from Industrial Commission, *Mining Conditions at Butte*, 3866. The associational ties of the four Irishmen who ran the ACM are from Emmons, *Butte Irish*, 21, 52–53, 83, 107–8, 144–46.

8. Hugh O'Daly, "Life History of Hugh O'Daly," 1945. Typescript, no page numbers, [156], [236]; Brondell to the *Catholic Sentinel*, October 3, 1888, Bishop John Brondell Papers, Diocese of Helena Office. The "Protestant Ore" reference is from Wayland Hand, "The Folklore, Customs, and Traditions of the Butte Miner," *California Folklore Quarterly* 5 (1946): 167.

9. The "cooperation with the more powerful" is from Bodnar, *Workers' World*, 65. David Ryan from AOH, Div. 3, *Minute Books* (hereafter MB), October 5, 1908. RELA, MB, November 14, 1907. Irish Collection, microfilm copy, University of Montana (hereafter IC).

10. RELA, MB, November 5, 1903; August 22, September 26, October 10, 1907. McCarthy's comment is from AOH, Div. 3, MB, April 19, 1913, IC.

11. AOH, *Constitution. 1886*; *Bylaws. 1887*; *Ritual and Manual of AOH. 1901*; AOH, "Black Books," n.d., n.p., RELA, Membership and Dues Ledgers. All in IC. Emmons, *Butte Irish*, 141–44, 170–71.

12. AOH, Div. 3, MB, July 9, 1910, IC.

13. *Helena Independent,* February 20, 1889. Hand, "Folklore," 178.

14. *The (Butte) Examiner*, June 15, 1895; February 27, March 19, April 19, October 31, 1896.

15. Wyman, *Hardrock Epic*, 115; Montana, Dept. of Labor and Industry, *Report. 1914* (Helena: Independent Co., 1915), 293, 295.

16. Industrial Commission, *Mining Conditions at Butte* (1915), 3874–79.

17. Butte/Silver Bow Archives has a convenient index of newspaper references to accidental deaths in the mines. Major disasters are listed in the *Anaconda Standard,* June 9, 1917; see also the edition of March 12, 1922. The cemetery population figure is from WPA, *Conner Came: Stories of the World's Greatest Mining Town. Butte. Montana* (New York: Hastings House, 1943), 163. Brosnan to father, February 18, 1917, Brosnan Letters, in possession of Professor Kerby Miller, University of Missouri. Constance Gore Booth (Countess Markievicz), *Prison Letters of Countess Markievicz, 1934* (New York: Krause reprints, 1970), 289.

18. U.S. Bureau of Mines, *A Preliminary Report of an Investigation on Miners' Consumption in the Mines of Butte . . . 1916–1919* by David Barrington and A.V. Lanza. Technical Paper 260 (Washington, DC: GPO, 1921), 11, 12, 14. Silver Bow County, "Mortuary Records, 1906–7," in Butte/Silver Bow Archives. See also *Anaconda Standard*, January 17, 1898; *Butte Mining Journal*, September 21, 1887.

19. Silver Bow Co., Board of Health, "Report on Sanitary Conditions in the Mines and Community, Dec., 1908–April, 1912," typescript, 6, 9, 10, 15, 25, 26, Montana Historical Society; Industrial Commission, *Mining Conditions at Butte* (1915), 3853.

20. Interviews with Kevin Shannon and John Curtin, University of Montana Archives.

21. Board of Health, "Report on Sanitary Conditions," 1–4, 6–7, 9, 11–13, 16–17, 19–21, 24.

22. Ibid., 1–4, 9–13.

23. Ibid., 1, 3, 6, 12, 16–17, 19–20.

24. Ibid., 24.

25. Ibid., 3, 31, 34. Industrial Commission, *Mining Conditions at Butte* (1911), 3914. Brown, *Hard-Rock Miners,* 69.

26. *Montana Socialist,* October 23, 1915.

27. For examples of manliness see Industrial Commission, *Mining Conditions at Butte* (1915), 3857, and Hand, "Folklore," 164.

28. For second-generation Irish avoidance of the mines, see Emmons, *Butte Irish,* 157–58, 176.

29. AOH, *Constitution. 1886;* MB, April 9, 1902. RELA, MB, March 27, 1884; November 22, 1906, IC.

30. For union sick benefits see J.C. Johnson to AOH, October 22, 1891, Correspondence, IC; *Anaconda Standard,* June 13, 1896; Industrial Commission, *Mining Conditions at Butte* (1911), 3917–18. AOH and RELA, MB, passim.

31. See Emmons, *Butte Irish,* 161, 177.

32. On the suspension of sick benefits see AOH, MB, July 20, August 3, 1887; June 19, 1889; February 27, 1901; AOH, Div. 3, MB, January 17, 1914; January 2, 1915. The reference to "generosity" and "financial embarrassment" are from AOH, MB, February 6, 1901, IC.

33. RELA, MB, December 12, 1907. AOH, Div. 3, MB, April 9, 1906, IC.

34. RELA, MB, passim, and May 12, 1892; December 12, 1895; November 14, 1903, IC.

35. Resolutions are from AOH, MB, March 1, 1899; February 22, 1899; RELA, MB, January 4, February 12, 1912, IC.

36. Emmons, *Butte Irish,* 165–66, 179. Kerby Miller, *Emigrants and Exiles: Ireland and the Irish Exodus to North America* (New York: Oxford University Press, 1985), 72–73, 325–27.

37. Hobsbawm, "Artisan and Labour Aristocrats?" in *Workers,* 259.

38. *Montana Socialist,* May 13, 1916.

CHAPTER EIGHT

CHILDHOOD MEMORIES OF SOUTH SLAVIC IMMIGRANTS IN RED LODGE AND BEARCREEK, MONTANA, 1904–1943

ANNA ZELLICK

The temper of the following article, which also treats miners in Montana, is quite different from what infuses David Emmons's study of the Butte Irish. Here, Anna Zellick draws on the memories of the children of South Slav immigrants—mostly Croats, Slovenes, and Serbs—who worked the coal mines in south-central Montana. Like Emmons's Irish, Zellick's South Slavs experienced great privation, horrendous working conditions, and the human drama that accompanies accident, disease, and death. Whereas Emmons discovered no sympathy between rival European ethnic groups, Zellick describes pleasant interaction, cooperation, and a spirit of helpfulness, occasional fights notwithstanding.

The article illustrates the intelligent use of oral interviews as source material. Zellick captures the simple speech of ordinary people recalling events that occurred sixty or seventy years earlier. Such memories must be used with care because they tell us what is remembered, never what is forgotten or omitted or in error. Memories are living things, and they often mellow with age. Memories tell us how people make sense of their own past experiences at the moment of recall, and hence reflect later values and attitudes. Memories necessarily evolve as life experiences accumulate.

Originally published in 1994 in Montana History, *Zellick's article appears here in a shortened and revised form without notes. Full transcripts of all the interviews are available in the Montana Historical Society in Helena.*

When South Slavic immigrants arrived in the United States early in the twentieth century, they heard of plentiful jobs in the mining industries of

Montana. The huge copper mines of Butte and the smelters of Anaconda were the most famous, but hundreds of southern Slavs—mostly Croats, Slovenes, Serbs, and Montenegrins—flocked with their families to the rich coal mines of Red Lodge and Bearcreek, located in the south central part of the state near the Wyoming boundary, where they lived amidst many other newcomers, including Scots, Irish, Finns, and Italians.

Like immigrants everywhere, the South Slavs found a very different life from what they had known in southern Europe. Today, many decades later, a few of their children remain to recall family experiences in adjusting to a wholly new environment. Their recollections, recorded in a series of interviews conducted by the author in 1991, are the basic source for the article that follows.

One of the interviewees was Eddie Blazina. He remembered how his father, Steve, born in Slavica Fuzina in Croatia, eventually was attracted to the Montana coalfields. With his father and two brothers, Steve Blazina immigrated in 1899, first to mines in Michigan and then three years later to the Northern Pacific coal mines in Roslyn, Washington. In 1904 he arrived in Red Lodge, where he worked as a coal miner until he retired in 1945.

Mike Dimich, a Serb from Gospic, Croatia, exemplifies a different occupational pattern. He found work in the coal mines when he first arrived in Montana, but in a few years went into the grocery business. According to his son, Danny, Dimich had some education and learned the English language. "My dad," Danny recalled, "went to school in Yugoslavia, which was quite a ways to go." Once he arrived in Montana, Mike Dimich went to night school and later obtained his American citizenship. Danny said his father was good at writing and "wrote a lot of letters to Europe for the Serbian people. My dad could write English. . . . He could speak English so much better than a lot of Serbian immigrants because a lot of them just worked in the mines and went home and read their Serbian papers."

South Slavs were also attracted to Bearcreek, which was a coal mining community in the Beartooth Mountains a few miles east of Red Lodge. Now a ghost town, Bearcreek was reached by the railroad in 1906. Two of the first South Slavs to arrive there were John and Frances Chesarek, Slovenians who met in Cleveland. "After a three month's courtship," their daughter, Mildred Chesarek Harbolt, recalled, "they married in 1903 and went to seek their fortunes in Aldrich, Montana, where there was a Slovenian settlement." After living in Aldrich for a while, the Chesareks moved to Weston, Colorado, where their second child was born. Hearing of the feverish coal mining activities in Bearcreek, however, they packed their belongings and moved to Montana in 1906. They remained in Bearcreek for the rest of their lives.

Eli Pekich was another South Slav who lived in Bearcreek. He came to the

United States from Shavnik, Montenegro, in 1904. A telegrapher by profession, Pekich was unable to pursue telegraphy in the United States because he did not know the English language. He became a miner instead, working first in silver mines in Nevada and then coal mines in Timber Line, and finally in Bearcreek, where he lived from 1907 to 1942. Laboring as a coal miner at first, Pekich in time became a merchant who ran a prosperous business with the help of his countryman, Mile Jankovich, who operated an adjoining bar. Pekich was highly regarded in Bearcreek and served on the local school board for many years.

Stana and Vaso Jurkovich came with their infant son to Bearcreek from Canada. Though both were young Serbian natives of Montenegro, they met in Canada, where Vaso worked as a coal miner with Stana's two brothers. Their marriage was prearranged, a common practice among the Slavic people. Although neither one had known the other, Stana and Vaso were happily married. Hearing about Bearcreek, they decided to relocate there in 1914.

As these examples show, South Slavs were willing to travel wherever jobs were available, regardless of the distance and the hardships they had to endure. Not only was coal mining a new and different occupation for them, it was also difficult and dangerous.

Alice Mallin remembered, for example, the hardships that her parents, John and Mary Trinaystich, had to endure. They came from Fiume, Croatia, and were married in Taylorville, Illinois. Mary had relatives in Red Lodge who encouraged the young couple to settle there, which they did in 1910. Alice recalled:

> My dad was hurt in the mine here in Red Lodge and had to have his leg amputated in 1912, which was the same year I was born. The coal fell on his foot and crushed it. He got gangrene from that. They couldn't save the leg so they had to amputate [it] below the knee. He was laid up for quite a while before he could do anything and then the mine company got him into being the check weightman. He sat in the office and weighed all the coal that came through the tipple [a structure made of chute and a screen]. He would write down [the weight] for every miner and they'd get paid for how much coal they dug.

Compensation for John Trinaystich's injury from the Northwest Improvement Company, his employer, was meager. "They paid his hospital bill," his daughter explained,

> and he had an artificial limb that every now and then he would wear out because they had leather tops that would split. He would have to get

112   Chapter Eight

another limb which they'd paid for about half, but that's about all. He never did get compensation for anything else.

It took John Trinaystich almost three years to recover. In the meantime his wife, Mary, had to provide a living for the family. Alice described her mother's work in detail. The company, she said,

had this slack from coal that they'd dump onto a little hill. Sometimes there would be chunks of coal with the slack. She would get the shovel and dig that coal out of there, and the people would come and buy that coal from her, filling gunny sacks, buckets, and even wagons.

Alice also described problems of child care. When she was a baby, Alice reported, her family occupied one side of a company house, located in the Italian part of Bearcreek, and a Finnish family lived on the other side.

My mother would leave me with this Finnish woman. My mother would take the other kids with her and they would play around the dump. . . . She [would] just work, oh, maybe five or six hours at a time because she had the children to take care of and cook for. So that's how she made our living at that time.

South Slav immigrants lived not only with hardship but with heartache. For example, John Kastelitz remembered that his father, Frank Kastelitz, had been killed in an accident at the Smith Mine at Bearcreek on Independence Day 1934. "He was working as a machine loader," John remembered.

He reached over to help put a rock on the conveyer belt and the roof caved in. He died that day. He died on the Fourth of July. I remember that real well. He went to the hospital with punctured lungs [and] broken bones. . . . He was conscious up to the time he died.

For men like Trinaystich and Kastelitz there was no worker's compensation and little or no assistance from their employers. More often than not, help came instead from the Croatian, Slovenian, and Serbian fraternal lodges, which paid 50 cents to $1.00 per day for disabilities, or the inability to work because of ill health. Death benefits ranged from $500 to $600. Monthly dues were about $1.00 or $1.25. Because the benefits were so low, memberships in two organizations was common.

There were eleven Slavic fraternal organizations. Three were Croatian and were affiliated with the Croatian Fraternal Union; six Slovenian lodges were linked to the Slovenska Narodna Podporna Jednota; and the Serbian National Federation had two lodges among the South Slavs of Montana.

Although they could provide only limited benefits, these fraternal organizations continued to serve a useful purpose long after the Montana legislature enacted a workmen's compensation law in 1915. As non-binding or voluntary legislation, it brought little or no relief, as the Michunovich family discovered.

A man of great endurance and strength, George Michunovich had walked from his native town of Niksic, Montenegro, all the way to Dubrovnik (a distance of more than two hundred miles) to catch his boat for the United States. Michunovich hurt his back while picking rock for the Smith Mine in Bearcreek and was forced into early retirement without compensation. The effect was devastating to his family. His son, John, remembered:

You were lucky if you had one pair of shoes. I learned as a young boy to make shoes out of tires. You took the tread off tires and cut them out in the shape of a shoe and put strings on them. That's what you did in the summertime because the only pair of shoes you had you saved for school. That's the way we were all raised.

Despite the difficulty, dangers, and tedium of employment in the coal mines, South Slavs liked their work. Mike and John Barovich recalled that their father, Sam, came to this country in 1908 at age seventeen. After working for four years in Texas and Nevada laying railroad track, Sam returned to his native Montenegro with the outbreak of the Balkan War in 1912. Being a patriot, he volunteered to fight against the Turks and then, during World War I, assisted the American Red Cross as a translator. While in Europe, he married and acquired a family. After the war he returned to the United States and arrived in Bearcreek in January 1921.

Barovich found immediate employment in the Smith Mine where, according to his son Mike, his duties included checking the roof of the mine

to make sure that it was safe and sound. Or if something had to be timbered up, he would check that. I don't think that he was actually involved in the mining of the coal itself. But his work was dangerous. Anytime you enter the ground, it's all dangerous. But once the miner got started down there, he would never change because it was nice down there. It's a nice temperature down in the mine. And they all seemed to go for it. They liked what they were doing.

114   Chapter Eight

There were considerable differences in pay. Steve Blazina's daily wage was $8.37, which was good money at the time, but George Michunovich, who picked rock out of the coal as it came out of the mine, was paid $2.00 per day.

South Slavs "did practically every kind of work in the mine," reported William Romek, hired in 1920 as the payroll clerk for the Smith Mine. But they seldom obtained choice positions, even though they quickly earned reputations for being reliable, dependable, and steady workers. According to Mildred Chesarek Harbolt, jobs such as superintendent, foreman, boss, and timekeeper were held by the Scots, people of influence who could speak the English language. Gratified that they even had jobs, South Slavs accepted their lots.

As avid gardeners, South Slavs had their own cows, chickens, and pigs. They only needed to purchase staples from merchants, who were usually their own countrymen. Daisy Pekich Lazetich recalled how her father, Eli Pekich, a Bearcreek merchant, always rewarded miners with a sack of oranges when they came to pay their bills on payday.

Inability to speak English was a disadvantage for all these immigrants. It not only barred them from responsible positions but also made it difficult for many of them to become American citizens. In addition to residency requirements, they had to pass an examination showing knowledge of the United States Constitution and of how the American government works. This all required study, and sometimes the examination had to be taken more than once. But once they gained citizenship, South Slavs remained forever faithful. Asked if South Slavs took their American citizenship seriously, John Barovich replied:

Did they ever! After becoming citizens, they voted. When I was living in Columbus, where I was employed as a teacher, my father, Sam Barovich, would drive down from Bearcreek to remind me to vote. He didn't have a phone so he would drive all the way down to make certain that we voted. Voting was very important to these people. You bet.

Learning how to speak and write in English was somewhat of an ordeal for the older children who emigrated with their parents. Referring to his own experience, Danny Dimich recalled:

When I went to school the first year, I had a hell of a time because I didn't understand. . . . I didn't know what I was really doing. I was in either the third or the fourth grade before I got to know the kids. I did get along with the kids after that.

Their teachers were often sympathetic. Two such teachers were Loretta and Lillian Jarussi, who came to Red Lodge with their parents from Italy in 1907. Remembering her own school days, Loretta recalled:

I had gone through that process [of learning English] myself the first two years. I had a terrible time. My mother would get me ready, and I would cry, "Mamma, I don't want to go to school." Mamma said, "You have to go to school." I'd say, "The teacher doesn't understand me, and I don't understand her." She'd say, "Well you watch and do what the other kids do so that you'll understand pretty soon." And that's the way it was. I don't know how my mother stood it with a crying kid every day.

Some Slavic youngsters encountered rough treatment during their first days of schooling. Recalling his school days in Bearcreek in January 1921, Mike Barovich remarked:

You know how kids are, the only thing you learn is cuss words. It seemed like the teacher said something to me and I probably cussed her, and I got the hell beat out of me because I didn't know what I was saying. I do recall that. I did have a few fights. I don't know what caused them. There were different kinds of settlements in Bearcreek. There was [one] called Chicken Town and they were all Serbs there. There was Stringtown that had mostly Austrians and Finlanders. Then downtown there were a lot of Italians. Over by the high school they were all Scotch, English, and Irish. There were different factions. It seemed always when I walked by there was a fight or two.

Inability to speak English separated the South Slavs from the English-speaking community. They were, after all, foreigners who were looked down upon socially, and that fact left a lasting impression with some of the children. Rose Jurkovich, daughter of Vaso and Stana Jurkovich, remembered growing up in Red Lodge:

The things that really hurt were that the American people [thought] that they could get the foreign people to work and slave for them for absolutely nothing. The girls especially cleaned the houses, did the ironing, and took care of the children. [I remember] one incident in particular. My sister went at eight o'clock in the morning and had all the ironing and the house cleaning to do. Then the people went out for the evening for entertainment. My baby sister sat until three o'clock in the morning. When they returned, they gave her fifty cents for all that work. Despite the fact that my sister was frightened to go home at that time, she flung the fifty cents at the lady and said, "You need this worse than I do." Frightened, she ran all the way home.

Strong family ties enabled these South Slav children to withstand the unhappy experiences they encountered outside their homes. They grew up in a tight family unit in which the father was the master of the household. "I still believe," declared Rose Jurkovich, that "as long as we were in the home that my father and mother provided, that we abided by their rules." As an example, she explained:

Whenever anyone went out to work, the paycheck was brought home to the parents. . . . It wasn't that "this was my money and I'm going to keep it." It went to the household. The older ones all contributed a lot to the betterment of the household in terms of material things and wanting to pursue education and all that.

While the father was sole or chief provider, the mother's domain was the home. Whether she was the wife of a miner or a prosperous merchant, she was usually a dutiful wife and mother and a very hard worker who always put her family ahead of herself. When seventeen-year-old Anga Jankovich arrived in Bearcreek in 1920 from Montenegro, she met and soon married Eli Pekich, the town's well known merchant. Their daughter, Daisy Pekich Lazetich, said of her mother:

She worked in her way just as hard as my dad did. He being a grocer and a butcher had to have white aprons, so my mother had [a] U-shaped copper boiler that she would put on [the] coal stove down in the basement. She would boil those clothes with strong soap because of the blood stains in the aprons. She laundered that particular laundry once a week. She tried to get the aprons as white as she could. That was hard work. She was just a good homemaker. She was always baking bread, and whenever we had any special days such as some of the Serb name days and my dad's name day, which was always on Halloween Day, she baked a big dinner.

Life in the new environment of Red Lodge required physical stamina that some of the young Slavic women did not possess. Mary Licac Naglich, a Croatian mother, was not quite sixteen when she had her first child. Her husband, John, whom she met in Walsenburg, Colorado, before they moved to Bearcreek in 1912, was also a Croatian. He had to give up mining because of tuberculosis. After he recovered he went into the dray business, and in order make ends meet, the family took in six boarders. To prepare their lunches and breakfast, Mary had to get up at four in the morning. Never strong after the birth of her first child, Mary had three more children. In the course of time she contracted cancer and died. She was only thirty-five years old. Her death left her teenage daughter, Rose, in charge of the household. Rose's initial responsibility was to cook and prepare the meals for her mother's funeral. As was customary with the Slavic people, her mother's body was brought home before burial. Rose described the traumatic events that followed:

When the casket was brought in, I ran outside. The undertaker came and got me. He was a nice man. He said, "I know what's the matter with you. You saw your mother how pale she looked and now you don't want to see her." I shook my head. He said, "She is beautiful. She looks like she is asleep." So he took me there and I looked at Mom and I went hysterical. Because she was so beautiful. She had a black dress with a V neck and she had no jewelry and I had a little crystal ball on that I just loved. It was on a sterling chain. I told the undertaker to take that chain off of me and put it on my mom. I wanted her to take something with her. And he did.

It took four days for her mother's brother to arrive by train from Portland. Rose described the wake.

Mom's body was there. There was a living room and dining room, all one combination. Adjoining was the kitchen. And I would look into the dining room and see Mom lying in the casket. And there I was trying to cook for everybody in the kitchen and everyone had gone to bed when I got up in the morning to cook. And there was Mom in the casket. After the service, I told Dad, "You should have had Mom in the Union Hall or the Lodge Hall, not the house." It was awful.

Rose became a mother to her sister and two brothers. They were now hers as they once were her mother's. With the added responsibility she had to give up her high school education.

South Slavic settlers in Bearcreek and Red Lodge valued education. Having attended schools in their own country, most of the men were literate when they arrived in the United States. They recognized that they were now citizens of a country in which English was the common language and that education was important for their children. For example, Steve Blazina encouraged his son Eddie to go to school so that he would not have to become a miner. Even though Frances Hodnik Chesarek was widowed with nine children varying in ages from twenty-one months to fifteen years, she managed to have seven of them go through to college.

Vera Marinchek Naglich, whose parents were natives of Slovenia who arrived in Red Lodge in 1912, remembered her school days with pleasure. "Growing up in Bearcreek was great," she said. She and her young friends had fun, for example, when they used boards, a stick, and a wheel to pretend that they had a car. "Afterwards in school," Vera recalled,

> I became interested in athletics, basketball, and track. We had track meets and things. There were a lot of Slavic kids that went to school. In Bearcreek we all intermingled. We were friends with everyone who was there. All of us kids were always together. . . . If there was a fight, we were the "hunkies" and they were the "wops" and there were the Scotch, but when the fight was over, that was it.

Athletics were especially important to the Slavic people of Bearcreek and Red Lodge, notably basketball. A great American sport, basketball offered tremendous opportunities to the sons of South Slavs because it did not matter whether the player was Slavic, Finnish, Italian, or Irish. What counted most was how good a player was. Furthermore, as a member of the team, he became "one of us" on equal terms with his fellow players. Basketball was democracy in action. It was enjoyed by parents, brothers, and sisters, as well as by the players themselves. John Barovich, who played for the Bearcreek Bears, talked about the fun and excitement—and opportunity—that basketball provided. Playing the game well could lead to a professional career. He reminisced about his high school days in Bearcreek:

> I was very interested in basketball and track. Those were the only two sports in Bearcreek. I worked hard at basketball and was on the team in 1932 when we placed second in the state. . . . We beat Great Falls, who were the Big Sixteen champions, and we beat Miles City and lost to Butte. I was one of five placed on the All-State team. I was an All-State center. I also vaulted and threw the discus, which gave me a scholarship to go to college. Otherwise I probably would be mining coal.
>
> Athletics played a number one role in my life because the only thing I wanted to be was an athlete. Because of that I didn't drink and I didn't smoke. I really worked at it. I practiced year around. We used to practice

basketball in the cold. I had a basket outside. Pretty soon the ball would get mushy. We would run into the house and put it behind the stove. It would puff up again because it had warmed up. Back out we would go, shooting the baskets. The basket was against the barn wall. We used to practice in the summertime. The Bearcreek boys didn't have an awful lot to do. Our parents mined coal. We didn't have to do any farming.

When I graduated from high school and my father found out that I was going into athletics, he had a fit. I was supposed to go to Montenegro and be a priest [Orthodox]. Like I told you, it was in the family. We had it forever. I don't know how come. He even tried to get the sheriff to send me. They were so gung ho that I was going to be a priest. I had no intentions along that line.

That young Barovich could not understand why his father wanted him to become a Serbian Orthodox priest clearly showed how he was being integrated into the American culture, a culture that did not place the same emphasis on religion as did that of the Serbs. In Serbia religion was an integral part of life. As soon as Serbs started to arrive in Montana, they were visited by traveling monks who came on horseback. The first Orthodox parish was organized in 1897 by Matj Stajacich, and the Holy Trinity Serbian Orthodox Church was built in 1903 in Butte. But due to difficult travel conditions, the priests traveled to Red Lodge to perform baptisms, funerals, and weddings only when it was possible.

South Slavs also expressed their religious faith in their observance of religious holidays, notably Christmas and Easter. Such times were great social affairs and were always held in the home where food and spirits were served in abundance. Everyone was welcome. Unlike the Catholics, the Orthodox adhere to the Julian calendar and celebrate their Christmas and New Year's on January 7 and 14 respectively. For Slavic settlers these were double holidays to be observed and enjoyed to the fullest. Rose Jurkovich remembered celebrating Christmas:

It seems to me that we were one of the few Montenegro families in Red Lodge as they were mostly Croatians and Slovenians. My people got along especially well with them. We celebrated our Orthodox Christmas at home on January 7. It was always a wonderful time because the Croatians were musically talented and happy, and they would come here and we would have a three-day celebration. They were here from morning until night eating and playing music and singing. We were always served barbecued lamb and pork. In preparation, mom and dad would strew straw all over the floor to resemble Christ's manger. The Christmas tree was brought in the night before, never before. Always Christmas Eve was known as "badjnak." To us it called for a ceremony.

Speaking of his youth in Bearcreek, John Barovich emphasized the importance of Easter:

At Easter time my mother would boil three, four, or five dozen eggs. We used vinegar and everything else to toughen them up. The men would start out in the morning from one end of town with a pot full of eggs. You would come to the house. You would have an egg contest. This party would hold his egg point up and you would hit point down and you better not miss the point up and cheat by hitting on the side. If you cracked the egg, you got it. This went on all day busting eggs. Then there would be a fist fight over the fact that somebody didn't hit the egg on the point. That's how serious we were about winning. It was only just Montenegrins who took part in this contest. The Croatians didn't do it, although we got along well. We also had great rapport with the Slovenians, as we did with the Finns, Italians and the Scotch.

Weddings were also special events. According to William Romek, one of the biggest parties ever held in Bearcreek was by a Montenegrin couple. Mile Jankovich sent for his bride, Mina, from Montenegro. The party was held after the marriage. Romek remembered that

The house was wide open. There was a banquet of every kind of meat, roasted pig, beef, ham, turkey, chicken, and everything to go with the entrees [and although it was prohibited] plenty of spirits.

Other events that brought these people together were Lodge Day, Labor Day, picnics, and barbecues. Attendance at lodge meetings, held once a month on a Sunday, was important because that was when dues were paid. Nick and Mary Zupan, two Croatians who were married in Waterloo, Iowa, in 1913 and came to Red Lodge in 1918, were members of a local Croatian lodge. Their son, Tony Zupan, remembered how his mother would remind his father "don't forget to pay the lodge dues."

Labor Day brought community-wide celebrations sponsored by the miners' union. William Romek said there always was a parade, and in Bearcreek the largest family received a ham for a prize. "Rado Jovanovich took the prize every year," Romek said.

I can still see Rado and his wife—she a little woman—leading their ten children in the parade proudly. Rado with a smile on his face as big as it could carry. Long speeches, races, and baseball followed the parade.

People loved to celebrate, even as they worked hard, and they never socialized without a drink, according to customs dating back many centuries. Romek recalled that in 1919 ten boxcar loads of grapes came to Bearcreek. "It wasn't brought to be eaten," he remarked, "but to be made into [something for] wine drinking purposes." As law-abiding as they were, South Slavs were willing to violate the law when it came to imbibing. As Tony Zipan noted:

One could walk down the streets in Red Lodge and just by sniffing one could tell where they were making whiskey. One time all of us kids were getting ready to go to school when there was a big explosion. Our still had exploded. It blew out the windows and cracked the walls, but we were lucky not to have a fire from it. I think the happiest day of my mother's life was when they raided our house. The revenuers came. I was playing with three or four of my friends when this official looking car drove up. And you know no one had a car in our neighborhood. All these men came out—one, two, three in their suits, and I knew it had something to with our bootlegging operation, so I said to my friends, "I think we better go play somewhere else." That is when they took the still and chopped it up.

All four groups—Serbians, Croatians, Slovenians, and Montenegrins—intermingled socially. In some instances ethnic relationships were close. John Michunovich described the spirit of mutual helpfulness:

We were Serbians. Our first neighbor was either Croatian or Slovenian. We were the best of friends. We shared. If you had a garden, you shared your vegetables. When they made bread or cookies, they would be shared. I grew up and didn't know the difference. When I went into the service in February 1941, I was asked what my religion was for my dog tag. I said I was Orthodox. They asked if I was Protestant or Catholic. I said, "I don't know; I'm Orthodox." I didn't know the difference.

South Slavs also joined each other's lodges. Some of the Serbs and Montenegrins, for example, joined the local Slovenian lodges as well as their own.

Over a span of forty years technological changes brought the coal mining industry to an end in Red Lodge and Bearcreek. The Northern Pacific Railroad closed its Sunset Mine in Red Lodge in 1924 and its Eastside Mine in 1932.

Chapter Eight

Destiny intervened in Bearcreek on February 27, 1943, when 74 miners lost their lives in the Smith Mine explosion, the worst disaster in the history of Montana coal mining. Sixteen of the miners were South Slavs. One was Sam Barovich, the father of Mike and John Barovich. Another was Ignace Marinchek, the father of Vera Naglich. Her husband, Joe, had just come off the night shift and her father went on the day shift, as usual. Vera Naglich remembered the day well:

> It was a sunny morning. It is real vivid to me. It was a wintry morning and yet it was starting to be warm. We were home visiting with my mother. Pretty soon Joe's dad came to the house saying, "There's something wrong." He knew that my dad was at work. Joe got into his truck and went to the mine and found out what had happened. My dad was gone. He was one of the few in the mine who knew how to get to the air course to try to get out. And he had gone there and there was a gate to get out, but there was a bunch of garbage against it. He lost consciousness and fell back on this garbage. Had he fallen forward to beneath the door, he would have gotten fresh air and he might have survived. They found him. They did resuscitation but he never came out of it.

Exactly how the explosion occurred has never been determined despite several official investigations. The only determination was the explosion was caused by methane gas. The tragedy nevertheless marked the end of coal mining in Bearcreek.

South Slavs contributed greatly to the development of Montana. They dug the coal that powered the mighty Northern Pacific locomotives and produced heat for the smelters and buildings at various mining centers. Their customs and traditions enriched Montana's heritage, and perhaps most importantly, their deep sense of values influenced their children, a new generation of Montanans, to remain forever grateful to their parents for their courage and stamina and for becoming American citizens.

CHAPTER NINE

ITALIANS IN SAN FRANCISCO: THE SECOND GENERATION

DINO CINEL

Like Anna Zellick, Dino Cinel also made use of interviews when he studied the children of Italian immigrants in San Francisco. Cinel asked a wider variety of questions about the second generation, and these led him to consult the records of welfare agencies, naturalization and marriage records, city directories, and other sources, in addition to interviews.

In this brief excerpt from his From Italy to San Francisco, *Cinel emphasizes the diaspora of the second generation out of the Italian settlements in North Beach and other Italian neighborhoods to the cities and suburbs around San Francisco Bay. By the mid-1930s this had become a mass movement. He relates geographical mobility to questions of parental opposition, time of marriage, birth order, occupations, and other variables, and he compares Italians to other immigrant groups.*

Although space restrictions do not permit reprinting here, Cinel also has profiled patterns of family formation among Italians of San Francisco before or after emigration, family size, and rates of marriage within the ethnic group, plus divorce, desertion, and other aspects of family sociology. He identifies what traditions the immigrants were able to preserve and what changes they were forced to make in the American environment. As in the earlier excerpt in this book from Cinel's From Italy to San Francisco, *notes have been omitted.*

THE CHILDREN OF THE IMMIGRANTS

The settlements were the creation of immigrants; their children grew up there, but eventually left. The children began leaving in large numbers in the

124   Chapter Nine

mid- 1930's, when they came of age, and the movement lasted for about three decades. By the mid-1960's the still considerable number of Italians in North Beach were mostly old people. The younger generation had moved across San Francisco Bay to Oakland and Berkeley, or south along the peninsula, or north to Marin County. Others left northern California, following economic opportunities in the Los Angeles area or elsewhere in the United States. The departure of the children obviously constituted a major change, but perhaps not as great as it looked.

Though the departure of Italians from the city became a mass movement by the mid-1930's, the pressure had been building for some time. Many of the immigrants' children grew up restless and rebellious, anxious to break out of the constricting world of their parents. In the records of the Italian Welfare Agency, the friction between immigrants and their children is probably the most discussed topic besides poverty. Social workers reported complaints of both parents and children. Parents almost invariably made the same points to judges, school principals, and social workers when their children got in trouble. The child had been properly raised, they said, and trouble started only when the child began to wander downtown or to associate with children of immigrants from other regions of Italy. Northern Italian parents, in particular, seem to have been unhappy about their children's associating with southern Italians.

The growing children found the places where they were unknown more alluring than the close Italian settlements. To social workers and judges, juvenile offenders almost invariably said that life was boring in North Beach but exciting downtown. Sam Capelli, a young man arrested twice by the age of seventeen, told a social worker: "There is nothing more boring than a Sunday afternoon at North Beach. Life at home is even more boring. My father and uncle get together over the weekend and the topic of conversation is always life in the Old World. For me life begins outside North Beach." Giacomo Clovelli told the social worker who asked him why he had missed classes almost every other day for three months: "I do it because it is considered smart to do it. If you go to school every day you are considered a sissy. Besides, it is the only time when I can go downtown. I know that my parents would not let me go otherwise."

The testimony in the records of the welfare agency, though important, must not be hastily extended to the entire Italian community, since it concerns only families with problems serious enough to need outside help. Confrontations between immigrants and their children, moreover, have to be seen as part of a broad inter-generational conflict that was not limited to Italians. It is important to notice, nevertheless, that this inter-generational conflict had to do with safe and unsafe places and with boring and exciting sections of San Francisco. The children were growing up with ideas of where they wanted to explore and where they felt safe that unsettled their parents.

The children were different from their parents; they had grown up in a different environment. Naturalization records of immigrants and marriage records of their children yield a profile of the children's lives. About 75 percent of the children of Italian immigrants were born in San Francisco, 15 percent in Italy, 6 percent elsewhere in California, and the rest in other states. The children of other immigrants were quite different: only 40 percent were born in San Francisco, another 8 percent in California, 10 percent in other states, and fully 42 percent in Europe. This is consistent with what we have already seen, that non-Italian immigrants came to San Francisco less directly than Italians, and it also implies that Italian children were less likely to have known other countries than the children of other immigrants. . . .

Almost all the children of the Italians grew up with their parents. The exceptions were a handful of children whose concerned parents sent them to live with their grandparents in Italy, especially if the grandparents owned land, when the depression came in 1929. Angelo De Martini, for instance, sent two of his three children back to Lorsica in 1932; they lived with their grandparents for three years. Southerners were less likely to send their children to Italy during the depression. Southern parents gave many reasons for not sending their children back: the health of the grandparents, the age of the child, the cost of the trip. But social workers reported another important reason, that immigrants did not want people back in Italy to think they had been unsuccessful in America. Carmelo Kosario, for instance, when his wife was hospitalized with a nervous breakdown, rejected the suggestion that he send his four children to Cinisi. "Carmelo is a proud man," a social worker noted, "and will never allow his parents to know that he needs them."

At the time most children of Italians married, they were still living in San Francisco with their parents. About 80 percent of the children were in that category; the rest had already moved out of their parents' house, and were living either in San Francisco or in other parts of northern California. Italian and Irish children seem to have been the least mobile among the large immigrant groups of the city. About 85 percent of the Irish children were living in San Francisco with their parents when they married, and the other 15 percent were still in the San Francisco Bay Area. The children of Russians and Germans were more mobile; about 40 percent of them had left the city by the time they married. Finally, only 30 percent of the children of British and Scandina-

126 Chapter Nine

vian immigrants were still in San Francisco when they married. As these figures indicate, the mobility of the children was remarkably similar to the mobility of their parents. . . .

The immigrants tried to control the lives of their American-born children in the same way their parents in Italy had controlled their lives. But what worked with the immigrants, who by and large had well-established family attitudes by the time they arrived in San Francisco, did not work with the Italo-American generation. The authoritarianism of the immigrant parents simply did not make sense to children born in the United States. It belonged to another world.

Though marriage records confirm that most immigrants' children lived with their parents up to the time of their marriage, three years later many had not only moved out of the house, but had moved out of the city. It is assumed here that if the name of a male child who married in a given year was not in the San Francisco city directory three years later, that child had moved out of the city. A search in this way for all the names of children who married between 1938 and 1961 indicates that about 40 percent of the Italo-Americans moved out of the city within three years after marriage. . . .

The movement of Italo-American children out of San Francisco was of course shaped by many social forces. The year the children of the immigrants married was important. Those who married in the 1940's were less likely to be out of the city within three years than those who married in the 1950's—only 25 percent in the 1940's compared with almost 50 percent in the 1950's. Obviously the Italo-Americans were subject to many of the same impulses in the 1950's that produced a broad movement out of American cities. Many of the Italo-Americans who married in the 1950's, for instance, were financially better equipped to leave the city for the suburbs than those who had married in the previous decade.

Many who wanted to leave in the 1940's, besides, encountered a stronger opposition from their parents than those in the 1950's. In the 1970's, when I interviewed older Italians in San Francisco, they often expressed pride in the economic success of their children, who were then living outside the city. But some of these old Italians admitted that they had opposed their children's leaving. For instance, in 1952 Angelo Lucchetti disapproved of the plans of his two children Mario and Aldo, both recently married, to leave him alone in his Columbus Avenue grocery store and move to Oakland to open a liquor store. The children confirmed that their parents had oppose their leaving the city; and those who had married in the 1940's generally recalled a stronger opposition. Arturo Vivante, for instance, said he could not count on financial help from his father, who was in a relatively good financial situation, when he moved to San Jose in 1948. Arturo's brother Vincent, however, met only mild resistance when he left San Francisco in 1955.

The older children were generally far less likely to leave within three years than the younger ones. Only 20 percent of the firstborn left the city within the three years, as against 45 percent of the others. Again we can speculate on several possible explanations. First, Italian parents traditionally counted on the support of the firstborn child in their senior years, and accordingly opposed the departure of the first child. Second, firstborn children were likely to marry before younger ones, and we have already seen that those who married in the 1940's were less likely to leave than those who married later. And third, younger children married at a time when their parents were likely to be more prosperous, and therefore better able to help them relocate out of San Francisco.

Another apparent influence was the occupation of the children's parents. There was a correlation in this area for non-Italians and Italians alike. Among non-Italians, those most likely to move were children of immigrants in the professions; next most likely came the children of immigrants in domestic and personal services; and finally came the children of immigrants in trade or transportation. . . .

Finally, geographical mobility can be viewed in the light of the occupations of the children themselves. For the children of non-Italians the pattern is fairly clear. About 50 percent of the children who had a profession by the time they married and 40 percent of those in skilled crafts left the city within the first three years. Only 10 percent of those in trade and transportation and 25 percent of those in domestic and personal services did so. For the Italo-Americans the following pattern emerges. About 60 percent of those in skilled crafts left and 25 percent of those in trade and transportation; those in domestic and personal services were less likely to move. So few Italo-Americans were in the professions that no firm pattern can be established. In general, however, professional people seem to have been the most likely to move, and the children engaged in trade seem to have been the most likely to stay.

To summarize, proportionately more immigrants of other nationalities left San Francisco than Italians. Among the children of non-Italians, the most likely to move were those whose parents had not come to San Francisco directly from their native countries and those who had been born in places other than San Francisco. The differences among the Italo-Americans of the nine groups can be at least partially explained by the differences in their parents' lives. The children whose parents came from communes that established multiple settlements were more likely than the children of parents who lived in nucleated settlements, which seem to have acted as a negative force against geographical dispersion. The movement out of the Italian settlements did not occur suddenly; it started slowly in the 1930's and accelerated in the 1950's. Finally, children whose parents had skilled occupations and those children who themselves had skilled occupations by the time they married were more likely to leave San Francisco than the children of other immigrants.

CHAPTER TEN

ETHNICITY, RELIGION, AND GENDER: THE WOMEN OF BLOCK, KANSAS, 1868–1940

CAROL K. COBURN

All too often the role of women in the development and maintenance of ethnic communities has been overlooked or ignored in the literature of immigration history. Carol Coburn, a professor of education at Avila College in Kansas City, Missouri, provides a corrective lens through which one may view women and families in restrictive ethno-religious societies.

Coburn offers an explicit theoretical framework for her analysis. Dismissive of constructs that separate male and female behavior, she clearly identifies the patriarchal character of her ethno-religious community but recognizes the complementarity of gender roles within four "networks of association"—church, parochial school, family, and the world external to the small ethnic community of German Lutherans in Block, Kansas, located a few miles from the Missouri boundary.

The author is herself descended from one of the families of Block. This enables her to penetrate the intricacies of this exclusive society; it infuses her account with an authenticity that would elude an "outsider." Like other authors in this book, she uses oral interviews to good effect: she knows precisely what questions to ask and who is likely to provide answers. Her analysis, though based on one community, describes gender relationships in hundreds of similar rural and small-town German-Lutheran communities in the American Midwest and West.

The article reprinted here originally appeared in Great Plains Quarterly *in 1988. A greatly expanded version was published as* Life at Four Corners: Religion, Gender, and Education in a German-Lutheran Community, 1868–1945 *(1992).*

130   Chapter Ten

Ethnicity, religion, and gender shape our past, providing a richness and texture to individual and group experience. This experience creates identities and communities that in turn educate the young and ensure the transmission of values, beliefs, and culture across generations. The women of Block, Kansas, provide an opportunity to examine the complex relationship of ethnicity, religion, and gender. Beginning in the late 1860s, this German Lutheran enclave used its ethnic heritage and its religious doctrine to create a separate, distinct community in south central Miami County, Kansas. Trinity Lutheran Church and School served as focal points in the development of this rural community.

To understand fully the role of ethnicity, religion, and gender in educating four generations of Block women, I have utilized an interdisciplinary approach combining aspects of history of education, social history, and women's studies. I use the term *education* in its broadest sense to include the acquisition of cultural knowledge, socialization, and the transmission of beliefs and values. By asking questions about ethnicity, religion, and gender, I intend this study to serve as a model for such interdisciplinary research. Specifically, how did the Block community transmit education to and through its female members? How did the religious institutions of church and parochial school serve as transmitters of education? How did the ethnic family function as educator? What role did the rural location and American cultural environment play in the transmission of education and culture?

To comprehend the lives Block women created for themselves in this male-defined community, it is necessary to develop a new theoretical framework which, unlike those used by many historians, does not assume a dichotomy between public (male) and private (female) spheres. While the public/private construct is useful in many contexts, it is not always helpful in describing rural or ethnic women's experiences because for many women a clear separation of worlds does not and never has existed. For historians to operate solely within such a polarized construct may render many past individuals' contributions and experiences invisible or insignificant or may lead scholars, following their own cultural biases, to view one side or the other as more valuable. Separating female and male behavior into competing and opposing ideologies does little to enhance understanding of the reciprocity needed to maintain any community. This is not to ignore gender differences nor to assume that reciprocal interactions ensure equality of opportunity or experience. Certainly the Block community was a social and theological patriarchy. Under this patriarchal umbrella, however, individual women and women's groups created their own consciousness and behavior, which the historian may better understand by setting aside preconceived notions about dichotomies and polarities.

To avoid entering the Block community from the front door of male domination/female victimization or the back door of female superiority/male indifference, I have attempted to construct a side door into the intricacies of the Block community. I will utilize a theoretical framework that was designed to examine women's "networks of association" and how these networks transmit education and culture. Historian Barbara Finkelstein's "networks of association" allow the researcher to analyze the transformation in networks of association, the structures of authority, and the character of women's activities.[1] This approach permits the historian to study the relationships between social structure and human consciousness within the context of a specific setting.

For the women in the Block community I have chosen four networks: church, school, family, and the outside world. Analyzing these networks gives me the opportunity to discuss formal as well as informal ways women functioned within this rural ethnic community. Within each of these networks, life cycle differences and continuity/change across generations can be assessed. This analysis also facilitates examining the influence of American technology and culture within the community.

The sources available for this interdisciplinary study are varied and rich. They include state and federal census data, official church records of births, baptisms, confirmations, marriages, and deaths, and minutes of all formal church meetings of male, female, and youth organizations. Also, official journals, booklets, and yearbooks published by the Lutheran Church–Missouri Synod provide insights into religious attitudes and prescriptive literature. "Alien Registration" documents required during World War I are repositories of information about immigration, occupation, literacy, and family of the German Americans at Block. Combined with these quantitative and literary sources are my interviews with twelve current or former Block women born between 1898 and 1920. Their stories, anecdotes, and memories enrich this study and give life to the reams of written material. Photos, personal correspondence, and newspaper accounts add to the documentation.

COMMUNITY BACKGROUND

Block is located in East Valley Township, eight miles southeast of Paola in Miami County, Kansas. It served as a hub for German Lutherans living on the periphery of four townships within the county. The first German-Lutheran immigrants came to the Block area in the 1860s, soon after Native American tribes in the area were sent to Oklahoma Territory and land became readily available for homesteading. Most of the immigrants were farmers from North-

132   Chapter Ten

ern Germany, many from Hanover province, who migrated in families and
made brief stopovers in Indiana, Missouri, or other midwestern states.

The Trinity Lutheran Church and School were organized in 1868, and by the
turn of the century the community boasted two general stores, a blacksmith
shop, a creamery, and a post office. Social and recreational activities focused on
church, school, and kinship networks. Church membership peaked in 1920
with 485 members, never dipping below the 400-mark through 1940.[2] Until
the advent of the automobile, travel was difficult and most members of the
community were geographically isolated from other German Lutherans and
from urban influences. The church was Missouri Synod, one of the most
conservative synods in American Lutheranism.

The Missouri Synod and its attitudes concerning women shaped the roles of
women in the Block community. Since its founding in 1847, the Lutheran
Church–Missouri Synod has charted its own course, often independently and
at odds with American Protestantism as well as with other Lutheran bodies. As
an immigrant church, it long insulated itself by the creation of its own parochial school system, use of the German language, and its claim to *reine Lehre* or
pure doctrine based on divinely inspired, inerrant Scripture.[3] The enemy was
American liberalism and a secularism that destroyed God's natural order and
threatened the very core of Lutheran doctrine and beliefs. According to historian Alan Graebner, "Synod leaders attempted to maintain a social structure
defined by ethnic and religious boundaries that was, save for politics and
economics, as self-contained as possible."[4]

This highly conservative, authoritarian structure compounded problems for
women in the church. Unlike their sisters in Catholicism who had a female
representative in the Virgin Mary, and unlike their Protestant sisters who could
participate in revivals and evangelical practices of preaching and teaching,
Missouri Synod Lutheran women operated within a structured, male-domi-
nated world. Synod theology made clear the complementary but different
callings of males and females. For women to challenge their maternal and
domestic roles was to question God's order and their natural subordination
brought about by the sins of Eve. Compounding the assumption of women's
innate inferiority, Synod doctrine exalted biblical directives of Saint Paul and
excluded women from speaking, holding office, or voting in congregational
affairs.[5]

Rural congregations such as Trinity Lutheran in Block exemplified this
closed, hierarchical system, content to maintain and insulate itself from outside influence and potential threats to its unity. Clergy/lay interactions were
based on this respect for authority, and the continued use of the German
language well into the twentieth century bolstered the local pastor's control

Carol K. Coburn   133

and power. According to *Protokoll* (voters' assembly minutes), all services at Trinity Lutheran were conducted in German until 1925, when English was introduced for one service per month. The last German service was held in 1950. An all-male voters' assembly, the formal male network in the church, and the all-male clergy ensured dominance in all governing bodies and church-related activities.[6]

CHURCH

Within a restrained, inclusive structure combining religion and ethnicity, how did the women of Block create a place for themselves, trapped between a perceived "hostile" outside world and a theology that seemed to offer few, if any, options? Block women had no opportunities to create a formal organiza-tion within the church until May 1912, when twelve women under the direc-tion of Pastor F. Droegemueller established the Trinity Lutheran Ladies Aid of Block, Kansas. These second-generation women, mostly middle-aged or older, molded themselves into an organized group with the stated purpose "to sew and quilt for orphanages, charitable institutions and such who are in need of help."[7] Their weekly gatherings included a business meeting with the re-mainder of the day spent in sewing, quilting, and socializing. Although the pastor was always present for the business meeting, the group elected its own officers and its president ran the meetings. Local secular women and other Protestant women had a long history of charitable work, but Block women had no female role models for conducting meetings or organizing themselves into a cohesive, formal network.[8]

After a tentative beginning, the Ladies Aid thrived in the 1920s and 1930s with the addition of younger women who expanded the group's activities and the organization's budget. Minutes over the years systematically documented the success of an expanding array of money-making activities. These included: sewing and making gifts for church charities; consignment work for dinners, quilts, and blankets; and monetary loans and gifts to the church, school, and synod.

Although the pastor's presence certainly affected the group's behavior, min-utes of the meetings throughout the 1930s demonstrate the group's growing autonomy. The group initiated its own money-making activities and accepted or rejected consignment offers for dinners or quilts. Young women learned to drive and were no longer dependent on husbands and sons to get them to meetings. By the 1930s, the group had its own savings account, recording secretaries began signing their own names, and women were no longer identi-

134   Chapter Ten

fied in the minutes by their husbands' names. The death of a member brought a eulogy in the minutes. The group planned birthday and anniversary celebrations for the teachers and clergy as well as its own twentieth anniversary celebration, which included the entire congregation.[9]

The character of the women's activities varied little from the domestic chores they performed for their family or the church. As with many secular women's organizations, however, domestic activities on behalf of the church often were "elevated" to formal status. Typically, interactions between women began in kinship networks or among neighbors caring for each other's children and sharing domestic tasks at home and church. Nora Ohlmeier Prothe described a women's tradition for the Saturday before Palm Sunday services.

> We'd get down and take our bucket, we'd walk to church. There they'd have a black kettle and a heap of water. We'd get down on our knees and scrub the floor and wash the windows in that old church.[10]

She went on to describe the activity as a social outing for women and children although the work was arduous and splinters were prevalent.

The formal organization of the Ladies Aid gave "women's work" some formal status but also provided opportunities to women who previously had been given little chance to participate in church affairs. Although the organization in no way challenged male authority, women now had a place to develop skills in leadership, money management, and group interaction. The Ladies Aid also gave individual women the excuse to spend time away from family concerns, socialize with each other, and donate their work to larger charitable institutions outside the local congregation. Their donations and handmade items were sent to synod-affiliated programs primarily in Kansas, Nebraska, and Colorado, but also to a black congregation in Alabama, a missionary hospital in India, and a German relief fund.

For women who had little opportunity to develop skills outside their homes, the Ladies Aid provided an expanding though informal educational network of a sort that scholars have often ignored or not viewed as educational at all. Ellen Condliffe Lagemann proposes close examination of women's nonschool activities, suggesting that, since women have been traditionally excluded from formal educational networks and since formal education may not be relevant to their own experience, informal educational settings (like the Ladies Aid) may be more important for continued growth and development, particularly for adult women.

As the autonomy and budget of the Ladies Aid increased, third- and fourth-generation women made an easy transition to Ladies Aid from the Walther

League, a formal youth program begun in 1924 to keep young people within the church, to encourage Bible study, to furnish opportunity for Christian education, to provide wholesome entertainment, and to assist in charitable endeavors. For Block girls age fifteen and older, Walther League provided a unique opportunity to participate and have equal voting power with boys in a formal church organization—an opportunity adult women rarely shared. Girls were elected as officers and committee members and served as debaters and lecturers on an equal footing with boys of the same age.

One night a month, the young people met in the schoolhouse for their business meeting and presentation of an educational topic. The church maintained a small library in the schoolhouse and presenters were expected to investigate their topics before they made their presentations. Another night during the month, they met for a social evening with entertainment of their own choosing. This included wiener roasts, ice-cream socials, outside speakers, and plays presented by the young people. These educational and social activities were particularly important since most girls did not attend high school and had little opportunity to develop such skills elsewhere.[13]

Trips to local and regional Walther League conferences exposed the girls to people and places they rarely had opportunities to visit. One interviewee stated these large gatherings were the most fun because you could "meet all the boys from other places" and see what other churches did differently.[14] For Block girls, most of them third- and fourth-generation German-American, the league served as a valuable network to interact socially and to develop skills in leadership, organization, and communication. With the addition of Walther League, girls now had a place upon completion of parochial school. This became an intermediary step for them before they began work in the outside world or married and joined their mothers in Ladies Aid.

SCHOOL

For girls the main network of association centered on the parochial school. The synod considered the school "an agency for ideal Christian training." Like the church, the school functioned to instill Lutheran doctrine and preserve ethnic culture and language, and theology was fundamental to the curriculum. Although the Block school taught the "3 R's," it emphasized religion, music, and the German language.[15]

Based on nineteenth-century German tradition, Lutheran schools were highly structured, authoritarian, and typically taught by male teachers. Unlike their peers in public schools, Block girls learned early that all authority in

136   Chapter Ten

church and school was male. Block did not hire its first female teacher until 1906, when school enrollment had reached seventy-six pupils. Women were hired throughout the following decades, but never to replace a male teacher, to teach the upper grades, nor to serve as principal.

Besides the formal doctrinal messages demanding female subservience, girls received informal messages concerning identity and appropriate gender behavior. As in public schools, gender differentiations were common. Boys and girls sat on opposite sides of the room and played together in separate groups at recess. Minnie Cahman Debrick described a special marching drill the children were to perform for the annual school picnic:

> We'd practice and we'd practice, and the boys carried the flag and we [girls] carried a broom over our shoulder. . . . I don't know why, I guess because the boys had the flags and the girls had to have something. So since girls done the housework . . . if you can figure out that puzzle, you can do more than I can.[16]

Lifelong female friendships began in the Block schoolroom and the experience of confirmation class solidified those early years of camaraderie. During the seventh and eighth grades, all children took special religious training to prepare for final adult confirmation into the church. Each day the oldest classes met with the pastor to memorize and recite doctrine. The activity most remembered with terror was *Christenlehre*. Each Sunday the students in the confirmation class would be lined up in the front of the church and asked doctrinal questions to be answered out loud in the presence of the congregation. An incorrect answer caused acute embarrassment long remembered by the humiliated child or parent.[17]

Confirmation was an important rite of passage for girls. They gained the right to partake in Holy Communion but also to leave school to earn money doing domestic work for other families or at least to take on more responsibility in their own homes. Until the late 1930s, when more Block girls began attending high school, confirmation and some adult status came at the age of fourteen.

FAMILY

As was true in most rural areas, the focus and main arena of activity for Block women was the family. The farm family functioned as both an economic and social unit, producing goods for home consumption and market while socializing children in cultural and gender-related roles.[18] Block families depended on each member to carry out certain roles and duties to ensure the overall welfare of the farm and home. Woman's role within the family focused on child-bearing, on child-rearing, and on the subsistence services necessary to feed, clothe, and nurture all family members. Nineteenth-century German ideology, defining woman's role as housewife, wife, and mother, ran deep, and the Block community certainly supported and maintained these attitudes.[19] Although young children of either sex performed many domestic duties, gender-defined activity became more prevalent as puberty approached and girls began an informal apprenticeship for future domestic roles.

As was true in many rural areas, in the early German-Lutheran families at Block uncles, aunts, and cousins served as sources of support, advice, and control for children. The elderly received respect and special treatment as they continued to contribute to the household as workers and storehouses of folk wisdom and cultural heritage.[20] Older women usually spent their widowhood in the home of a daughter or son where they performed domestic tasks until physically unable to do so.

Child-rearing practices varied widely among families, but both parents usually disciplined children. My interviewees often described their fathers as stern and quite willing to use corporal punishment and their mothers, in contrast, as often talking with children and using a more "tender-hearted" approach. Marie Dageforde Monthey told of her mother calling her and her misbehaving siblings into the kitchen for a talk. "She took us out into the kitchen. She said, 'You've all got me today yet but many a little child would be happy if they could have me as [their] mother.' We all broke down and cried."[21]

A girl's adult experiences began with marriage and childbirth. The average marital age for women in Block was 22.2 years and for men 26.6 years. Even third- and fourth-generation women typically chose German-Lutheran husbands from the Block area or from another German-Lutheran community closely associated with the Block Germans.[22] After marriage, motherhood and childbirth epitomized adult womanhood and its duties and responsibilities.

Midwifery was extensively practiced in Block until Gesche Mahnken Block, one of the community's original settlers, died in 1911. Highly respected and affectionately known as Grandma Block, she emigrated from Germany as a young wife in the 1850s. She and her husband, Dittrich Block, had sold the property to the church for its original buildings and the community was named after the Block family. When Grandma Block delivered babies, doctors were called only if she felt the mother might experience serious complications. Women essentially controlled the birth room when a midwife was present, but the growing availability and prestige of male doctors discouraged young women from taking over from the aging midwives of the nineteenth century.[23]

138   Chapter Ten

Accompanying this shift in birth practices, family size was beginning to decrease and by 1920, when the community was at its population peak, Block women were having fewer children. Third-generation Block women had smaller families than their mothers or grandmothers.[24]

Throughout the female life cycle, kinship ties were important, fostering strong family and community bonds. Work sharing was not uncommon. Often a woman performed one task, such as sewing, for the entire family while other female family members divided the other domestic chores. In Marie Block Prothe's family her oldest daughter sewed, another assisted her in the kitchen, and the youngest daughter lived with and worked for a married sistered.[25]

Sunday afternoons regularly became social events for kin and non-kin alike. On Sunday afternoons an entire family would visit another household for dinner, bringing together three generations for relaxation, recreation, and conversation. Annual mission festivals, similar to a long-practiced German custom, brought the church community together for worship services, guest speakers, and a basket dinner.[26] Family events such as baptism, confirmation, marriage, and death carried even more meaning when church ceremonies celebrated these passages.

Such social activities were ordinarily closed to "outsiders"—the term commonly used to describe individuals not in the Missouri Synod fold. For women at Block, whose activities were already narrowly defined, this synodical warning against the "hostile" secular world kept them effectively isolated from women outside the Block community. Only in economics and politics was the secular world tolerated and customarily these were domains of fathers, husbands, and sons. Theologically and socially, outside interaction was discouraged for all members well into the twentieth century. Mildred Block related a story her mother told her about "outsiders."

> Pastor taught Mom and them in the school that if you weren't a Lutheran you shouldn't have anything to do with them or go to Hell. That was his philosophy. Wasn't that something?[27]

RELATIONS WITH THE OUTSIDE WORLD

Although outside contact was minimal, Block women and girls were heavily involved in domestic production on the farm, and this created a pathway to the outside world. Women produced goods for their families, neighbors, and friends, with the surplus going to Block, Paola, and neighboring general stores that sold their products to consumers. At times, the demand for domestic goods may have outstripped the supply.[28] Sometimes goods were bartered and at other times sold for cash. The sale of women's domestic production was a reciprocal exchange that took place so often, usually weekly, that money was rarely deposited in banks or documented in legal transactions. Women, unlike men, were not involved in exchanges of large amounts of cash that resulted from annual harvest or periodic sale of livestock. Although women's domestic goods brought in small amounts of money, the value of women's production lies in the fact that it provided a steady, continuous income even through the depression years.

First- and second-generation women varied in their ability to control their own production. Husbands and fathers initially took the domestic goods to market, although many wives went along and the task was performed together. Women who married after 1920 and learned to drive cars began taking their own goods to town, bartering and collecting the cash themselves. The experience of Lydia Prothe Schultz is typical of the transition between second- and third-generation women. Lydia's father taught her to drive the family car when she was seventeen, and she often ran errands to town alone. Her mother never learned to drive either a car or the family's horse-drawn wagons.[29]

Domestic service provided women with a slow transition into the outside world. Initially, girls worked for the immediate family or relatives in the community. By the end of the nineteenth century, the neighboring town of Paola began advertising for live-in domestic servants or hired girls. Hiring out became a girl's rite of passage to womanhood and marriage.

The importance of exposure to the outside world cannot be overemphasized, particularly in its power to assimilate girls into American culture. Some scholars convincingly argue that because of this live-in experience, German-American girls had better English skills and assimilated more quickly than their brothers.[30] For girls from Block, hiring out exposed them to their first financial and social independence. They used their wages for clothes, trips home, or for building their trousseaus.[31] The opportunity to be in town with the excitement of new faces, shops, and movie theatres was simultaneously frightening and thrilling but always highly educational.[32]

For girls coming of age after 1920, domestic service in Kansas City provided higher wages and better educational opportunities. The contrasts in community size and lifestyle loomed large for girls who had rarely if ever been away from home and family. For Irene Minden Prothe, her hired girl experience included her first train ride, her first streetcar ride, and exposure to kitchen appliances and foods she never knew existed.[33]

Train travel home once a month provided a continuous link with Block and

140   Chapter Ten

the family. Although most young women returned home after two or three years in Kansas City, some stayed and married men in Kansas City. Most, however, returned home to care for ill parents, help the family, or to marry local men. Hiring out definitely gave these women new perspectives upon themselves and the outside world. The combination of urban lifestyle, financial independence, and living in the homes of non-Lutherans afforded a broad, rich experience unparalleled in the lives of their mothers or grandmothers.

In 1917, the outside world came to Block. The United States entered World War I and anti-German sentiment escalated nationally. In February 1918, the local newspaper announced President Wilson's order for registration of "alien enemies," or all German-born men who were not American citizens. In June, all German-born women and women born in this country but married to German-born men were also required to register as "Enemy Females." Eighteen women from Block, including six American citizens born in the United States, came to the Paola post office to be interviewed, fingerprinted, and photographed. Threatened with deportation solely because their husbands had been born in Germany, they were doubly stigmatized by gender and ethnicity. American-born husbands of German women were not required to register.[34] Esther Prothe Maisch reported that her American-born mother was so angry about the registration that she refused to give the family extra copies of the required photograph even though they pleaded for it as a keepsake.[35]

The Block community had no major incidents of violent anti-German behavior during the war years. While nationally the Missouri Synod was under heated attack, the Block community struggled internally with issues of assimilation and particularly with the use of the German language. Attitudes about the war varied from anger and resentment to outward patriotic displays of American loyalty.[36] Even as grandsons, sons, and brothers were drafted for military service, Block women were forced to deal with marginal status in the outside world where being female did not protect them from ethnic and religious bigotry.

CONCLUSION

The women of Block, Kansas, created and participated in networks of association that shaped and molded four generations of German Lutheran women. Church, school, family, and outside networks each played a role in the transmission of beliefs, values, and culture. The institutions of church and school functioned with unparalleled authority in the lives of girls and women. The networks of family and the outside world provided the most opportunity for change and growth.

Church networks were gender defined, and age determined the entry and exit patterns of girls and women. The hierarchy of authority remained solidly male in a church that firmly believed in the subordination and silence of women and children. Women and eventually adolescent girls defined a place for themselves by creating church-related activities that justified separate associations. The Ladies Aid operated at the discretion of the male voters' assembly, but in time the women achieved independence of action and governance. These women successfully combined social gatherings with domestic activities, and the girls in the Walther League combined Bible study and educational activities with social activities and trips. In true American entrepreneurial spirit, each organization learned to parlay these activities into money-making endeavors that increased their importance and assured their existence. It can even be argued that girls in Walther League enjoyed a closer parity to their male peers than did adult women.

Of all the networks, the church was affected least by Americanization and the passage of time. For more than seventy years, its formal networks, structure of authority, and character of activities changed only by degree. It is not difficult to understand the lack of female visibility and power. In a hierarchical world where men were often reluctant to challenge the authority of the pastor, it is no wonder that change came slowly for women and girls.

The school gained authority through its close association with the church, and girls received strong messages concerning beliefs and behavior. Young girls learned social and gender roles in conjunction with religious doctrine, firmly linking appropriate gender behavior to religious imperatives. Male authority, like the church itself, was to be unquestioned. In distinction from public schools, girls saw few female role models in the classroom. The much acclaimed "melting pot" of the public schools remained remote and had little effect until Block girls started attending public high school in the late 1930s.

Aided by rural isolation, Block's protective and insular institutions staved off religious and cultural threats. Even if young women were tempted by the outside world, Block's institutions remained unwavering in their authority and "truth." For some, the protection was unwanted and resented, but for many it offered strength, assurance, and unfailing support from birth to death. Unlike some urban environments that created dissociation and conflict between families and generations, the rural environment buffered the cultural shock many first- and second-generation Germans faced in large American cities. According to Frederick Luebke, "it seems that immigrant institutions operative in the rural

142   Chapter Ten

and small town environment were fairly successful in easing the process whereby the newcomer was assimilated, mostly, perhaps, by slowing it down."[37]

Family networks functioned as productive work units and provided the arena for all manner of interactions. Women and girls worked together. As in other rural environments, when girls and women worked with males it was typically perceived as "helping out." Because of the complexity, variability, and privacy of family life, the structures of authority are difficult to assess. Bolstered by religious doctrine, patriarchy was unmistakable; however, the German reverence for motherhood placed women squarely in the core of family interactions. Women's public deference to their husbands in no way determined the private interactions of husband and wife or parent and child. In assessing women's experience, Claire Farrer suggests that historians may assume that public roles are dominant over private ones simply because they are more accessible to the scholar.[38]

As women ventured into the outside world, outside networks changed family dynamics and individual behavior. Outside activities played a large part in expanding the role and activities of Block women. Continued need for salable and consumable domestic goods kept women in the mainstream of family productivity. Improvements in transportation allowed young women to work in Kansas City as hired girls and increased their mobility through their use of the automobile. Twentieth-century Block women, like many rural women, functioned as both producers and consumers much longer than their urban counterparts.[39]

Questions remain to be answered concerning religion, ethnicity, and gender. How representative are Block women when compared to other rural ethnic women? Nineteenth-century Kansas was replete with small rural/ethnic settlements. What made Block different from other ethnic enclaves? In many ways, Block was not different. Many such rural communities developed around an ethnic church and espoused traditional family values. Some differences, however, are evident. For a Missouri Synod Lutheran, religion and ethnicity were inseparable. As Robert M. Toepper has pointed out, the rural immigrant character of the synod, its well-organized parochial education system, and its explicit linkage of theology and the German language, bound the Missouri Synod into "the most compact German culture group in the United States . . . perhaps the only separate culture-group which has a perfect organism for self-perpetuation on such a high and well-rationalized plane."[40]

Even if ethnic communities had foreign language or parochial schools, most did not experience the longevity or religious exclusivity of Missouri Synod schools. In many ways, Missouri Synod communities, like Block, were one pole in a continuum running from them through ethnic communities that created parochial schools but had a more mixed ethnic population to ethnic groups who sent their children to heterogeneous public schools.

Although the study of gender remains a difficult task in traditionally male-defined communities, it continues to deliver rich rewards. Additional ways must be devised to uncover the attitudes and activities of women in a strongly patriarchal community. Block women had limited personal and work options and, unlike other Protestant women, they could not resort to evangelical causes to assert their independence and worth. And, for busy rural women, reform societies such as suffrage or temperance organizations were a luxury when domestic work had to be done and families fed and clothed. Numbers alone provide limited information, particularly when much quantitative analysis has been based on male work or urban female work patterns. Also, the public/private construct fails to provide a meaningful format when discussing rural or ethnic women's experiences. More research must be focused on finding objective and subjective ways to assess rural women's work experience and attitudes.

By looking at networks of association, I have drawn a composite portrait of four generations of women in the Block community. The purpose of this study was not to create a story of female victims or rebellious heroines fighting for recognition, although individually they may be found. I chose to examine four generations of women and the nature of their everyday lives. Historian Gerda Lerner stated, "The true history of women is the history of their ongoing functioning in a male-defined world on their own terms."[41] The powerful combination of religion, ethnicity, and gender provides a fascinating backdrop for such a study.

NOTES

1. Barbara Finkelstein, "Casting Networks of Good Influence, in *American Childhood: A Research Guide and Historical Handbook*, ed. Joseph Hawes and N. Ray Hiner (Westport, CT: Greenwood Press, 1985), 111–52. Although Finkelstein uses the concept of "networks of association only in analyzing history of childhood, I believe the concept is adaptable to women's history and provides a way to view women's interactions in a male-defined culture.

2. *Statistical Yearbook of the Lutheran Church-Missouri Synod 1924* (St. Louis: Concordia Publishing House), 172 and *Statistical Yearbook* (1940), 83.

3. See Carl S. Meyer, *Moving Frontiers: Readings in the History of the Lutheran Church–Missouri Synod* (St. Louis: Concordia Publishing House, 1964) and a series of articles by Heinrich H. Mauer in *American Journal of Sociology* 30–34 (1924–28).

4. Alan Graebner, *Uncertain Saints: The Laity in the Lutheran Church–Missouri Synod, 1900–1970* (Westport, CT: Greenwood Press, 1975), 113.

5. Ibid., 17–18.

6. For specific information on church governance see Carl S. Mundinger, *Government in the Missouri Synod* (St. Louis: Concordia Publishing House, 1947).

7. *Constitution* of the Trinity Evangelical Lutheran Church Ladies Aid (Block, KS: Trinity Lutheran Church [TLC] Archives), 1. Although the first Ladies Aid in the synod began in St. Louis in 1852, the organization in small rural congregations did not become common until after the turn of the century.

8. The nineteenth-century Lutheran Church in Germany did not have a long history of women's philanthropy. See Catherine M. Prelinger, "The Nineteenth Century Deaconessate in Germany, in *German Women in the 18th and 19th Century: A Social and Literary History*, ed. Ruth-Ellen Joeres and Mary Jo Maynes (Bloomington: Indiana University Press, 1986), 215–29.

9. Ladies Aid Minutes, 6 April 1932, p. 90.

10. Author's interview with Nora Ohlmeier Prothe, 24 June 1986, Block, Kansas.

11. Ellen Condliffe Lagemann, "Looking at Gender in Women's History, in *Historical Inquiry in Education: A Research Agenda*, ed. John Hardin Best (Washington, DC: American Educational Research Association, 1983), 251–64.

12. *Constitution* of the Trinity Lutheran Walther League (TLC Archives), p. 192. Walther League was a national organization begun in the 1890s in St. Louis. The name came from C.F.W. Walther, who served as one of the primary founding fathers of the Missouri Synod.

13. Rural bus service did not become available in Block until 1937. Until then, the completion of eighth grade at the parochial school marked the end of most children's formal education.

14. Author's interview with Ada Ruth Schultz Coburn, 6 October 1986, Paola, Kansas.

15. Walther H. Beck, *Lutheran Elementary Schools in the United States* (St. Louis: Concordia Publishing House, 1939), 101. No lesson plans have survived to reveal Block's exact curriculum, but since schools had synod-trained teachers it is reasonable to assume the curriculum was similar to synod recommendations presented in official school journals and teacher training books. See Beck, *Lutheran Elementary Schools*, 379–80.

16. Author's interview with Minnie Cahman Debrick, 23 September 1986, Paola, Kansas.

17. All my interviewees mentioned *Christenlehre* and many told of anxious moments and nightmares before Sunday morning services.

18. Karin Hausen, "Family and Role-Division: The Polarisation of Sexual Stereotypes in the Nineteenth Century—An Aspect of the Dissociation of Work and Family Life, in *The German Family*, ed. Richard J. Evans and W.R. Lee (Wenonah, NJ: Barnes & Noble Books, 1981), 52.

19. Juliane Jacobi-Dittrich, "Growing up Female in the Nineteenth Century," in *German Women in the Nineteenth Century: A Social History*, ed. John C. Fout (New York: Holmes & Meier, 1984), 199.

20. Charles H. Mindel and Robert W. Habenstein, eds., *Ethnic Families in America: Patterns and Variations* (New York: Elsevier, 1976), 420.

21. Author's interview with Marie Dageforde Monthey, 16 August 1986, Block, Kansas.

22. *Trinity Lutheran Church Recordbook* Marriages (TLC Archives). These figures are

average marital ages compiled from 1885 to 1940. There were marriages before 1885 but ministers did not begin recording ages until that year. Church minutes repeatedly describe clerical and holiday exchanges with German Lutheran churches from Franklin County and Crawford County. The *Paola Western Spirit* lists many social exchanges, including marriages, with the Palmer Germans in Washington County.

23. My interviewees born after Grandma Block's death or who had younger brothers and sisters born after 1911 referred less to midwives and women helpers and more to male doctors who came by car to deliver babies. See also Judy Barrett Litoff, *American Midwives: 1860 to the Present* (Westport, CT: Greenwood Press, 1978).

24. Church records of birth and baptism generally confirm this decrease in fertility (TLC Archives). In addition, records of the sixteen first- and second-generation Block women required to register as "Alien Females in 1918 reveal large families. Two-thirds of the women had home at least six children and three had borne ten or more ("Alien Enemy Registration, Box 17, Federal Archives, Kansas City Branch, Kansas City, Missouri). Of the twelve third-generation women I interviewed, more than half came from families with at least seven children. None of the third-generation women had more than four children and six had only two children.

25. Author's interview with Lydia Prothe Schultz, 26 January 1985, Paola, Kansas.

26. Mission festivals were celebrated yearly as noted in *Protokoll* minutes from 1888 through 1940 (TLC Archives).

27. Author's interview with Mildred Block, 22 November 1985, Fontana, Kansas.

28. In 1900, the Peiker-Wishropp grocery store in Paola printed a large front-page advertisement in the newspaper asking "to take all produce our county customers can offer. *Paola Western Spirit,* 24 August 1900.

29. Author's interview with Lydia Prothe Schultz, 13 February 1982, Paola, Kansas.

30. Doris Weatherford, *Foreign and Female: Immigrant Women in America, 1840–1930* (New York: Schocken Books, 1986), 148, and Laurence A. Glasco, "The Life Cycle and Household Structure of American Ethnic Groups: Irish, Germans and Native-Born Whites in Buffalo, New York, 1855," in *A Heritage of Her Own,* ed. Nancy F. Cott and Elizabeth H. Peck (New York: Simon and Schuster, 1979), 288.

31. Block women who had worked as hired girls all told me that they kept their own money and either saved it or bought items for themselves. The family did not expect their daughters to send money home but to take care of their own financial and personal needs.

32. Sylvia Lea Sallquist, "The Image of the Hired Girl in Literature: The Great Plains, 1860–World War I," *Great Plains Quarterly* 4 (Summer 1984): 166–77. Although Sallquist focuses most of her analysis on fiction, she wrote that the hired girls' memoirs mention "education as a motive for being a hired girl" and the "opportunity to be in town."

33. Author's interview with Irene Minden Prothe, 18 July 1986, Block, Kansas.

34. *Paola Western Spirit,* 1 February 1918, explained "Alien Enemy" registration, and 21 June described the registration of "Enemy Females."

35. Author's interview with Esther Prothe Maisch, 25 June 1986, Block, Kansas.

36. *Protokoll* minutes from 1918 until 1950, when German was officially discontinued, describe the anxiety, anger, and frustration of the church in dealing with English. My

146   Chapter Ten

interviewees confirm the wide range of attitudes and emotions brought about by World War I. Many second- and third-generation residents were ready to assimilate at a faster rate but others consistently attempted to slow the process and succeeded for decades.

37. Frederick C. Luebke, *Immigrants and Politics: The Germans of Nebraska, 1880–1900* (Lincoln: University of Nebraska Press, 1969), 35.

38. Claire Farrer, "Women and Folklore: Images and Genres," *Journal of American Folklore* 88 (January/March 1975): ix.

39. See Joan M. Jensen, *Loosening the Bonds: Mid-Atlantic Farm Women* (New Haven: Yale University Press, 1986), 91.

40. Robert M. Toepper, "Rationale for Preservation of the German Language in the Missouri Synod of the Nineteenth Century," *Concordia Historical Institute Quarterly* 41 (February 1968): 167. Toepper cites Heinrich H. Mauer, "Studies in the Sociology of Religion," *American Journal of Sociology* 31 (July 1925): 49–50.

41. Gerda Lerner, *The Majority Finds Its Past: Placing Women in History* (New York: Oxford University Press, 1979), 148.

CHAPTER ELEVEN

LAND, LABOR, AND COMMUNITY IN NUECES: CZECH FARMERS AND MEXICAN LABORERS IN SOUTH TEXAS, 1880–1930

JOSEF J. BARTON

Much recent research in immigration history seeks to avoid the dangers that accompany an excessive reliance on so-called elitist sources. Older studies tended to depend heavily on the records left by ethnic-group leaders in politics, economic activity, or cultural achievement. Their object was to demonstrate that immigrants, too, had contributed much to American history. This meant, however, that little attention was given to ordinary people—the large numbers of faceless folk whose experiences were often markedly different from those of the elite. As a remedy for such historical astigmatism, scholars have developed quantitative methodologies that permit systematic comparisons between one immigrant group and another in different times and places.

In the following article, Josef Barton compares European immigrants—a group of Czech farmers—with immigrant laborers from Mexico in a single environment—Nueces County, Texas.

Barton's main purpose is to illustrate, by means of comparative analyses, how group responses were conditioned by ethnic culture. Both Czech farmers and Mexican field workers were highly transient and both were united by bonds of family and religion. But Czechs were linked by generational lines and Mexicans by lateral ties or a concentric order of alliances. Czechs were often landowners; Mexicans were a landless rural proletariat. Czechs united to secure credit, purchase equipment, and provide for mutual aid; Mexicans, whose needs were more urgent, formed defensive associations to negotiate wages and hours and to organize strikes.

Barton bases his elegantly organized study on a remarkable array of sources: agricultural statistics, census data, county mortgage records,

148   Chapter Eleven

*church records, diaries, letters, and newspapers. He works in several
languages, mostly Czech, Spanish, and English. His voluminous notes
are omitted here but are available in his original version as published in
Frederick C. Luebke, ed.,* Ethnicity on the Great Plains *(1980).*

Nueces County is part of a barbarously large country, alternately drab and
dazzling, spectral and remote. South of San Antonio, the plain veers to the
southeast, driving the timber line to the Gulf of Mexico at Matagorda Bay.
Here, in a diamond-shaped territory bounded by that bay, by the mouth of the
Rio Grande, by Laredo, and by San Antonio, lay all the requirements of
ranching: Texas grasslands, Spanish stock, Indian horses, and American cow-
boys. Hungry cities and eager railroads assured markets, northern capital and
Texas management spurred expansion. Between the end of the Civil War and
1885, while an astonishing swarming of cattle covered the Great Plains, the
Nueces country was the seat of the cattle kingdom.

Toward the end of the nineteenth century, as the pull of market demand
raised the value of produce and so of land, an agrarian transformation swept
this corner of the Great Plains. Production of sheep and cattle for cash drove
the first engine of change. The number and value of sheep reached a peak
between 1874 and 1876, that of cattle between 1882 and 1889. Values of land first
lagged behind, then caught the tempo of stock raising; prices doubled between
1876 and 1879, again between 1881 and 1884. Accompanying the steep rise in
value was enclosure, begun on small scale around 1870 and accomplished by
1885, by means of which big ranchers secured their hold over the most productive land. The Nueces countryside came under a regime of agrarian capitalism:
a consolidation of private control over land, and the consequent ease of its
conversion from one use to another and of its movement into the hands of
owners eager to extract a maximum of revenue.

Cotton drove the second engine of change. The extension of railroads
throughout Texas in the late 1870s opened new territory; cotton acreage rose
from two to seven million acres between 1879 and 1899. In an already spe-
cialized economy, cotton farming worked another transformation of south
Texas. While ranching remained the dominant activity in Nueces County until
the early twentieth century, cotton patches appeared on marginal lands in the
1880s. A decade later, 120 farms, on which farmers produced five hundred bales
in a good year, dotted the county. Clearing began in earnest in 1899; gangs of
Mexican and black laborers changed stretches of land from mesquite clumps to
vast open fields. The major part of the country remained in enormous ranches
of 100,000 to 200,000 acres in 1910, but now divided into hundreds of cleared
farms of 20 to 200 acres. Simple statistics illustrate these dramatic changes:

between 1910 and 1930, the number of holdings grew from 945 to 1,947; the proportion of cultivated land rose from 3.5 percent to 76 percent, the proportion of arable land in cotton from 6.6 percent to 88 percent. In 1929, Nueces led the counties of Texas in cotton production, in 1930, the counties of the entire United States.

The drive to raise production sprang partly from new farmers' notions of the good life, more from habits of enterprise and risk taking. A large proportion of the cotton farmers came from east and central Texas, Louisiana, Arkansas, and Mississippi; of two samples of twenty new farmers with 600 or more acres, in each of two five-year periods (1910–15 and 1920–25), fifteen came from counties in which cotton accounted for more than half the farm acreage. Like two Louisiana farmers who arrived in Nueces in 1911, J.B. Womack and W.T. Munne, they routinely committed three-quarters of their improved acreage to cotton and, when opportunity came, leased great tracts from old landed families and made ranches into cotton lands. New landowners quickly married into old families as they gained the best lands and so gave new life to what passed for an old social structure. Everywhere in the cotton fields appeared the signs of the new planters' presence: machinery, white-suited purchasing agents for southern mills, Missionary Baptist and Southern Methodist churches. A new elite had, by the end of World War I, worked a revolution on this bleak, flat land.

A new force of labor emerged as King Cotton overthrew the stock regime. Ranching had fitfully drawn upon herders and hands from ranches and farms on the periphery of the great holdings. A small proportion of the rural population worked steadily on the ranches in herding and fencing. During times of more intense demand, from April to August, big ranchers hired men from the two hundred tiny ranches in the county, but even then few worked for stretches longer than three weeks. Cotton demanded a new formation of the rural labor force, a complex pattern of farmers, tenants, and laborers. Immigrant farmers on less than 50 acres, half of them Czech, operated a third of the cotton farms in 1910. A regiment of tenants, at first largely Mexican and later mostly southern black and white, carved out small farms of 20 to 80 acres; they accounted for one-third of all farms in 1910, three-fourths in 1930. Alongside tenants, during the sixty days of peak demand from mid-July to mid-September, worked an army of laborers; almost wholly of Mexican origin, this rural proletariat made up a third of the population in 1919. On farms of 600 acres, where ten laborers ordinarily worked, the labor of chopping and picking required forty. This fourfold increase in demand drew hundreds of families to Nueces and created a reserve of mobile labor. A sudden spurt of growth created a characteristic formation of rural labor which, by the mid-1930s, accompanied

150   Chapter Eleven

large-scale agriculture not only in the cotton Southwest, but also in the cotton and sugar South, on the sugar operations of Puerto Rico and Cuba, and in the factories in the fields of southern California.

Three related themes—the origins, development, and maturation of ethnic communities in a modernizing rural society—concern me here. I take up each of these themes and bring my considerations to bear on a question, Why did Czechs and Mexicans choose to be *Czech* farmers and *Mexican* laborers and not just farmers and laborers? If the term *ethnicity* is to be given palpable meaning and its social and cultural implications uncovered, the connection between ethnic identity and such developments as capitalist forms of agricultural organization, the growth of voluntary associations, the emergence of new classes, and a whole host of other social realities must be discovered. My contribution to this large task depends upon an entrance into the landscape and history of a place, and upon my sense of connection with two farming populations, their cultures and their interests. What I seek are the particulars of a situation, for an exploration of context and choice in ethnic allegiance winds through a thicket of observations.

The twentieth century arrival of immigrant peoples in Nueces marked the last stages of two movements. In the 1760s the Spanish had pushed north to the Nueces River, where they claimed great landholdings until the Texas War of Independence. Spanish grantees abandoned their lands during the war and, between 1840 and 1848, transferred seven of fifteen original grants to Anglo-Americans. The sale of the last Spanish grant to an Anglo-American in 1883 left only patches of land in Mexican hands. The resurgence of Mexican movement into south Texas in the mid-1870s came as Anglo-American ranchers consolidated their control of the land. The migration of Mexican ranch hands and their families proceeded through Laredo and then into rural areas around Zapata and San Ygnacio, northward to San José and Concepción, finally to San Diego and so to Nueces. A steady stream flowed from the northern Mexican states of Tamaulipas and Nuevo León around the hundreds of islands of Mexican families in the ranching country between the Rio Grande and Nueces Rivers.

Czech immigrants began a southward movement from central Texas during the same years. Latecomers to the cotton counties, they found them already crowded. German farmers had established agricultural colonies in the 1830s and 1840s, then spread southward after the Civil War in a segmentary belt of settlement through the cotton counties. These communities matured in the 1870s, whereupon the second generation again scattered southward deeper into the coastal plain. Polish farmers also moved southward from their settlements near San Antonio into coastal counties, where they established dispersed cotton farms in the 1880s and 1890s. When Czech farmers shifted south and west, from the mid-century settlements of Praha and Dubina, on to the 1870s settlements of Frydek and Wied, and to the turn-of-the-century settlements of Siner and Panna Maria, they followed well-worn paths.

Newcomers to Nueces were a mix of first- and second-generation immigrants. Mexicans entering the county between 1900 and 1920, so far as I can learn from a sample of two hundred people, were three-fifths of them born in Mexico, two-fifths in Texas. Their Mexican origins lay in the agglomerations of laborers on haciendas in the states of Tamaulipas, Nuevo León, and Coahuila, from which 95 percent of them came. The rapid development of large-scale agriculture in the North, and the consequent shortage of labor, created a mobile rural proletariat. Caught in fitful cycles of development, families sought employment in both Mexican and Texas agriculture. Already in motion when Villa's revolution burned over the North, great numbers streamed northward into Texas.

Czech peasants left an old countryside in transition. A third of Czech newcomers, in a sample of seventy-seven, were born abroad, in two clusters of southern Bohemian and eastern Moravian villages. Although living in mountainous areas to which agrarian transformation came late, these peasants nonetheless became in the 1860s part laborers and part cultivators. Expanding local markets, stimulated by the industrialization of Bohemia, drove agricultural productivity forward in the latter part of the century. In these villages a system of wage work gained ascendancy, the use of machines began, and an old organization of work gave way to new forms of capitalist management. In response to their displacement, young men and women sought work in highly commercialized agricultural areas of Bohemia and Poland, then whole families started out for Texas.

Czech farmers quickly acquired land in Texas, learned to plant cotton and established households. There followed a characteristic development of parishes, mutual benefit societies, and farmers' unions—in short, of communities. But in the early twentieth century, the lands of central Texas were already crowded, with little room left for the continuing stream of newcomers; in 1906, for example, three of every five Czech families in Williamson County were sharecroppers. Hence began another exodus, of whole families, from Williamson County in particular and central Texas in general.

Mexican laborers moved north gathering in the cattle basins of small ranches and farms around the great estates of south Texas, alternately herding their own sheep and cattle and working on big ranches. Households clumped around rural Catholic chapels where families assembled once or twice yearly

152   Chapter Eleven

for confession, baptism, first communion, marriage, and requiem. Never was theirs a settled life, for families moved constantly in search of work and shelter; and so they arrived in Nueces County.

After lives of extraordinary transiency, Czech and Mexican newcomers reached Nueces. Their constant movements, first from changing homelands and then from Texas settlements, made them uprooted peoples. Yet if we follow their movements long enough, we find prior ties of locale and kinship among the migrants. All the foreign-born Czechs in my sample (one-third of the newcomers) came from six villages, one wholly Catholic cluster in Bohemia, another wholly Protestant in Moravia. Among second-generation Czechs (two-thirds of the arrivals), two of three came from Williamson County, of families whose parents had left the same Bohemian and Moravian villages a generation earlier. Three-quarters of the Czech newcomers, then, belonged to moving communities. What bound them was more than memories of place, for two-thirds of the newcomers belonged to vertically extended families of three generations. At first glance an uprooted people, the Czech immigrants are seen on closer examination to be bound together by common origins and kinship.

The Mexican families also shared ties of locale and kinship. Three-quarters of the Mexican-born newcomers (two-thirds of the newcomers to Nueces) came from five contiguous haciendas south of Bustamante, in Tamaulipas, and from three neighboring haciendas near Cadereyta Jiménez, in Nuevo León. Of the Texas-born (one-third of the newcomers), 60 percent came from a string of six ranches south of San Diego. More than origins bound them: a third of the newcomers moved in the company of brothers and sisters, another third with other kindred. Both origins and kinship, then, linked Mexican families on the move.

What strikes the observer of both Czech and Mexican immigrants is the durable bonds of place and blood. The persistence and proliferation of personal relations, among the members of two groups in which we expect disruption and insecurity, require further comment. In the case of the Czechs, what initially linked newcomers was lineal families of three generations' depth, a kind of segmentation of kinfolk into lineal units. In the case of the Mexicans, what early bound was a web of crosscutting relationships among kinfolk. Czech immigrants, in short, allied themselves in families of three generations, Mexican newcomers in families of lateral kindred. This fundamental difference in patterns of initial bonds had cardinal importance in the subsequent development of the two communities. The locus of membership and alliance in the Czech community was the lineal unit of the family; for the Mexican community, the armature of belonging and association was the lateral network of kindred. In order to grasp the character and consequences of this difference, we look now at the agrarian realities of the peoples' lives.

The fortunes of the Czech and Mexican newcomers stand out in bare summary. As both groups moved into the county around 1910, the take-off of cotton production made places for them. But what different locations! Of the ninety-nine Mexican families resident for three decades, only Juan Saldaña was able to scratch together a thousand dollars to buy a twenty-acre patch. Another sixteen families bought small lots in Robstown and Bishop. Of the sample, 80 percent were landless, without title to farm, garden, or lot. Eight families among the propertyless secured sharecropping rights to farms or gardens for short times, but not one climbed the agricultural ladder. The great part of the Mexican families—three-quarters—entered and endured lives of agricultural labor.

The steady drift of Mexican families into Nueces before the massive migration of 1907–17 provided tenant farmers for the young county. On their tiny plots of ten or twenty acres they picked four or five bales of cotton. The Sánchez family, for instance, entered a sharecropping arrangement with W.B. Croft and W.W. Meek in 1900, cultivated five acres of cotton, and expanded their farm to one hundred acres by 1903. Two brothers, Paulino and Rafael Cadena, jointly worked fifty acres of cotton under a crop lien to Croft and Meek in 1903. Tenancies, however, rarely led to ownership. Occasionally a family like that of León Galván acquired a planter, middle buster, cultivator, and harrow, but its hold on such machinery was precarious. Moreover, the rapid influx of southern tenants at the end of World War I forced Mexican tenants off the most productive farms and onto marginal lands. By the early 1920s, all eight Mexican tenants in my sample had lost access to land, their places taken by black and white southerners.

That left only agricultural labor for three of every four Mexican families. July's surge of workers, come to chop and to pick, left behind new families at September's ebb. Every large cotton farm provided seasonal work for two or three families. Laborers' shacks thickened the countryside and eventually raised whole towns on the plain. The movement into towns marked the maturation of a landless, wage-earning, store-buying, rural proletariat. The Mexican community now formed a mobile labor force whose major problem was to survive the dead times. "I'm going to Pennsylvania to escape the vagrant's lot," ran a famous *corrido* of south Texas: "Farewell, Texas, with your planted fields, I'm going to Pennsylvania so I won't have to pick cotton." So rapid a proletarianization threw families into an unending struggle to get through slack months and eventually to join seasonal migrations to other areas of large-scale farming.

154   Chapter Eleven

The contrast of Czech with Mexican families leaps to the eye. Of the thirty-five families in my sample that remained three decades, two-thirds acquired farms. The holdings were modest, the median size barely exceeding eighty acres. The remainder of the families held long-term cash leases from family or relatives.

Czech families secured land largely because they had their own reserves of labor. Six families, five of whom came as families of three generations, with a little capital, a knowledge of cotton, and, most important, abundant labor, initially held 160 acres or more. All six endured into the second generation. Families starting out with 120 acres or less commonly lacked generational extension: ten of these sixteen families were young, lacked capital, and commanded only the husband's and wife's labor. The outcome of such beginnings was brutal: among the nine families with tiny farms of 20 to 40 acres, five lost everything before ten years passed, four clung to their farms by means of heavy mortgages. The successful establishment of a household depended upon a large labor force and upon the slow consolidation of resources over the cycle of a family's life. Only by fully exploiting their reserve of labor did families survive for two generations upon the land.

The consequences of familial strategies over the long run show up in the passage from generation to generation. Now the first generation sorted sons and daughters into heirs and disinherited, into advantaged and disadvantaged. The eleven families that had come with mature children succeeded in ten cases in establishing at least one son. Like the family of Stanislav Procháska, by purchase, by gift, by will, they settled a new generation upon the land. Procháska moved to Nueces in 1909, when his family already counted two sons of fourteen and seventeen; Vlasta Mrázek bore him three more sons and a daughter. Procháska and his two eldest sons, Emil and Frank, worked a tenant farm of 80 acres between 1909 and 1921, then bought a farm of 160 acres in 1922; Ladislav and Anton settled on a new farm of 160 acres in 1926; Timothy, the youngest, briefly farmed 80 acres in 1929, then left this farm to his father. In his will, Procháska left the big farm to Emil and Frank and divided his farm equipment between them; each, in turn, chose one of his sons as major heir. Contrast Procháska with Anton Krušinsky, who came with his wife and one son in 1923, purchased 79 acres of cotton land, and conveyed 40 acres by deed of gift to his son in 1930. Often forced to enter chattel mortgages for operating expenses, Krušinsky and his family worked 39 acres for three decades, until at his death he divided his patch into five equal portions and gave them to his five children. Within a few months all but Rosa had sold their lands; she kept the old house and grew onions on her 8 acres. Like the Krušinskys, nine of the eleven families in similar circumstances were extinguished as farming families.

Czechs came to Nueces to keep a customary way of farming and to maintain their united families and the kind of future they wanted for their families. They wanted to escape the changing agriculture of central Texas, so they moved on to another frontier where they hoped to renovate old forms of security. The families of this little community possessed several resources, of which the most significant was the labor force. Those families that realized their aim of assuring another generation's livelihood arrived in the county just as their children one after another reached maturity and provided a rising curve of labor. But those families without such working capacity largely disappeared from farming within ten years. And so was set in motion yet another migration, of the sons and daughters of extinguished farmers, now toward the cities.

Immigrant families formed a complex pattern of farmers, tenants, and laborers. Czech farmers settled on the land; some held on to farms for at least two generations and thereby established a lineage in a situation of considerable uncertainty. Each successful family was a little community of labor and land. Although the accumulation and inheritance of land appears a wholly domestic affair, it had a crucial public dimension, for it created the conditions for the recruitment of a core population and hence maintained a Czech community. Mexican families met with extraordinary changes in these few years, for as tenants they were members of a little community of families, while as laborers they were as much participants in the wider society as members of a local community. They lost even their access to tenancies, hence their landlessness was no longer concealed. Mexican laborers, like Czech farmers, could not make things happen except collectively, though, unlike the farmers', the Mexican laborers' experience of labor demonstrated every day that they must act collectively or not at all.

One thing becomes clear from the realities of the Czech and Mexican immigrants' lives. The departures from old situations and arrival in new rendered the past problematic. The past of Mexican haciendas and Czech villages ceased to be the soil in which these peoples had their roots and from which they drew life. At least they no longer did so in the matter-of-course manner of old. With special reference to their need for continuity, for stability—in a word, for culture—the fit between the world the immigrants lived in and life as they lived it, on the one hand, and the forms and institutions that their ancestors had used to order it and make it meaningful, on the other, had gone.

In order to grasp the distinctive attempts of Czech and Mexican newcomers to place their new worlds in some frame, we must seize upon the particular ways in which they used old forms in confrontation with altered conditions of life and how, out of that confrontation, came ethnic cultures that shaped and

156   Chapter Eleven

sustained their lives and communities. "For most individuals," Sidney Mintz and Richard Price remind us in their discussion of Afro-American cultures, "a commitment to, and an engagement in, a new social world must have taken precedence rather quickly over what would have become, before long, largely a nostalgia for their homelands." People ordinarily long, not for an abstract heritage, but for immediately experienced personal relationships, evolved in specific cultural and social settings, that any deracination such as migration may destroy. Hence a culture, in this sense, becomes closely linked to the social contexts in which ties of kinship and friendship are experienced. I have trained my analysis thus far on the realities of economics and stratification by which the newcomers were restricted, and on the particular frameworks within which their new lives were fabricated. I turn now to a brief consideration of the manner in which cooperative efforts became institutions, of the ways in which religion became a bond of community, and, finally, of the means by which men and women transformed ritual associations into resources for collective action.

The Czech and Mexican families endured and, having endured, reached beyond their households to bind themselves in little communities. Some shreds of evidence suggest that Mexican immigrants entered cooperative efforts soon after their arrival in Nueces County. Gang laborers on clearance projects formed a mutual benefit society in the mid-1880s; tenant farmers organized three similar societies between 1897 and 1905. Such voluntary networks of mutual aid widened after 1907 to include rural laborers; in the two following decades at least seventeen laborers' societies appeared. Formed sometimes among families already linked by kinship, more often among households in burgeoning rural settlements, mutual benefit societies translated private relations of trust into public cooperation. And in so doing, Mexican laborers made kinship and friendship, ritual and ceremonial—dimensions of old communities they had left—into passageways toward new communities.

Czech families entered similarly reciprocal relationships. The springs of such cooperative acts were, in the case of Roman Catholics, the saints' societies of native villages, in which expectations of mutuality took visible form. From Williamson County eight families carried an image of St. Joseph that their parents had brought from the homeland; other allied families gathered under the patronage of St. Isidore. By the mid-1920s, eleven such societies, each numbering nine or ten families, pulled the Czech Catholics of Nueces into a round of organized life. Protestants also created societies of mutual aid, often as their first cooperative act. Among the Protestant heads of households were five men who had founded benefit societies upon their arrival in Texas, and now in Nueces their first response was establishment of a lodge of Podporná jednota (Mutual Aid Society). Wider than the circle of kindred but drawing upon the obligatory mutuality of kinship, such societies practiced the rituals of reciprocity without which a community cannot long endure. Such artificial families became the cores of both Czech and Mexican communities.

The weave of small decisions of family and association also formed patterns of religious life. Institutional development flowed from the choices of many ordinary families as they reached beyond their own households for aid and support and, in so doing, forged some sense of the ordering of their world. "In the morning," noted an itinerant priest during a month's journey through the Mexican communities of Nueces in 1876, "Mass at about 7. Then on horseback to the next ranch, in the evening after supper Catechism, Rosary, a little instruction to the people, next day the same as the day before." In the two decades following, the dispersed communities of the region built chapels with such names as Concepción, Jesús María, Santo Tomás, Dolores, San Juan, Los Reyes, Las Animas. Priests visited these missions sometimes once a year, most often once every six months. The religious life of Mexican parishes, then, was a life of lay confraternities and sodalities in which the priest's role was sporadic and peripheral.

The Catholicism of rural communities responded to the needs of Mexican families in that it made a ritual statement about social relationships and obligations. My scraps of evidence indicate early lay initiative in the establishment of confraternities and sodalities, and a subsequent development of a complex and integrated religious framework. The proliferation of saints' societies, each encompassing families already bound by kinship, marked the emergence of community life, for now such families became associated in enactments of the Catholic calendar. In the parish of San José, for instance, newly arrived Mexican sharecroppers founded three saints' societies in 1898; gang laborers from a hacienda in Tamaulipas established a confraternity in honor of their patron saint in 1904; rural laborers created many such societies in 1914 and 1915. Such associations, set within networks of ongoing social relations, became the heart of parishes. At La Cejita, sixty families of rural laborers living within a few minutes' walk of each other formed six sodalities and confraternities between 1907 and 1916. They petitioned their bishop for a chapel in 1917, "in order better to manifest our good will and to secure our children's good, to practice more regularly our Catholic religion, and to receive proper instruction." The maturing communities of laborers built their own religious institutions, which the bishop and clergy served to sanction, not to control. The families' sense of making institutions on their own was expressed in the 1920s in petition after petition to their bishops in which hundreds of men and women resisted the efforts of clergy to exercise control over lay societies. Nowhere was this sense more urgently expressed than in a new parish of some two hundred laboring families in which members of several saints' societies successfully thwarted their priests' authority for five years. In practicing the ceremonials of togetherness in this world and procuring the salvation of their members in the next, saints' societies created a ritual method of living rich in human relationships.

While Mexican Catholicism was expressive of concentric circles of social relations, Czech religious life formalized tangential circles of familial relationships. Czech Catholics quickly formed saints' societies, but with an important difference from Mexican societies; the charter members of Czech societies, in every case for which documentation survives, restricted membership to lineal and affinal kin, and thus created closed corporate groups. Such associations were the linchpins of parochial life, for their marches, vigils, and feasts drew families into representations of solidarity. The saints' day, customarily celebrated in the household of the oldest family in the society, periodically enacted the little dramas of Catholic life.

Czech Protestants of the Jednota bratrska (Unity of the Brethren) created a similar framework for religious life. The heads of large families were the heart of the church; "Grant thy peace to this household and its heirs," prayed the pastor at the funerals of men, "even as Thou takest this thy son to thine own house." In such households the itinerant pastor administered ceremonies of baptism and confirmation, of marriage and burial, rites of personal and familial passage. Within this congregation were articulated relationships among members of the Czech Protestant community: the Elders, whose task was the maintenance of good order; the Christian Sisters, whose charge was charitable acts; and the Sunday school class, whose preparation was for passage through confirmation into adulthood.

Out of the exigencies of lives predominantly hard and unendowed, Czech and Mexican immigrants evolved an unexpectedly mature pattern of sanctions and responsibilities. An assessment of the transition of peasants and laborers to modern agriculture depends upon a firm knowledge of ordinary peoples' lives, of the interaction of family, farm, and community, of older and new attitudes, and of particular places. Czech and Mexican families entered an unsettled rural world with distinctive cultures, but those cultures were more than backgrounds. Their cultures had their own meanings, expectations, definitions of purpose; they had their own rituals of reciprocity and rites of passage. After other impressions fade, this one remains: along with the loss of any felt cohesion in these communities, Czech farmers and Mexican laborers built for themselves new domestic and familial ties, new cooperative relationships, and new religious institutions.

The achievement of contrasting solidarities—of a lineal order of familial and associational alliances among Czechs, of a concentric order of alliances among Mexicans—shaped different forms of collective action. In the Czech settlement, families fastened upon farmers' unions, which were gatherings of the heads of households, as a means of communal control of resources. The advantaged families—the landed core—found in this union sources of credit, cooperative arrangements for the purchase of equipment, and mutual aid in times of drought and low prices. A communal form of collective action, the Czech unions succeeded only sporadically in making alliances beyond the local circles of families. Yet the union, a kind of local brotherhood, was the effective expression of Czech farmers' aspirations, for it assured continuity of lineage and property.

In the urgency of their needs, Mexican laborers reached beyond households, beyond mutual aid and religious associations, outward to solidary unions. The early stage of the movement was defensive and consisted of leagues of laborers bound together in opposition to landlords and foremen. Such defensive associations soon claimed not merely old but new rights, the most important of which was the right to organize. Agricultural laborers on one great Nueces cotton farm organized a defensive league in 1911; two years later they refused to work without a contract for wages and hours. The ferment of action and organization was alive in the county: gang laborers on clearance projects struck in 1907; teamsters walked off their jobs in 1910; rural laborers organized several locals between 1926 and 1937 and tried to form an agricultural workers' union in south Texas in 1937. The failure of Mexican laborers to provide a centralized expression of their resistance should not obscure the importance of their constant stirrings; in opposition to their labor and their masters, rural laborers drew upon the resources of their communities to give political expression to their needs and aspirations.

To return to my initial question, Why did Czechs and Mexicans choose to be *Czech* farmers and *Mexican* laborers, and not just farmers and laborers? In their new world of modernized agriculture, these immigrants pursued two mingled yet distinct ends, the one a search for identity, the other a pursuit of decent and secure lives. Both demands led families beyond their households into communal association and, in the case of Mexican laborers, into labor organization. Ethnicity was, then, an expression of primary but extrafamilial identity, and a protean resource for collective action. Yet these contrary impulses produced ironic consequences. The little community of Czech farmers endured from generation to generation by securing the continuity upon the land of a few children and by disinheriting the others, hence the greater part of

160   Chapter Eleven

each generation had to find livelihood elsewhere. The community of Mexican laborers achieved a measure of solidarity, yet the maturation of that solidarity required alliance with other working-class organizations. Thus was set in motion processes of integration whose implications for these rural communities are still unfolding.

CHAPTER TWELVE

STEINBACH AND JANSEN: A TALE OF TWO MENNONITE TOWNS, 1880–1900

ROYDEN K. LOEWEN

In the essay that follows, Royden Loewen introduces another kind of comparative analysis. Instead of contrasting two ethnic groups in one location, as Josef Barton does in the preceding article, Loewen compares the adaptive strategies of one small ethnoreligious group in two different settings.

Loewen's people are Kleine Gemeinde Mennonites, a tiny sect of German-speaking farmers who emigrated from southern Russia. Pietistic, separatistic, and theologically very conservative, they formed agricultural colonies in Manitoba and Nebraska in the 1870s and 1880s. Although both locations share many physiographic characteristics of the Great Plains, their social, economic, and political environments were rather different. Steinbach, Manitoba, was an isolated community, preeminently a Mennonite town; Jansen, Nebraska, though founded by a Mennonite and named for him, was a railroad town, loud and bawdy, not an ethnoreligious island. Like Steinbach, it had some Mennonite merchants, but most Kleine Gemeinde families lived in the surrounding countryside.

Loewen's Mennonites emigrated to North America to conserve old customs and traditional values; their method was to reformulate familiar strategies or evolve new ones. Contrasting adaptations are at the heart of this article. They demonstrate how history emerges from the interaction of culture and environment over the passage of time.

This article is an adaptation of chapter 8 in Loewen's book, Family, Church, and Market: A Mennonite Community in the Old and New World *(1993).*

162   Chapter Twelve

Historians have depicted Mennonite communities in North America as isolated rural sectarian settlements *par excellence*. Among Mennonites, those of Dutch and North German ancestry who emigrated from Russia during the 1870s to settle on the American and Canadian plains have especially been lauded for successfully transplanting rural cultural features. Kansas and Nebraska Mennonites have been noted for their close-knit communities, cadre of ethnic institutions and Russian-based agricultural practices, especially that of Turkey Red wheat production. Manitoba Mennonites have been credited with an even purer transplantation, including the medieval open-field system, complete with the farm-operator village, the *Strassendorf* (street village) and an attending communitarian government. The Mennonite story, however, is also intersected with that of town life. And it was not a simple one-way relationship, with the town representing a conduit for new and destabilizing ideas. The town could represent starkly different options. It could act as the Achilles heel of assimilation; it could also act as the very defense of traditionalism.[1]

Two towns, Jansen (Nebraska) and Steinbach (Manitoba), are representative of two ends of the spectrum of change and continuity. Both towns were located in the heart of conservative Mennonite farm communities that had been founded in 1874 by Kleine Gemeinde (little congregation) Mennonites, a small sub-group of Mennonites noted for their strict lifestyles, tight social boundaries, and church-centered communities. Steinbach is located 35 miles southeast of Winnipeg, in what was once the exclusive Mennonite block settlement of the East Reserve; Jansen is situated in Cub Creek township, Jefferson County, 60 miles southwest of Lincoln. Both towns served as the dominant service centers in their respective agricultural districts. In 1900 Steinbach had a population of 349 persons in 96 households, Jansen 273 in 55 households.[2] Both towns introduced potentially destabilizing forces into the tight, exclusive Kleine Gemeinde communities. They provided access to markets for commercial farmers, jobs for landless wage earners, and residential options for the elderly, just as merchants introduced a growing cash nexus into the local economy. All such forces expanded opportunities for members of the Kleine Gemeinde to interact with outsiders.

Steinbach and Jansen, however, were also remarkably different towns, in cultural ambience, social structure, and governing values. Steinbach evolved into a service center after having been founded as just another East Reserve *Strassendorf* in September 1874. Jansen had its beginning in October 1886 as a commercially-oriented railroad town. Their disparate beginnings would shape diverse developments. Jansen was founded by progressive Mennonites out of step with the rural sectarian community and developed quickly into a loud, bawdy railroad town, boosted by land speculators and peopled with non-

Mennonite merchants seeking quick profits. Steinbach was less of a departure from established ways. Its developers were respected members of the Kleine Gemeinde; the town maintained the solidaristic, communal-oriented, closed nature of the immigrant Mennonite community. Its business enterprises had roots in the craft industries of the communities in Russia. Its laborers were young, highly mobile and determined to becoming landed farmers.

A comparison of Jansen and Steinbach reveals the ways of life and values of the descendants of the 1874 Kleine Gemeinde settlers from two different perspectives. In Steinbach the settlers saw a town that could safeguard old values; in Jansen they saw the opposite—a town that was a threat to their community, and a social entity that required the development of more sophisticated approaches to securing social distance from the town's "American" milieu.

I

In 1874 Steinbach was a typical Mennonite *Strassendorf* that took its basic design from farm villages in South Russia and West Prussia. It was founded by 18 farm households and laid out along a stream on the eastern edge of the East Reserve (known, after 1883, as the Rural Municipality of Hanover). Farmers settled along one side of the street and organized the rich arable land around the village as an "open field." Following Russian ways, several of the farmers practiced craft industries to supplement household income. Within a few years of settlement the Steinbach farm economy was diversified with the presence of a blacksmith, a flour miller, a sawyer, and a merchant. In this respect the village differed little from its namesake in Russia, the village of Steinbach in Borosenko Colony. Here local Mennonite farmers had engaged in sideline enterprises—Klaas R. Reimer in his blacksmith shop, Abram S. Friesen with his roller mill, Peter Buller at his wind-powered flour mill, and others who worked as hardware and clothing retailers, carpenters, and teamsters.[3]

Steinbach began to change in the late 1870s, but its character did not differ much from the larger Mennonite towns in South Russia. The business which led the Manitoba town's growth was a wind-powered flour and sawmill, erected in 1877. The mill, owned by local farmer, Abram S. Friesen, resembled one in the old Steinbach, in Borosenko, Russia. Just as diaries from Borosenko recount the excitement of November 1873 when the Butler mill was dismantled and hauled from the village in Russia, memoirs of Manitoba pioneers in Steinbach recount the excitement in February 1877 when the long oak beams and milling stone were hauled into Steinbach from Winnipeg and erected by Peter Barkman, the millwright from Borosenko. Just a year later, however,

164   Chapter Twelve

Friesen sold the windmill and grinding stone, purchased a steam engine, and turned exclusively to saw-milling. To fill the void left by this sale, local merchant Klaas Reimer and millwright Peter Barkman built a three-story flour mill and fitted it with a steam engine. Steinbach received a third commercial enterprise in 1877 when Klaas Reimer began to sell merchandise on consignment for a Winnipeg merchant.[4]

The community acceptance of these businesses was immediate. One Steinbach farmer noted in December 1880 that "things are very lively here at the sawmill and business is also increasing in size and scope at the general store." Steinbach's growth as a service center continued during the 1880s. In the mid-1880s Klaas Reimer's son, Heinrich, opened an even more substantial hardware store. In Russia retailing had been regarded as disgraceful, but it was now accepted as a "necessity" by the most conservative community members. The other businesses were patronized too. Farmers came from distances of 25 miles to trade at the Reimer–Barkman mill where they acquired not only flour, but a variety of animal mashes, with specific mixes for beef cattle, hogs and chickens.[5]

It was not till the 1890s, however, that Steinbach took off. In 1881 Steinbach still had fewer households than did some of the neighboring Mennonite villages and each of its households was still engaged primarily in agriculture. Between 1891 and 1898 this changed as Steinbach's population almost doubled from 208 to 361 and the number of landless households increased almost fivefold from 10 to 48.[6]

At the foundation of Steinbach's growth was the continued development of farm service enterprises. Some of the ventures were new. In 1889 Klaas W. Reimer, another of merchant Klaas Reimer's sons, built a cheese factory to produce a commodity hitherto not a part of the Mennonite economy. In its first year of operation, the factory produced 50,000 pounds of cheese and yielded a $1000 profit; within seven years the young Klaas opened two more cheese factories in two other villages. By 1896 he was running a small empire that produced 150,000 pounds of cheese annually. Also in 1889 two young entrepreneurs established a successful farm implement dealership.[7]

Old services grew as well. When the Reimer–Barkman flour and feed mill burned to the ground in August 1892, a new five-story mill powered by a larger steam engine was constructed. In the same year, Abram S. Friesen opened his new, two-story shop to repair steam engines, forged plow shares, constructed straw blowers, and experimented with primitive versions of the combine harvester. Friesen's business also owned a sawmill at Pine Hill, 25 miles to the east in the forests of the Canadian Shield, and sold lumber from its yardsite in Steinbach. By the turn of the century two other entrepreneurs operated smaller mills at nearby Pine Hill, one of whom, Peter W. Reimer, shipped firewood and fence posts by railroad to his retail outlet in Winnipeg.[8]

The businesses that experienced the greatest growth were Steinbach's two general stores. By the early 1900s the stores had combined annual sales of over $56,000. Of the two stores, "K. Reimer and Sons" was the more ambitious. In 1893 Reimer offered to sell the store to a relative from Russia, but when this sale did not materialize, Reimer expanded the scope and size of his enterprise. In a single month, February 1895, Reimer sold $1000 worth of merchandise from his store; operated his mail order service that sold everything from prayer shawls and needles to moose horns and wild cherries; hired a convoy of French and English teamsters to ship 1060 bushels of oats and 4700 pounds of beef and pork 50 miles south of town to a sawmill camp; struck a deal with a Jewish merchant from Winnipeg for the sale of 4000 pounds of butter; and began his annual shipment of eggs to Winnipeg. The business continued to grow and by 1906, when Reimer died, his total personal worth exceeded $72,000.[9]

Steinbach's growth in the 1890s attracted attention from the wider world. It was praised in several German-language newspapers. "Steinbach is . . . a large, beautiful village and is inhabited by very enterprising people," wrote one traveler in the Winnipeg-based *Nordwesten* in 1894. He described it as a factory town with "the puff and clatter of steam engines as rarely seen out in the countryside." In 1898 Heinrich Kornelsen, the Steinbach reporter for the Indiana-based newspaper, *Mennonitische Rundschau*, added to this impression: "Here in town is a roller flour mill, a feed mill, a steel and wood works center, a tannery, two blacksmith and repair shops, a sheet metal shop, a saddlery, three general stores and several food dealers, and two guest houses with stables for travellers; the only requirements we still have are for a doctor and a shoemaker."[10]

Despite Reimer's innovations and Kornelsen's boosterism, Steinbach was a recreation of an "old world" village. Unlike other prairie towns, Steinbach had neither a railroad nor outside infusions of merchant capital. Its first businesses had their roots in Borosenko Colony in Russia. Its later businesses, although interacting regularly with the outside world, were geared to meet the aims of the Mennonite agrarian household. Most important, perhaps, in guaranteeing continuity in Steinbach was that its very growth was based on a transplanted social hierarchy.

Among scholarly explanations for Steinbach's remarkable growth is one that argues that the town was favored with "poor" but "ambitious, hardworking men" and another that Steinbach was a "strategically located" service center.[11] Neither was true. Indeed, Steinbach was located on the southeastern edge of the East Reserve's grain growing area, guaranteeing that little Winnipeg-bound

166   Chapter Twelve

traffic would pass through Steinbach. And if geography was not a factor in Steinbach's growth, neither was the "Horatio Alger" spirit of Steinbach's "poor men." In fact Steinbach's merchants were not poor men at all. In Russia they had been among Borosenko's most successful farmers and craftsmen. Indeed, in the East Reserve's first recorded tax assessment in 1881, merchant Klaas Reimer and miller Abram S. Friesen represented the Reserve's most highly taxed individuals. Clearly these men had been able to transfer sufficient capital from Russia to invest in the expensive steam engines and two- and three-story business enterprises.[12]

What differentiated Steinbach from its neighboring villages in Manitoba was not simply the presence of prosperous men. Each village had its wealthy farmer. Steinbach was unique in that its rich and its poor were separated by a larger gap in wealth than the rich and poor of any other Kleine Gemeinde village. Despite the presence of the well-to-do Reimer and Friesen families, Steinbach was on the whole the poorest of the Kleine Gemeinde villages on the East Reserve. The presence of Steinbach's poor was evident in the comparative sizes of Steinbach's first houses, farms and tax assessments. Its first residents lived in houses averaging 419 square feet, compared to 878 and 677 square feet for those in neighboring Gruenfeld and Blumenort respectively. Its farmers cultivated an average of 16.1 acres in 1881, compared to 16.9 in Gruenfeld and 28.2 in Blumenort. Its households had an average tax assessment in 1883 of $522, compared to $624 in Gruenfeld and $720 in Blumenort. An economic differentiation was also apparent in the municipal tax assessment of 1883. Although the top 10 percent of the households in Blumenort and Gruenfeld were assessed 21 percent and 24 percent of the village taxes respectively, the 10 percent of the wealthiest households in Steinbach (3 of the 34) were appraised 42 percent of their village's taxes.[13]

This combination of poor farmers, seeking alternative sources of income, and well-to-do farmers, who transferred significant capital pools from Russia, served to turn Steinbach into a regional market center. Steinbach possessed men with surplus capital for off-farm commercial investments and men whose households depended on wage labor. Just as poor farmers in Russia had readily engaged in non-farm labor during the off-season, underemployed farmers in Steinbach served as a labor pool for local merchants and miners. Some farmers worked as winter loggers—a regular activity by the 1880s. Other poor farmers worked as teamsters for local merchants, allowing merchant Klaas Reimer to advance his trade with Winnipeg in the 1880s without the aid of a railroad. Farmer Gerhard Kornelsen's diary records 438 miles of travel in the winters of 1880 and 1881, 200 of which represented nine trips to Winnipeg or Niverville in the employ of Klaas Reimer. Kornelsen clearly welcomed this opportunity, for his farm comprised only 19 cultivated acres and three milch cows. A three-day sleigh run from Steinbach to Winnipeg, for instance, provided Kornelsen with a gross income of five dollars.[14]

The combination of underemployed farmers and monied merchants ensured Steinbach a concentration of wealth strong enough to counter the competition of the railroad towns when they did come. Giroux, for instance, was founded in 1897 when the Manitoba and Southeast Railroad bypassed Steinbach seven miles to the east. By 1897, however, Steinbach had a well-established merchant elite, willing and able to turn Giroux to its own advantage. The Reimer family alone owned three general stores, 75 percent of the flour mill, four cheese factories, and a sawmill and together they provided 45.5 percent of the town's taxes.[15] Thus, unlike less established prairie towns which simply disintegrated when a railroad bypassed them, Steinbach was able to counter the Giroux challenge. The Steinbach merchants merely redirected their teamsters from Winnipeg to Giroux and increased their shipments of cheese, butter and eggs to the Winnipeg markets. Because of their proximity to Giroux and its railroad station, Steinbach merchants were also able to secure a post office. Indeed, Giroux enabled them to swing the economic axis of the East Reserve by 180-degrees, so that its geographic entrepot now became Steinbach. Symptomatic of this switch was the fact that the village of Chortitz, the seat of the Rural Municipality of Hanover, which had received its mail from St. Pierre, lying to the west of the East Reserve, now received its mail from the east, via Steinbach and Giroux.[16]

Undergirding Steinbach's growth was a traditional concern, its merchants' ability to meet the needs of small, mixed farm operators of the East Reserve. Unlike the cash-and-carry stores of some towns in wheat-production districts, Steinbach merchants fashioned their businesses to the requirements of mixed farms. In fact, Steinbach merchants allowed farmers the means of obtaining supplies by barter instead of cash, exchanging household-produced commodities for supplies of clothing and tools. Farmer Abram R. Friesen's diary entry of March 1883 illustrates the process: "To Steinbach with seven dozen and five eggs. Took one pair of shoes for $1.50, three yards cloth for 90 cents, one dozen matches for 25 cents, one dozen cups at 65 cents. The eggs brought $2.22, so I had to pay $2.00 cash." Among the barterers were the poor, like widow Elisabeth Reimer Toews, who paid 63 percent of her bin with farm products and her sons' labor. The merchants clearly benefitted from these payments in kind. The bartered commodities were resold for profit in either Winnipeg or turned over within the store. Moreover, merchants charged higher prices from clients relying on farm products for payment than those paying in cash.[17]

168   Chapter Twelve

II

Steinbach's merchants thus did not undermine the self-reliant Mennonite agrarian household, nor did they end the conservative, communitarian nature of village society in Steinbach. Assertions that "trading centers . . . served as the bridgeheads for the assimilation of the Mennonites into prairie society" did not explain Steinbach's experience during its first generation.[18] Such claims seem to underestimate the resilience of cultural values and the complex strategies that ethnic group members employed to seek cultural and social continuity. Evidence suggests that the worldviews of Steinbach's leaders, the values of its villagers, the social structure of the growing town, and the continued presence of conservative churches in village affairs, ensured that Steinbach people would not assimilate to the wider Canadian society during this period.

Steinbach's social make-up was one sign of continuity. It is true that the town comprised an increasing number of landless households, especially after 1900 when free arable land disappeared and cultivated land became too expensive for many young couples. Indeed, between 1891 and 1898 the percentage of households owning no farmland increased from 26 percent to 63 percent. Nearly 46 percent, 27 of 58 household heads, declared themselves to be general or skilled laborers, that is, blacksmiths, machinists, miners and cheese makers.[19] Yet there was nothing new about the rise of this population group. Many Steinbach residents could still recall the cottages of the "Anwohner," the landless in the Mennonite colonies in Russia during the 1860s. Like the "Anwohner" in Russia, the landless of Steinbach rented cottage lots, near the farmyards of the landowners. By the 1890s the west side of Steinbach's central street was rapidly filled with the rented houses of young Mennonite families and German Lutheran immigrants who worked as wage earners and craftsmen.[20]

The youthfulness of these workers, however, ensured that they would not come to constitute a permanent working class. They were the sons of farmers or recently arrived German immigrants, who hoped to establish their own farms. Their average age of 28.1 years was considerably lower than the average age of 41.5 for Steinbach's landed farmers. They also were mobile; only one of the 32 wage-earning household heads of 1898 still worked as a laborer in 1906. By 1906 the majority of the 1898 workers had founded farms in the parkland, south and east of Steinbach, or had joined one of the colonization efforts in Alberta and Saskatchewan.[21]

Steinbach's solidaristic nature was also assured by resilient social boundaries. It is true that the merchants interacted frequently and regularly with outsiders. Heinrich W. Reimer, for instance, had a standing account with 20 different Winnipeg wholesalers in 1890; moreover, 15 percent or 31 of his 199 clients for

1890 were non-Mennonites, mostly Anglo-Canadians from the nearby Clear-spring settlement and a few Franco-Manitobans. During the 1890s the number of non-Mennonite patrons increased as German Lutherans arrived in the area. By 1898 fully 13 percent of households in Steinbach itself were non-Mennonite. Still, the interactions with non-Mennonites did not affect the primary relationships within the churches and families. Endogamy rates, for example, remained high. In the dozen marriages involving a Mennonite and a non-Mennonite between 1890 and 1905, only one was performed outside the auspices of a Mennonite church. Most of these marriages resembled that of Karolina Kneller and Gerhard Reimer. Karolina was a German Lutheran immigrant from Poland who worked as a servant for Peter W. Reimer in the early 1890s; in 1895, at the age of 19, she was baptized in the Kleine Gemeinde church and married to Peter's brother, Gerhard.[22]

Conservative church leadership in Steinbach also ensured that the town would not become a typical prairie market center during these years. The leadership of the Kleine Gemeinde, the largest Steinbach congregation, worked steadily to counter practices and ideas that could undermine the closed, ascetic nature of Steinbach. It continued the old teachings that commerce could lead to greed. In 1884 when Heinrich W. Reimer built his general store in Steinbach church leaders objected. "As the congregation never had had a business of such size in its midst," noted one farmer, "it was greatly opposed and considered a downfall by the church leaders and most of the brethren."[23] The church leadership eventually came to accept Heinrich Reimer's new store as a necessity for the community, but it still did not believe that its growth should go unchecked.

In 1895 church leaders raised a concern that Klaas R. Reimer's store, worth five times the value of most farms, was not conducive to Christian simplicity and exemplified greediness as defined by Anabaptist writers. When the leaders visited Reimer they criticized his "business dealings." Reimer became defensive: as he saw it, church leaders "keep forgetting how much unrighteousness occurs because of poverty, when the sheriff is used to help [foreclose on property]." Although church leaders ceased action against Reimer, they continued to admonish local merchants, especially after 1896 when the economy strengthened. There were reports that profiteering from the sale of land, timber and cattle had become acceptable in Steinbach. The church was uneasy. Among the special church business meetings in which the problem of Steinbach's "big businesses" came up for discussion was the meeting of May 14, 1905. Here leaders denounced those "evil businesses" which are "always growing larger."[24]

To ensure the continued conservative nature of Steinbach, the Kleine Gemeinde church also vociferously opposed the coming of a railroad to Stein-

170   Chapter Twelve

bach. The Southeastern Railroad had bypassed Steinbach in 1897 and by 1905 some Steinbach businessmen were lobbying for a spur line to connect the town with the railroad. Church brotherhood minutes for January 6, 1905 reveal why the spur line was never built: "We . . . discussed the building of the railroad with which some of the brethren are working and seeking signatures for a petition. . . . [but we] strongly opposed this . . . as there is danger in it for us and our children in that we might become like the world in business and life-style. . . . and the [present] businesses, which already seem too big, would grow even larger."[25]

Cultural continuity in Steinbach is best exemplified in the personal history of its foremost merchant, Klaas R. Reimer. Reimer's diary and letterbook for the early 1890s reveal a conservative, communitarian man. He maintained close, personal ties with an intricate network of relatives and fellow Mennonites in other settlements. The numerous letters Reimer received requesting personal favors, expressed relationships that were rooted in common understandings and loyalties. Letters came requesting jobs, rides to Winnipeg, extensions of credit, the use of his oxen, and outright requests for charity. Emotional ties also shaped Reimer's sense of community. The very thought of travelling far from the community, he wrote in 1886 caused "a lot of tears to fall, for by nature I am quite soft-hearted." And those who emigrated from the close-knit Steinbach district were chided by Reimer. In 1889 when one of Reimer's sons left to study cheese-making in Winnipeg, Reimer responded with sadness: "I had not given him the permission [and warned him] that education often results in pride. . . . I wrote three sheets full, advising him to come back." Reimer's conservative values were even apparent in the will he left when he died in 1906. He could have bequeathed his widow enough cash for a life of middle-class ease. Instead he left her the same amount of money as each of his 17 children, $2309.46, plus the farmyard, the chickens, 220 acres of farm land and the necessary livestock, equipment and tools to farm it. And he left her the family's religious literature: "The Martyrs' Book, the Menno Simons Book, and one Bible." The fact that his funeral drew an estimated attendance of 500 mourners, 200 more than the funeral of the Kleine Gemeinde bishop eight years earlier, indicates not so much that people had chosen an entrepreneur as their true leader, but that this merchant had continued to symbolize conservative values.[26]

III

The town of Jansen in Cub Creek township, Jefferson County, Nebraska, stands in stark contrast to Steinbach. It was founded in October 1886 by Peter

Jansen when the Chicago, Rock Island and Pacific Railroad was built from St. Joseph to Denver and passed through southeastern Nebraska. Jansen was a typical railroad town.[27] Like the other places on the line, Jansen was founded by a well-to-do individual with close ties to the railroad and a vision for a booming town. In some ways Peter Jansen resembled his more conservative Mennonite brethren; he was probably no wealthier than his Canadian second cousin, merchant Klaas R. Reimer. Moreover, Jansen had derived his initial wealth not from merchant or proto-industrial activities, but from operating a farm that during the 1880s sustained 25,000 sheep annually and cultivated more than 400 acres.[29]

Unlike Reimer, however, Jansen was not a member of the conservative Kleine Gemeinde Mennonites. He was the son of Cornelius Jansen, a former German consul, grain trader and urban-dweller of Berdyansk, Russia. As such Peter had learned English before coming to America and was under no commitment to a solidaristic community or traditionalist church. Once in the United States, Jansen quickly became an assimilated American. Even in 1874, when Jansen led the Kleine Gemeinde delegates through Jefferson County, local newspapers marvelled that "Jansen, himself a Mennonite, [was] so much Americanized that his consanguinity with his companions would not be suspected."[29] Jansen, in fact, spent his life proving his American patriotism: he made a personal decision "to use the English language," sought to remain a "consistent Republican," became a justice of the peace in 1880, served as a delegate to the National Republican Convention in 1884, and was elected to the Nebraska legislature in 1898. He prided himself on his business acumen, buying up tracts of land for speculation, and operating his sheep ranch in an "atmosphere of bigness."[30] His own siblings noted Peter's sense of ambition and even his sense of self-importance: "His own ego keeps him from [deferring to his father]" was the frank analysis of his sister in 1877, for "he cannot stand that somebody else should be honored in his place."[31]

Peter Jansen's town-building activities reflected a progressive and entrepreneurial mind. He secured plans for a railroad town even before the line was constructed. Jansen later recalled that "I took quite an active part in the preliminaries, buying right of way, voting bonds, etc." In August 1886 he purchased 80 acres from two Kleine Gemeinde farmers in the southern part of Cub Creek, surveyed a town site, named it after himself and began town boosting. He advertised in local newspapers and printed circulars offering "lots for improvement . . . at low prices and on favorable terms." He invited newspapers to feature the new town, declaring that "our town is booming" and that "everybody [is] invited to invest in Jansen before it is too late, and all the lots are gone." And as other town boosters he also attempted to provide the town

172   Chapter Twelve

with a respectable image; to ensure that it would be alcohol-free, he placed on each deed a caveat noting that "intoxicating liquors shall not be manufactured, sold or given away . . . on said premises. . . . "[32]

During the winter of 1886 and 1887 the town of Jansen experienced a building boom. In January 1887, John P. Thiessen, a local Mennonite and the town's first hardware merchant, reported that a railroad "station, elevator, steam-powered mill to make mash, a hotel and a private guest house are presently being constructed." On April 3 the first passenger train passed through Jansen and a new era dawned in Cub Creek township. By September 1887 the new town could claim 13 business establishments including Peter Jansen's bank, a lumber yard, a grain elevator, a hotel, an implement dealership, a clinic, a barber shop and five stores, a shoe shop, a drug store, a carpentry supplies store and two general stores.[33]

Over the course of the next 20 years Jansen grew steadily. By the turn of the century it was inhabited by 57 families and had a population of 273. New businesses continued to come to town. Amongst those businesses, much to Jansen's chagrin, were three saloons, two located outside the original town boundaries, and one on a lot that had been deeded on without Jansen's prohibition clause. But most of the additions were standard retailing outlets. A 1902 report sounded an optimistic note: "four new brick-constructed stores were built here last summer and increased the business of our town quite considerably." And the first business establishments continued to increase in size and scope. In 1904 the Jansen elevator expanded its capacity by 10,000 bushels at a cost of $2000 and by 1906 a total of 36 stores and shops, including several saloons, were open for business.[34]

As in Steinbach, the development of the town of Jansen advanced the commercialization of local agriculture. The elevator and train station fulfilled that promise and farmers began to produce more corn for export and more cattle for the stockyards in Omaha, St. Joseph, Kansas City and Chicago. The daily rail service also brought regular mail and diaries indicate that farmers viewed the town positively for this service: in June 1894 farmer Jacob Classen noted the joy of having received a letter from a Canadian cousin and then added, "usually when one receives a letter that means one has been to Jansen."[35] Farmers no longer received mail only when business took them to Fairbury, six miles to the west. And now too, they could subscribe to the services of the Nebraska Telephone Company that built a telephone line from Beatrice through Jansen to Fairbury and began selling subscriptions for $36 a year. Old-timers recalled in later years how these facilities provided the farmers with a direct line of communication with the larger centers such as Lincoln, from which parts for farm implements and drugs for cattle could be ordered and received within a day.[36]

The town may have helped farmers secure the economic base for their sectarian, farming community, but it was also a social threat. Sociologist Paul Miller has argued that Jansen ended the isolation of the conservative Cub Creek Mennonites. He points to the number of saloons in town which drew youth from miles around and led to frequent street fights and vandalism. He refers to the travelling circuses and medicine shows that visited town. During the 1890s theatre companies like the "Uncle Tom's Cabin Company" and the "Quaker Botanical Medicine Company" passed through Jansen and attracted huge audiences including, at one point, the bishop of the Kleine Gemeinde church.[37] Threatening old boundaries, too, were the number of Mennonite families who made Jansen their home in its first year and the former Kleine Gemeinde farmers who turned into Jansen businessmen. John P. Thiessen who held shares in a Fairbury lumber yard and implement dealership, now opened a hardware store in Jansen and N.B. Friesen and his brother operated a town-based implement store. Indeed, amongst the owners of the 13 first businesses were six former Cub Creek Mennonite farmers.[38]

In addition to these Kleine Gemeinde–descendant town merchants were a number of Kleine Gemeinde–descendant wage laborers. By 1900 some of the town residents included people such as 57-year-old Peter Friesen who, "as farming became too difficult, rented out the farm and built a nice little house in town." But they also included people like 23-year-old John Friesen who, finding himself without land when he married in 1899, moved into a rented house in town and began work as a carpenter. By 1900, 14 of the 23 Mennonite households in Jansen were engaged in a variety of occupations: in cottage industry such as broom making and cream separating; in civic jobs such as schoolteaching or post delivery; or in wage labor, such as carpentry and steam engine operation. The fact that 70 percent of the Mennonite households in Jansen owned their houses and that the average age of a Mennonite male householder was 39.9 years, indicates that both workers and businessmen now considered townlife a permanent arrangement.[39]

Despite the Mennonites' participation in the town of Jansen, its prevailing German nature ameliorated its potentially disruptive nature. Indeed, while 30 of the 55 households were non-Mennonite in 1900, only 13 household heads had not been born in Germany or in one of the German colonies of southern Russia. At least two-thirds of the households in Jansen spoke German.[40]

Given this critical mass, Jansen Mennonites bravely maintained their German-language schools. In some ways they had no greater official pressure to

174   Chapter Twelve

Anglicize their schools than did their brethren in Manitoba. When, in 1890, Nebraska nativists introduced a compulsory English-school attendance bill into their state legislature, vociferous opposition from non-Anglo populations ensured that the bill did not come into force. In this context, German-language parochial schools continued to exist in Cub Creek throughout the first generation. Jansen Mennonites even braved the derision of Anglo-American neighbors and opened a German school in town. There was strong opposition, climaxing in 1901, to the Jansen Mennonite School. By this year the German school had out-grown its old building and its teacher, J.W. Fast, rented a large vacant house from an Anglo-American. Seemingly, only after the school children moved into their new premises did the landlord realize that his house was being used for German education. He immediately evicted Fast, declaring that "Dutch" had no place in America. Instead of closing the school, an alternative building was located and the Mennonites confidently continued to maintain their ethnic institution. Indeed, they defended their German school with some racism of their own. One Mennonite resident claimed that "these sort of people who purport to be reformers of the Germans and boast that this country could not go on without the Yankees are, themselves, so often in such financial straits that the sun must be ashamed to shine on them."[41] The German schools were complemented by other Mennonite institutions that bolstered Mennonite networks and espoused traditional values of asceticism and communalism. These included the Kleine Gemeinde, Bruderthaler and Krimmer Brethren churches located in or near Jansen, and the Mennonite fire insurance agency which in 1905 elected to extend insurance coverage to town dwellings as well as farm buildings.[42]

The strategy of most Cub Creek Mennonites, however, was to maintain a "social distance" from the town of Jansen. In this way they ensured that the town would not substantively affect their ways of life during the 1880s and 1890s. True, farmer Jacob Classen's diary indicates at least weekly visits to the town, but each was to use the town services for the advancement of the Mennonite community and household. It was a place to which to haul corn or sell hogs, and purchase and repair farm equipment. And it was a place to patronize Mennonite merchants—a pound of coffee, lemon extract, a horse brush at Thiessen and Co., or a gallon of syrup, underwear and calico print at Peter Fast's. It was also the site that provided elements of the very ground of the Mennonite community, such as lumber for a coffin after a sister-in-law died and the depository for grain donated to a "Colorado farmer" and the place for "paper and slate for school." Each such encounter undergirded rather than threatened the Mennonite community.[43]

Few Mennonites made Jansen their home and site for primary relations.

Indeed, only 18% of the 673 Mennonites in Cub Creek lived in town. Even half of the 40 landless Mennonite households continued to live in the countryside where they rented farms or worked as farm laborers. Many of these landless families were able to remain aloof from the urban milieu by joining colonization efforts around 1905. Landed Mennonites who lived in the rural parts of the township, were even better able to maintain old social boundaries. This end was served by the high retention of the Low German dialect (Plautdietsch) in the rural Mennonite households. Census records indicate that by 1900, all Mennonite men in rural Cub Creek had learned to speak English (likely through their market ties), but that only 57 percent of their wives were able to speak English. The strongest indication that Low German continued to be the language of the rural household is that only 17 percent (10 of 58) of rural Mennonite children between the age of three and six spoke English. Figures for Mennonites in the town of Jansen differ significantly: here 88 percent (22 of 25) of the Mennonite wives and 43 percent of pre-school Mennonite children spoke English.[44]

High endogamy rates also indicate the continuation of social distance between Cub Creek Mennonites and the wider American milieu. Only two of the 102 Cub Creek Mennonite families in 1900 represent an inter-ethnic marriage. Both of these marriages involved a German-speaking person who was born in South Russia and who migrated to the United States in the 1870s. It is even possible that these non-Mennonites may have been servants or foster children of a Mennonite family. Endogamy rates changed little in the decade following 1900; in 1910 only one of the 37 urban Mennonite households and only one of the 49 rural Mennonite households represented inter-cultural marriages.[45] Ironically, the Manitoba Kleine Gemeinde Mennonites, who had fewer non-Mennonite neighbors, had a lower rate of endogamy. Clearly the Cub Creek Mennonites were engaging in a defensive strategy of boundary maintenance.

IV

Steinbach and Jansen helped to change the Kleine Gemeinde communities in Manitoba and Nebraska. Both towns served to develop a commercial agricultural economy by providing improved access to markets and services and greater access to farm technology. Both towns also nurtured a class of Mennonite merchants as well as a corps of youthful Kleine Gemeinde wage laborers. The very existence of Steinbach and Jansen reminded Mennonite households that only new agrarian colonies could guard against the ultimate urbanization of Kleine Gemeinde descendants.

176   Chapter Twelve

Yet, Steinbach and Jansen stood in sharp contrast to each other. Steinbach evolved from a transplanted *Strassendorf*, comprised of farm households pursuing familiar craft industries. It continued to be governed by an assembly of Mennonite landowners and its culture was shaped by the conservative Mennonite churches and their bishops. Its workers continued to venerate the ideal of farming one's own land and its business elite were strong defenders of traditional social boundaries. Jansen, on the other hand, was an externally-imposed railroad and elevator town. As such it was a more representative prairie town with a main street perpendicular to and residential side streets parallel with the railroad. Its founder was a wealthy town booster who lured land speculators and merchants to Jansen, and who attempted to develop the simultaneous image of greatness and sobriety. Unlike Steinbach, the majority of Jansen residents remained non-Mennonites and the spirit of the town was more "American." Jansen represented for its Kleine Gemeinde neighbors the epitome of "worldly society" and compelled them to maintain their "social distance."

Steinbach and Jansen were the symbols of the different contexts in which the Canadian and American Kleine Gemeinde found themselves. Steinbach was clearly the consequence of conservative values implanted in a bloc settlement where critical mass favored the Mennonites. Jansen was as clearly a North American frontier town. Continuity for Kleine Gemeinde Mennonites was attained only by developing radically different approaches to these two kinds of urban existence.

Notes

1. For depictions of rural Mennonites see: Oscar Handlin, *The Uprooted* (Boston, 1951), 76, 95; D. Aidan McQuillan, *Prevailing Over Time: Ethnic Adjustment on the Kansas Prairies, 1875–1925* (Lincoln: University of Nebraska Press, 1990); John Warkentin, "The Mennonite Agricultural Settlements of Southern Manitoba," *Geographical Review* 49 (1959): 342–68.

2. Hanover Tax Roll, 1898, Rural Municipality of Hanover [hereafter RMH], Steinbach, MB; U.S. Population Census, Jansen, 1900, Nebraska State Historical Society [hereafter NSHS], Lincoln, NE.

3. Abram F. Reimer, "Tagebuch, 1870–1874," Evangelical Mennonite Conference Archives [hereafter EMCA], Box 14, Steinbach, MB.

4. Peter T. Barkman, "Mitteilungen aus dem Pionierleben," ed., K.J.B. Reimer, *Das 60 jaehrige Jubilaeum der mennonitischen Einwanderung in Manitoba, Canada* (Steinbach, MB, 1935), 34; Klaas Reimer to Jacob Willms, March 1, 1890, Klaas R. Reimer Papers [hereafter KRR], Peter J. Reimer, Steinbach, MB.

5. *Mennonitsche Rundschau* (Elkhart, IN), 5 December 1880; 5 February 1881; Gerhard Kornelsen, "Tagebuch," Gerhard K. Kornelsen Papers [hereafter GKK] Dave Schellenberg,

Steinbach MB, 1884; Peter Unger, "Denkschrift, 1882–1929," EMCA; A.R. Friesen, "Tagebuch," EMCA, Boxes 4 and 29; A.M. Friesen, "Tagebuch," EMCA, Box 104.

6. R.M. of Hanover Tax Rolls, 1881, 1891, 1898.

7. Klaas Reimer to Peter Friesen, 9 September 1890, KRR; *Der Nordwesten* (Winnipeg, MB), 5 September 1890; 6 May 1891; 13 January 1893; 28 September 1899.

8. *Nordwesten,* 26 August 1892; 15 August 1892; Peter W. Reimer to Gerhard Kornelsen, 12 March 1904, GKK.

9. R.M. of Hanover Council Minutes, 1902, RMH; K. Reimer Store Account Books, 1905, Mennonite Heritage Village [hereafter MHV], Steinbach, MB; Reimer, "Memoirs," 27 February 1895, KRR; 15 April 1895; *Rundschau,* 11 April 1906.

10. *Rundschau,* 27 June 1894; 8 April 1898.

11. E.K. Francis, *In Search of Utopia: The Mennonites in Manitoba* (Altona, MB, 1955), 187; John Warkentin, "The Mennonite Settlements in Southern Manitoba: A Study in Historical Geography" (Ph.D. diss., University of Toronto, 1960), 162; Frank Epp, *Mennonites in Canada, 1786–1920: The History of a Separate People* (Toronto, 1974), 222.

12. R.M. of Hanover Tax Rolls, 1881.

13. Homestead Patent Applications, 7–6E, 6–6E, 5–56E, Provincial Archives of Manitoba [hereafter PAM], Winnipeg; R.M. of Hanover Tax Rolls, 1881 & 1883.

14. Kornelsen, "Tagebuch," 135 and 136; 20 January 1885.

15. Abram F. Reimer, "Tagebuch"; Klaas Reimer, "Memoirs"; R.M. of Hanover Tax Rolls, 6–6-E, 1898.

16. Abe Warkentin, Reflections on Our Heritage: A History of Steinbach and the R.M. of Hanover From 1874 (Steinbach, 1971), 44 and 49.

17. A.R. Friesen, "Tagebuch," 17 March 1883; H.W. Reimer, "Store Account Book," 1891.

18. John Warkentin, "The Mennonite Settlements in Southern Manitoba," 147.

19. R.M. of Hanover Tax Roll, 6–6E, 1881, 1891, 1898.

20. John C. Reimer, ed., *75 Gedenkfeier der Mennonitischen Einwanderung in Manitoba, Canada* (North Kildonan, MB, 1949), 155; Gerhard Kornelsen, "Steinbach Einst und Jetzt," *Steinbach Post,* March and April, 1916.

21. R.M. of Hanover Tax Rolls, 1898, 1906.

22. H.W. Reirner Store Account Book; Peter R. Dueck, "Tagebuch, 1901–1919," Dec.18, 1904, EMCA, Box 184; Jan. 6, 1905; East Reserve Kleine Gemeinde "Seelensliste," EMCA; Johan G. Barkman, "The Diary of John G. Barkman, 1858–1937," trans. Waldon Barkman (Steinbach, MB, 1988), 63.

23. Unger, "Denkschrift," 2.

24. Klaas Reimer, "Diary: 1880–1900," trans. P.U. Dueck, P.J. Reimer, Steinbach, MB, 4 February 1895; 17 March 1895; Peter Dueck, "Tagebuch," 14 May 1905, EMCA.

25. Ibid., 6 January 1905.

26. Reimer to Friesen, 15 April and 9 March 1895, KRR; to Warkentin, 8 March 1890; to G. Willms, 2 March 1886; to Harms, 1 February 1890; to Rempel, 1 February 1890; to Mrs. Esau, 15 February 1890; to Peter Fast, 10 July 1890; to H. Unrau, n.d. 1890; *Rundschau,* 1 March 1906; P. Dueck, "Tagebuch," 13 February 1906.

178   Chapter Twelve

27. Fred Stafford, "Jefferson County and Fairbury, Nebraska,1850–1900" (Master's thesis, University of Nebraska, 1948), 50.

28. Peter Jansen, *Memoirs of Peter Jansen: The Record of a Busy Life* (Beatrice, NE, 1921), 44ff.; U.S. Agricultural Census, Cub Creek, 1880 & 1885, NSHS.

29. *Beatrice Express,* 6 August 1874, in Clarence Hiebert, *Brothers in Deed to Brothers in Need: A Scrapbook About Mennonite Immigrants From Russia, 1870–1885* (Newton, KS, 1974), 166.

30. Jansen, *Memoirs,* i, 33, 54, 55, 57; Gustav E. Reimer and G.R. Gaeddert, *Exiled By the Czar: Cornelius Jansen and the Great Mennonite Migration, 1874* (Newton, KS, 1956), 131.

31. Anna Jansen, "Diary, 1874–1878," trans., n.n., Mennonite Library and Archives [hereafter MLA], Newton, KS, 24 August 1877.

32. Jansen, *Memoirs,* 52; M.B. Fast, *Mitteilungen von etlichen der Groszen unter den Mennoniten in Russland und in Amerika: Beobachtungen und Erinnerungen von Jefferson Co., Nebraska* (Reedley, CA, 1935), 39; *Rundschau.* 9 March 1887; 22 September 1886; Reimer and Gaeddert, *Exiled,* 137 and 138; D. Paul Miller, "An Analysis of Community Adjustment: A Case Study of Jansen, Nebraska" (Ph.D. diss., University of Nebraska, 1953), 100.

33. *Rundschau.* 5 January 1887; September 1887.

34. Reimer and Gaeddert, *Exiled,* 138; *Rundschau,* 1 January 1903.

35. Jacob Classen, "Tagebuch: 1894–1897," trans. Ben Hoeppner, Delbert Plett, Steinbach, MB and Mildred Ediger, Sanger, CA.

36. Jansen, *Memoirs,* 52; Stafford, "Fairbury," 54; interview with John Kroeker, Jansen, NE, October 1987.

37. Miller, "Jansen," 103 & 261.

38. *Rundschau,* 29 July 1885, 27 January 1904.

39. Ibid., 1 February 1904; Population Census, Cub Creek, 1900, NSHS.

40. Population Census, Jansen, Nebraska, 1900, NSHS.

41. *Rundschau,* 20 March 1901; see also Henry Fast, "The Kleine Gemeinde in the United States of America," in *Profile of the Kleine Gemeinde, 1874,* ed. Delbert F. Plett (Steinbach, MB, 1987).

42. Paul Miller, "The Story of Jansen's Churches," *Mennonite Life* (1955): 37–40.

43. Classen, "Tagebuch," January–June 1894.

44. Population Census, Cub Creek, 1900.

45. Ibid.

SELECT BIBLIOGRAPHY

Many hundreds of books, articles, dissertations, and theses have been written on European immigrants in the American West. The following list includes the most important books on this topic in terms of coverage, methodology, and historiography, mostly published in the past two decades, plus a few articles that seem special or unique to me. I have generally omitted books that do not concentrate on the American West. Thus, general studies in American immigration history are not listed here; they can be readily identified elsewhere. For a comprehensive bibliography, see Florence R.J. Goulesque, *Europeans in the American West since 1800: A Bibliography*, Occasional Papers No. 6 (Albuquerque: University of New Mexico, Center for the American West, 1995).

For introductions to individual ethnic groups, see Stephan Thernstrom, ed., *Harvard Encyclopedia of American Ethnic Groups* (Cambridge: Harvard University Press, 1980). The best atlas is by James P. Allan and Eugene James Turner. *We the People: An Atlas of America's Ethnic Diversity* (New York: Macmillan, 1988).

Athearn, Robert. *Westward the Briton*. New York: Scribner, 1953.
Baker, T. Lindsay. *The First Polish Americans: Silesian Settlements in Texas*. College Station: Texas A & M University Press, 1979.
Bernard, Richard M. *The Poles in Oklahoma*. Norman: University of Oklahoma Press, 1980.
Bicha, Karel. *The Czechs in Oklahoma*. Norman: University of Oklahoma Press, 1980.
Bjork, Kenneth O. *West of the Great Divide: Norwegian Migration to the Pacific Coast, 1847–1893*. Northfield, MN: Norwegian-American Historical Association, 1958.
Blessing, Patrick. *The British and Irish in Oklahoma*. Norman: University of Oklahoma Press, 1980.
Bohme, Frederick G. *A History of Italians in New Mexico*. New York: Arno Press, 1975.
Broken Hoops and Plains People. Lincoln: Nebraska Curriculum Development Center, 1976.

180   Select Bibliography

Brown, Kenny L. *The Italians in Oklahoma.* Norman: University of Oklahoma Press, 1980.

Burchell, Robert A. "British Immigrants in Southern California, 1850–1870," *Southern California Quarterly* 53 (1971): 283–301.

Burchell, Robert A. *The San Francisco Irish, 1848–1880.* Manchester, UK: Manchester University Press, 1979.

Carman, J. Neale. *Foreign-Language Units of Kansas,* vol. 1: *Historical Atlas and Statistics.* Lawrence: University of Kansas Press, 1962.

Chudacoff, Howard. "A New Look at Ethnic Neighborhood: Residential Dispersion and the Concept of Visibility in a Medium-Sized City," *Journal of American History* 60 (June 1973): 76–93. [Treats Omaha.]

Cinel, Dino. *From Italy to San Francisco: The Immigrant Experience.* Stanford, CA: Stanford University Press, 1982.

Cline, Scott. "Creation of an Ethnic Community: Portland Jewry, 1851–1866," *Pacific Northwest Quarterly* 76 (April 1985): 52–60.

Coburn, Carol K. *Life at Four Corners: Religion, Gender, and Education in a German-Lutheran Community, 1868–1945.* Lawrence: University Press of Kansas, 1992.

Conzen, Kathleen Neils. "Peasant Pioneers: Generational Succession among German Farmers in Frontier Minnesota." In *The Countryside in the Age of Capitalist Transformation,* edited by Steven Hahn and Jonathan Prude, 259–92. Chapel Hill: University of North Carolina Press, 1985.

"The Czech Experience." *Nebraska History* 74 (Fall/Winter 1993). [Entire issue devoted to Czech-American history.]

Doerries, Reinhard. "Church and Faith on the Great Plains Frontier: Acculturation Problems of German-Americans." *Amerikastudien/American Studies* 24 (1979): 275–87.

Douglas, William A., and Jon Bilbao. *Amerikanuak: Basques in the New World.* Reno: University of Nevada Press, 1975.

Emmick, Nancy L. "Bibliographical Essay on Irish-Americans in the West." *Journal of the West* 31 (April 1992): 87–94.

Emmons, David M. *The Butte Irish: Class and Ethnicity in an American Mining Town, 1875–1925.* Urbana: University of Illinois Press, 1989.

Eterovich, Adam S. *Croatians from Dalmatia and Montenegrin Serbs in the West and South, 1800–1900.* San Francisco: R & E Research Associates, 1971.

Etulain, Richard, ed. *Basques of the Pacific Northwest.* Pocatello: Idaho State University Press, 1991.

"European Folk Islands in Northwest Texas." *Panhandle–Plains Historical Review* 56 (1983). [Entire issue devoted to various ethnic groups: Poles, Italians, Czechs, Germans, and Germans from Russia.]

Faulkner, Virginia, and Frederick C. Luebke, eds. *Vision and Refuge: Essays on the Literature of the Great Plains.* Lincoln: University of Nebraska Press, 1982.

Fierman, Floyd S. *Guts and Ruts: The Jewish Pioneer on the Trail in the American Southwest.* New York: Ktav, 1985.

Select Bibliography 181

Gerlach, Russel L. *Immigrants in the Ozarks: A Study in Ethnic Geography*. Columbia: University of Missouri Press, 1976.

"The German-Speaking Immigrants of Utah." *Utah Historical Quarterly* 52 (Fall 1984). [Theme issue.]

Gish, Theodore, and Richard Spuler, eds. *Eagle in the New World: German Immigration to Texas and America*. College Station: Texas A & M University Press, 1986.

Gjerde, Jon. *From Peasants to Farmers: The Migration from Balestrand, Norway to the Upper Middle West*. New York: Cambridge University Press, 1985.

Goldberg, Robert. *Back to the Soil: The Jewish Farmers of Clarion, Utah and Their World*. Salt Lake City: University of Utah Press, 1986.

Gonzalez, Nancie L. *The Spanish-Americans of New Mexico: A Heritage of Pride*. Albuquerque: University of New Mexico Press, 1969.

Green, Frank L. *Captains, Curates, and Cockneys: The English in the Pacific Northwest*. Tacoma: Washington State Historical Society, 1981.

Hale, Douglas. *The Germans from Russia in Oklahoma*. Norman: University of Oklahoma Press, 1980.

Halseth, James, and Bruce Glasrud, eds. *The Northwest Mosaic: Minority Conflicts in Pacific Northwest History*. Boulder, CO: Pruett, 1977.

Heitman, Sidney, ed. *Germans from Russia in Colorado*. Ann Arbor, MI: Western Social Science Association, 1978.

Hendrickson, Gordon O., ed. *Peopling the High Plains: Wyoming's European Heritage*. Cheyenne: Wyoming State Archives and Historical Department, 1977.

Hostetler, John A., and G.E. Huntington. *Hutterites in North America*. New York: Holt Rinehart Winston, 1967.

Hostetler, John A. *Hutterite Society*. Baltimore: Johns Hopkins University Press, 1974.

"The Irish in the West." *Journal of the West* 31 (April 1992). [Theme issue.]

Jackson, Jack. *Los Mesteños: Spanish Ranching in Texas, 1721–1821*. College Station: Texas A & M University Press, 1986.

Jackson, W. Turrentine. *The Enterprising Scot: Investors in the American West after 1873*. Edinburgh: Edinburgh University Press, 1968.

Jones, Oakah L. *Los Paisanos: Spanish Settlers on the Northern Frontier of New Spain*. Norman: University of Oklahoma Press, 1979.

Jordan, Terry G. "A Century and a Half of Ethnic Change in Texas, 1836–1986." *Southwestern Historical Quarterly* 89 (April 1986): 385–422.

Jordan, Terry G. *German Seed in Texas Soil: Immigrant Farmers in Nineteenth-Century Texas*. Austin: University of Texas Press, 1966.

Juhnke, James C. *A People of Two Kingdoms: The Political Acculturation of the Kansas Mennonites*. Newton, KS: Faith and Life Press, 1975.

Kann, Kenneth L. *Comrades and Chicken Ranchers: The Story of a California Jewish Community*. Ithaca: Cornell University Press, 1993.

Kedro, M. James. "Czechs and Slovaks in Colorado, 1860–1920." *Colorado Magazine* 54 (1977): 93–125.

Select Bibliography

Kilpinen, Jon T. "Finnish Cultural Landscapes in the Pacific Northwest." *Pacific Northwest Quarterly* 86 (winter 1994–95): 25–34.

Kloberdanz, Timothy J. "In the Land of Inyan Wosleta: Plains Indian Influences on Reservation Whites." *Great Plains Quarterly* 7 (1987): 69–82.

Kroes, Rob. *The Persistence of Ethnicity: Dutch Calvinist Pioneers in Amsterdam, Montana.* Urbana: University of Illinois Press, 1992.

Lamar, Howard. "From Bondage to Contract: Ethnic Labor in the American West, 1600–1890." In *The Countryside in the Age of Capitalist Transformation: Essays in the Social History of Rural America,* edited by Steven Hahn and Jonathan Prude, 293–324. Chapel Hill: University of North Carolina Press, 1985.

Leonard, Stephen J. "The Irish, English, and Germans in Denver, 1860–1890." *Colorado Magazine* 54 (1977): 126–51.

Levinson, Robert E. "American Jews in the West." *Western Historical Quarterly* 5 (July 1974): 285–94.

Levinson, Robert E. *The Jews in the California Gold Rush.* New York: Ktav Publishing House, 1978.

Levinson, Robert E. "Jews and Jewish Communities on the Great Plains." *Red River Valley Historical Review* 5 (fall 1980): 55–70.

Lindgren, H. Elaine. "Ethnic Women Homesteading on the Plains of North Dakota." *Great Plains Quarterly* 9 (summer 1989): 157–73.

Loewen, Royden K. *Family, Church, and Market: A Mennonite Community in the Old and New Worlds, 1850–1930.* Urbana: University of Illinois Press, 1993.

Lowenstein, Steven. *The Jews of Oregon, 1850–1950.* Portland: Jewish Historical Society of Oregon, 1987.

Luebke, Frederick C. "Ethnic Group Settlement on the Great Plains." *Western Historical Quarterly* 7 (October 1977): 405–30.

Luebke, Frederick C., ed. *Ethnicity on the Great Plains.* Lincoln: University of Nebraska Press, 1980.

Luebke, Frederick C. *Germans in the New World: Essays in the History of Immigration.* Urbana: University of Illinois Press, 1990. [See especially chapter 3, "Legal Restriction on Foreign Languages in the Great Plains States, 1917–23," 31–50.]

Luebke, Frederick C. "Ethnic Minority Groups in the American West." In *Historians and the American West,* edited by Michael Malone, 387–413. Lincoln: University of Nebraska Press, 1983.

Luebke, Frederick C. *Immigrants and Politics: The Germans of Nebraska, 1880–1900.* Lincoln: University of Nebraska Press, 1969.

Machann, Clinton, and James W. Mendl. *Krasna Amerika: A Study of the Texas Czechs, 1851–1939.* Austin: Eakin Press, 1983.

Marschall, John P. "Jews of Nevada: 1850–1900." *Journal of the West* 23 (January 1984): 62–72.

May, Dean. *Three Frontiers: Family, Land, and Society in the American West, 1850–1880.* New York: Cambridge University Press, 1994.

Select Bibliography   183

McQuillan, D. Aidan. "The Mobility of Immigrants and Americans: A Comparison of Farmers on the Kansas Frontier." *Agricultural History* 53 (July 1979): 576–96.

McQuillan, D. Aidan. *Prevailing Over Time: Ethnic Adjustment on the Kansas Prairie, 1875–1925.* Lincoln: University of Nebraska Press, 1990.

Meinig, Donald. *Imperial Texas: An Interpretive Essay in Cultural Geography.* Austin: University of Texas Press, 1969.

Notarianni, Philip F. "Utah's Ellis Island: The Difficult 'Americanization' of Carbon County." *Utah Historical Quarterly* 47 (Spring 1979).

Ostergren, Robert. *A Community Transplanted: The Trans-Atlantic Experience of a Swedish Immigrant Settlement in the Upper Middle West, 1835–1915.* Madison: University of Wisconsin Press, 1988.

Ostergren, Robert. "European Settlement and Ethnicity Patterns on the Agricultural Frontiers of South Dakota." *South Dakota History* 13 (1983): 49–83.

Ostergren, Robert C. "The Immigrant Church as a Symbol of Community and Place in the Upper Midwest." *Great Plains Quarterly* 1 (Fall 1981): 225–38.

Palmer, Howard. "Escape from the Plains: The Icelanders in North Dakota and Alberta." *Great Plains Quarterly* 3 (Fall 1983): 219–33.

Papanikolas, Helen, ed. *The Peoples of Utah.* Salt Lake City: Utah State Historical Society, 1976.

Papanikolas, Helen. "Toil and Rage in a New Land: The Greek Immigrants in Utah." *Utah Historical Quarterly* 38 (1970): 99–203.

Parish, William J. *The German Jew and the Commercial Revolution in Territorial New Mexico, 1850–1900.* Albuquerque: University of New Mexico Press, 1959.

Pickle, Linda Schelbitzki. "Rural German-Speaking Women in Early Nebraska and Kansas: Ethnicity as a Factor in Frontier Adaptation." *Great Plains Quarterly* 9 (Fall 1989): 239–51.

Qualey, Carlton. "Ethnic Groups and the Frontier." In *American Frontier and Western Issues: A Historiographical Review*, edited by Roger L. Nichols, 199–216. New York: Greenwood, 1986.

Riley, M.P. "Hutterites and Their Agriculture: 100 Years in South Dakota," Bulletin #669. Brookings, SD: Agricultural Experiment Station, South Dakota State University, 1974.

Rischin, Moses, "Beyond the Great Divide: Immigration and the Last Frontier." *Journal of American History* 55 (June 1968): 42–53.

Rischin, Moses. "Immigration, Migration, and Minorities in California: A Reassessment." *Pacific Historical Review* 41 (1972): 71–90.

Rischin, Moses, and John Livingston, eds. *Jews of the American West.* Detroit: Wayne State University Press, 1993.

Rohrs, Richard C. *The Germans in Oklahoma.* Norman: University of Oklahoma Press, 1980.

Rolle, Andrew. *The Immigrant Upraised: Italian Adventurers and Colonists in an Expanding America.* Norman: University of Oklahoma Press, 1968.

184   Select Bibliography

Sallet, Richard. *Russian-German Settlements in the United States.* Translated by L. Rippley and A. Bauer. Fargo: North Dakota Institute for Regional Studies, 1974.

Saloutos, Theodore. "Cultural Persistence and Change: Greeks in the Great Plains and Rocky Mountain West, 1890–1970." *Pacific Historical Review* 49 (February 1980): 77–103.

Saloutos, Theodore. "The Immigrant in Pacific Coast Agriculture, 1880–1940." *Agricultural History* 49 (1975): 182–201.

Sarbaugh, Timothy J. "Celts with the Midas Touch: The Farmers, Entrepreneurs, and Millionaires of Spokane's City and County Pioneer Community." *Journal of the West* 31 (April 1992): 41–51.

Satterlee, James. "The Hutterites: A Study in Cultural Diversity," Bulletin #717. Brookings, SD: Agricultural Experiment Station, South Dakota State University, September 1993.

Schach, Paul, ed. *Languages in Conflict: Linguistic Acculturation on the Great Plains.* Lincoln: University of Nebraska Press, 1980.

Schock, Adolph. *In Quest of Free Land.* San Jose: San Jose State College, 1964. [On Germans from Russia.]

Schulte, Janet. "'Proving Up and Moving Out': Jewish Homesteading Activity in North Dakota, 1900–1920." *Great Plains Quarterly* 10 (Fall 1990): 228–44.

Scott, Larry E. *The Swedish Texans.* San Antonio: Institute of Texan Cultures, 1990.

Sensi-Isolani, Paola A., and Phyllis Martinelli, eds. *Struggle and Success: An Anthology of the Italian Immigrant Experience in California.* New York: Center for Migration Studies, 1985.

Shannon, James P. *Catholic Colonization on the Western Frontier.* New Haven: Yale University Press, 1957.

Shepperson, Wilbur S. *Restless Strangers: Nevada's Immigrants and Their Interpreters.* Reno: University of Nevada Press, 1970.

Sherman, William C. *Prairie Mosaic: An Ethnic Atlas of Rural North Dakota.* Fargo: North Dakota Institute for Regional Studies, 1983.

Sherman, William C., and Playford V. Thorson, eds. *Plains Folk: North Dakota's Ethnic History.* Fargo: North Dakota Institute for Regional Studies, 1988.

Skrabanek, Robert L. *We're Czechs.* College Station: Texas A & M University Press, 1988.

Soike, Lowell J. *Norwegian Americans and the Politics of Dissent, 1880–1924.* Northfield, MN: Norwegian-American Historical Association, 1991.

Taylor, Philip A.M. *Expectations Westward: The Mormons and the Emigration of Their British Converts in the Nineteenth Century.* Ithaca, NY: Cornell University Press, 1966.

Tobias, Henry J. *The Jews in Oklahoma.* Norman: University of Oklahoma Press, 1980.

Toll, William. "Ethnicity and Stability: The Italians and Jews of South Portland, 1900–1940." *Pacific Historical Review* 54 (May 1985): 161–89.

Toll, William. *The Making of an Ethnic Middle Class: Portland Jewry over Four Generations.* Albany: State University of New York Press, 1982.

Vigil, Ralph, Frances Kaye, and John Wunder, eds. *Spain on the Plain: Myths and Realities of Spanish Exploration and Settlement on the Great Plains.* Niwot, CO: University Press of Colorado, 1994.

Vorspan, Max, and Lloyd P. Gartner. *History of the Jews of Los Angeles.* San Marino, CA: Huntington Library, 1970.

Weber, David J. *The Spanish Frontier in North America.* New Haven: Yale University Press, 1992.

Wheeler, Wayne. *An Analysis of Social Change in a Swedish-American Community: The Case of Lindsborg, Kansas.* New York: AMS Press, 1986.

White, Sid, and S.E. Solberg, eds. *Peoples of Washington: Perspectives on Cultural Diversity.* Pullman: Washington State University Press, 1989.

White, W. Thomas. "Race, Ethnicity, and Gender in the Railroad Work Force: The Case of the Far Northwest, 1883–1918." *Western Historical Quarterly* 16 (July 1985): 265–83.

Winther, Oscar O. "English Migration to the American West, 1865–1900." *Huntington Library Quarterly* 27 (1964): 159–73.

Wirsing, Dale R. *Builders, Brewers, and Burghers: Germans of Washington State.* [Tacoma]: Washington State Bicentennial Commission, 1977.

Woods, Lawrence M. *British Gentlemen in the Wild West: The Era of the Intensely English Cowboy.* New York: Free Press, 1989.

Zeidel, Robert F. "Peopling the Empire: The Great Northern Railroad and the Recruitment of Immigrant Settlers to North Dakota." *North Dakota History* 60 (Spring 1993): 14–23.

INDEX

advertisement: of Butte, Montana, 54–57; of new settlements, 22–23. *See also* information flow

"Alien Registration" documents, 131

Allamakee County, Iowa, 23–24

Alpine, Utah, English Mormons in, 33–47

Amalgamated Copper Mining Company, 93

Americanization: German Lutherans and, 141; Italians and, 72–73; Mennonites and, 169–71. *See also* children of immigrants; exclusivity

American Protective Association, 95

American West (Hine), vii

Anaconda Copper Mining Company, 93–97

Ancient Order of Hibernians, 92, 101–4

aristocracy, labor, 92–93

artisans: Jews as, 78–79; miners as, 92

association networks, women and, 129–43

associations, Irish, 52, 59–61, 62n8, 91–92, 101–4

associations, personal, and settlement patterns, 28, 30

associations, voluntary, 75; for Czechs, 156–59; for farm workers, 156; for Jews, 76, 81–86; for Mexicans, 156–58; for women, 85–86, 133–35, 141; youth, 135. *See also* clubs, merchants'; lodges, fraternal; so-

cieties, benevolent; societies, burial; societies, saints'

Atherton, Gertrude, quoted, 55

Austro-Hungarian Empire, in census data, xiv

banking, 78, 83

Baptist church, in Dalesburg settlement, 20

Barkman, Peter, 164

Bartlett, Richard, quoted, xviii, n3

Barton, Josef, 147–60

Bearcreek, Montana, South Slavs in, 109–22

Benavides, Alonso, 5

birth order, and mobility, 127

birth practices, 137

Block, Kansas, German Lutherans in, 129–43

B'nai B'rith, Order of, 83–84, 86–87

Bohemia, 151–52

Bonilla, Francisco, 3

Borosenko Colony, Russia, 163

Bowden, Henry Warner, 1–14

British, in census data, xiv, xv

Brockett, Linus, quoted, 55

Brody, David, quoted, 61

Brondel, Bishop John, 59; quoted, 94

Brosnan, Father Patrick, quoted, 51, 54–55, 97

187

188   Index

Buller, Peter, 163
businesses, Mennonite, 163–65, 167–69
Butte, Montana, Irish in, 49–61, 91–105
Butte Miners' Union, 93–94

Cabeza de Vaca, Álvar Núñez, 2
California Commission on Immigration
    and Housing, 67
Catholicism, 9–10, 151–52, 156–58
census data: for Butte, Montana, 56–57, 59;
    limitations of, xii–xiv; for Portland,
    Oregon, 79; for San Francisco, 66–67
ceremony, religious, Pueblos and, 6
chain migration: family-based, 59–61; Ital-
    ians and, 71–72; Jews and, 77
charities. See societies, benevolent
child care, 112
child-rearing practices, 137
children of immigrants, 123–28; dispersion
    of, 123–28; friction with parents, 124–26;
    German Lutheran, 137; as laborers, 168;
    mobility of, 123–28, 155, 168; recollec-
    tions of, 109–22
Christianity, Pueblos and, 3, 5–14
churches, 40–41, 43, 46, 132–35, 141. See
    also names of churches; synagogues, for-
    mation of
church membership, 15, 28–30, 132
Cinel, Dino, 65–74, 123–28
citizenship, U.S., South Slavs and, 114
Classen, Jacob, quoted, 172
Clay County, South Dakota, 16–31
clubs, merchants', 86–88
Coburn, Carol, 129–46
Cohen, Benjamin I., 78
colonists: Spanish, 4–5; vs. immigrants, 1
colonizers, 1–2
community, Mormon, centrality of, 43, 46
compartmentalization, Pueblos and, 13–14
Concordia Clubs, 87
conquistadores, 2
conversion: to Mormonism, 42, 46; of
    Pueblos, 5–6

Coronado, Francisco Vásquez de, 2–3
Cortez, Hernando, 2
cost of living, in Butte, Montana, 63n.21
cotton production, in Nueces County,
    Texas, 148–50
Council Bluffs, Iowa, 24
Croatian Fraternal Union, 113
culture group associations, and settlement
    patterns, 26–28
cultures, ethnic, immigrants and, 155–58
Czechs, in south Texas, 147–60

Dalesburg settlement, South Dakota, 16–31
Daly, Marcus, 49, 53–54
death, Butte miners and, 100–101
Dessery, Edna, quoted, 73
Dickens, Charles, quoted, 35–36
Dillingham Commission, xi–xii
discrimination: claims of, 95; against Ger-
    man immigrants, 140; against Italians,
    72
diseases: of miners, 97–98; Pueblos and, 11
dispersion, of Italians in San Francisco, 66–
    69. See also mobility
dissension, religious, in Dalesburg settle-
    ment, 20
domestic service, 139, 145n31
drinking: barred in Jansen, Nebraska, 171–
    72; Mennonites and, 173; South Slavs
    and, 121. See also saloons
drought, and Pueblo revolt of 1680, 11
du Maurier, Daphne, Hungry Hill, 51
Durkheimer, Julius, 77

education: South Slavs and, 114–15, 117–18;
    women and, 130, 134–36, 141
emigration: from England, 34–38; of fam-
    ilies, 31n.8, 59–60; from Germany, 76–
    77; Pueblos and, 13; from Sweden, 20–24.
    See also migration; migration patterns
Emmons, David, 49–64, 91–108
employment, temporary, 72
England, Mormon migration from, 34–38

Espejo, Antonio de, 3
Estevanico, 2
ethnicity, 150, 159–60; and worker solidarity, 92–96
exclusionary policies, Irish miners and, 92–96
exclusivity, in German-Lutheran community, 138–43

family: artificial, 157; Czech, 152–53, 158; emigration of, 31n8, 59–60; extended, 60, 136–38; farm, 136–38; German Lutheran, 136–38, 142; as influence on immigration, 59–60, 71; Italian, 124–26; Jewish, 79–81; Mexican, 152–53; Mormon, 42–44; nuclear, 60; as source of farm labor, 154–55; South Slav, 116; vertically extended, 152–53; as women's "network of associations," 136–38, 142
family network, Irish, 59–61
family size, among German Lutherans, 138, 145n.24
farmers: Czech, 147–60; English Mormon, 35–38, 46; German, 150; German Lutheran, 131–32; as labor pool, 166; Polish, 150–51; tenant, 149, 153
farming: commercialization of, 164–65, 172; gender roles in, 136–39
farm production, in Alpine, Utah, 39–40
farm size, in Alpine, Utah, 39, 46
Far West and the Great Plains in Transition. . .(Paul), vii
fertility rates, among Jews in Portland, 81
Finkelstein, Barbara, 131
food supply, for Montana coal miners, 114
Frank, Sigmund, 77
friendships, among women, 136
Friesen, Abram S., 163–64, 166
frontier, histories of, vii
fund-raising, by Lutheran women, 133

gender relationships, 129–43
gender roles, 130, 136–38, 141

genealogy, of Irish immigrants, 50–51
German Lutherans: in Block, Kansas, 129–43; relations among, 144–45n22; in Steinbach, Manitoba, 168–69
Germans, xiii, xv, 69, 150
Germany, emigration of Jews from, 76–77
Goldsmith, Bernard, 78; quoted, 77
government, Spanish: and Pueblo revolt of 1680, 11–13; in Rio Grande Valley, 4–5, 12
Graebner, Alan, quoted, 132

Hawikuh pueblo, 2
health care, 83, 85, 101–3, 111–13, 137
Hine, Robert V.: American West, vii; quoted, xviii, n4
hiring out, 139–40, 145n31
hiring practices, in Butte mines, 92–96, 99–100
Hirsch, Sol, quoted, 78–79
histories: ethnic, xvi; labor, viii; "new western," viii–ix
Hobsbawm, Eric, quoted, 104
holidays, South Slavs and, 119–21
Hopis, 13
host kin, 60
household: landless, in Steinbach, 168; Mormon, 42–43
housing: in Butte, Montana, 57; for Italians in San Francisco, 69–71
Hudson, John, 16
Humana, Juan de, 3
Hungry Hill (du Maurier), 51

identity, personal, Pueblos and, 8–9
immigrants, European: as forgotten people, vii–ix; marital status of, 23; numbers of, ix–xiii; vs. colonists, 1. See also Czechs; German Lutherans; Germans; Irish; Italians; Jews; Mexicans; Mormons; Poles; South Slavs; Swedes
immigration, viii, 57–58
Immigration Commission. See Dillingham Commission

immigration rates, self-sustaining, 58
indigenous peoples, and colonizers, 1
industrialization, 36–38, 54–57, 78
information flow: about new settlements,
    22–23, 31n9; and Butte Irish, 52, 58–59
interviews, 109–29
Ireland, 50–51
Irish: associational, 93–94; in Butte, Mon-
    tana, 49–61, 91–105; in census data, xv;
    economic insecurity of, 93; in San Fran-
    cisco, 69; unaffiliated, 95
Irish World, 59, 64n27
Italia, L', 71–73
Italians, in San Francisco, 65–74, 123–28;
    relations among groups, 124

Jansen, Nebraska, Mennonites in, 161–63,
    170–76
Jansen, Peter, 170–71
Jednota bratrska, 158
Jews: in census data, xiv; in Portland,
    Oregon, 75–88
Judaism, 82–83

Kansas, German Lutherans in, 129–43
Kansas City, Missouri, 139–40
Kelley, Cornelius, quoted, 93
Keokuk, Iowa, 24
kinship ties: among Czechs, 152; among
    German Lutherans, 138; among Mexi-
    cans, 152; and settlement patterns, 31n.10
Kleine Gemeinde Mennonite church, 169–
    70, 173
Kornelsen, Gerhard, 166–67
Kornelsen, Heinrich, quoted, 165

labor, organized, 72, 159
laborers, 51, 149, 153, 159; immigrants' chil-
    dren as, 168; Mexicans as, 147–60. *See
    also* workers
labor history, 91–105
Lambertenghi, Consul Francesco, quoted,
    73

land-seeking parties, 26
language, English: German Lutheran
    church and, 145–46n36; Mennonites
    and, 171, 175; Pueblos and, 14; South
    Slavs and, 110–11, 114–16
language, German, 132–33, 135, 140, 173–75
language, Spanish, 5, 10, 13
languages, native, 4, 13
Legacy of Conquest (Limerick), viii
Lerner, Gerda, quoted, 143
letters to home, as influence on immigra-
    tion, 58
life expectancy, of Butte miners, 100
Limerick, Patricia Nelson, *Legacy of Con-
    quest,* viii
living conditions, of Butte miners, 98–99
lodges, fraternal: for Jews, 83–84; for South
    Slavs, 112–13, 120
Loewen, Royden, 161–78
Lubin, Simon, 67
Luebke, Frederick, quoted, 141–42
Lutheran church, in Dalesburg settlement,
    20, 30
Lutheran Church (Missouri Synod), 129–43
Lynch, Dan, quoted, 57

Manitoba, Mennonites in, 161–70, 175–76
Markievicz, Countess, quoted, 97
marriage: among German Lutherans, 137;
    among Jews, 80–81; among Mennonites,
    169, 175; among South Slavs, 120
Marvels of the New West (Thayer), 55
May, Dean, 33–48
mechanization, of mining, 92
Meier, Aaron, 77
Mennonites, 161–76
Mennonitische Rundschau, 165
merchandising network, Jewish, 77
merchants: Jewish, 76–78; Mennonite,
    163–68, 170, 174
methodologies, comparative, xvi
Mexicans, in south Texas, 147–60
Mexico, 150, 152

Michigan, copper mines, 51–52
middle-class status, and declining fertility
    rates, 81
Middleton, Idaho, 39–45
midwifery, 137
migration: direct *vs.* indirect, 22–26, 31n.9,
    71–72, 125; internal, 73; seasonal, 153;
    speed of, 22, 26
migration patterns, 15; of South Slavs, 110–
    11; study of, 16–17, 30–31n2, 49; Sweden
    and, 20–22
Miller, Paul, 172–73
miners: Irish, 49–61; South Slav, 113–14
mining: coal, 109–22; copper, 56, 91–105;
    occupational hazards of, 96–101, 111–13,
    122
Mintz, Sidney, quoted, 156
Mission Covenant church, in Dalesburg
    settlement, 20
missions, Franciscan, 2–14
mobility: of immigrants' children, 123–28,
    155, 168; of Irish miners, 52; of women,
    139–40, 142
Montana: Irish in, 49–61, 91–105; South
    Slavs in, 109–22
Montana Historical Society (Helena), 109
morality, Pueblos and, 9
Moravia, 152
Mormonism, xv, 40–44
Mormons, English, 33–47
mortality: infant and child, 85–86; in min-
    ing industry, 96–97, 100–1
Murphy, Clyde, quoted, 55

naturalization records, 67
Nebraska, Mennonites in, 161–63, 170–76
networks of association, women and, 129–43
Niza, Marcos de, 2
Nordwesten, 165
North Dakota, 16; immigrant population
    of, x, xi
Northern Pacific Railroad, 121
Northwest Improvement Company, 111

Nueces County, Texas, Czechs and Mexi-
    cans in, 147–60

occupations, and mobility, 127
O'Dwyer, Riobard, 50–51
Omaha, Nebraska, 24
Oñate, Juan de, 3–4
Oregon, Jews in, 75–78
Ostergren, Robert C., 15–32
Oxford History of the American West, ix

Padilla, Juan de, 2–3
patriarchy, Jewish family as, 80
Paul, Rodman, *Far West and the Great
    Plains in Transition. . .,* vii
peddlers, Jewish, 77
Pennsylvania, coal fields, 51–52
place, ties of, 152–53
Podporná jednota, 156
Poland, 82–83, 151
Poles, xiii–xiv, 150–51
polygamy, 42–43, 45
Popé, 12–13
population: of Italians in San Francisco,
    66–67, 69; of Jews in Portland, 79; of
    seventeenth-century Pueblos, 13
population patterns, xiv–xv
Portland, Oregon, Jews in, 75–88
poverty, of Mennonites in Steinbach, 166
Price, Richard, quoted, 156
promotion, of Butte, Montana, 54–57
prosperity, perception of, as influence on
    immigration, 58–59
Protestantism, 156, 158
Prussia, 82
Pueblo Indians: and Franciscan missions,
    3–14; revolt of 1680, 11–13

quantitative methodologies, 147–60

railroads: entering Butte, Montana, 57; ex-
    tension of, 148; as link with home, 139–
    40; Steinbach's lack of, 165–67, 169–70

railroad town, Jansen as, 170–75
ranching, 148–50
recruitment: of immigrant miners, 54; military, 104–5
Red Lodge, Montana, 109–22
Reimer, Klaas, 163–66, 170
Relief Society (Alpine, Utah), 44–45
religion, Pueblo, 6–8, 14; Franciscans and, 10–11
repatriation: Irish and, 58; Italians and, 72
residential pattern, in San Francisco, 69
Rio Grande Valley, Franciscans in, 3–14
Robert Emmet Literary Association, 92, 94–96, 101–4
Rodríguez, Agustín, 3
Russia, 162–63
Ryan, David, quoted, 94

saloons, 99, 173
San Francisco, Italians in, 65–74, 123–28
San Francisco Housing Association, 70–71
Santa Fe, New Mexico, 12
Santo Domingo, Franciscan mission at, 5
Scandinavians, in census data, xv
schools: Jewish, 82; Lutheran, 135–36; Mennonite, 173–74; for South Slavs, 117–18; as women's "network of associations," 135–36
self-perceptions, immigrants', 28–30
Selling, Ben, 77–78
seniority system, for Butte mines, 100
Serbian National Federation, 113
Serbian Orthodox church, 119–20
settlement patterns: in Bearcreek, Montana, 115; of Italians in San Francisco, 66–69, 73
settlement process, in Dalesburg, 26–28
settlement studies, 16–17
Silver Bow County, Montana, 50
Sioux City, Iowa, 24
Slovenska Narodna Podporna Jednota, 113
social life: among German Lutherans, 138; among South Slavs, 119–21

societies, benevolent, 44–45, 83, 85, 101–4, 112–13
societies, burial, 81–82, 103–4
societies, saints', 157–58
Sosa, Gaspar de, 3
sources, historical, 16–17, 30–31n2, 31n4, 49, 109–29, 131, 147–48. *See also* census data
South Dakota, Swedes in, 15–31
South Slavs, 109–22; as miners, 113–14; relations among groups, 121
spheres, public *vs.* private, 130, 142–43
sports, 118–19
Steinbach, Manitoba, Mennonites in, 161–70, 175–76
Strassendorf, Mennonite, 163
strikebreakers, immigrants as, 72
Sublimity, Oregon, 38–45
subsistence levels, in Alpine, Utah, 46
surnames, Irish, 50
Sweden, emigration from, 20–24
Swedes, in Dalesburg settlement, 15–31
synagogues, formation of, 82–83

Taos pueblo, 11–12
Taylor, P.A.M., 38
Texas, Czechs and Mexicans in, 147–60
textile industry, British, 37
Thayer, William, *Marvels of the New West,* 55
Thiessen, John P., 173; quoted, 172
Three Frontiers (May), 33
Toepper, Robert M., quoted, 142
Toll, William, 75–90
tourism, Irish and, 59
town life, Mennonites and, 163–75
tradition, preservation of, Italians and, 73
transportation. *See* railroads
Trinity Lutheran Church and School (Block, Kansas), 130, 132
Trinity Lutheran Ladies Aid (Block, Kansas), 133–35
"turnover" studies, 16

underemployment, farmers and, 166
Union Pacific Railroad, 55
unions, 93–94, 159
Utah, English Mormons in, 33–47
Utah County, Utah, 41

Vermillion, South Dakota, 26
voluntarism, Mormons and, 44–45

wages, miners', 55–57, 114
Walther League (Block, Kansas), 134–35, 141
Wasserman, Philip, 78
West: histories of, vii–viii; image of, 54–55
white, in census data, xii
Williamson County, Texas, 151–52
Winckler, Gus, 78
women: in Block, Kansas, 129–43; and domestic production, 138–39; as laborers,
112; and Lutheran Church (Missouri
Synod), 132–33; mobility of, 139–40, 142;
Mormon, 43–45; South Slav, 116–17
workers: Mennonites as, 173–74; as pioneers, 36–38
worker solidarity, ethnicity and, 92–96
working class, 49, 96
working conditions, in Butte mines, 97–99
world views, competing, 1, 6–9
World War I, and anti-German sentiment,
140

Young, Brigham, quoted, 34

Zellick, Anna, 109–22
Zuni, 2

CONTRIBUTORS

JOSEF J. BARTON is an associate professor of history at Northwestern University, Evanston, Illinois.

HENRY WARNER BOWDEN is a professor in the department of religion at Douglass College, Rutgers University, New Brunswick, New Jersey.

DINO CINEL is a historian living in New York. He received his doctorate from Stanford University.

CAROL K. COBURN is an associate professor of education and history at Avila College, Kansas City, Missouri.

DAVID M. EMMONS is a professor of history at the University of Montana, Missoula.

ROYDEN K. LOEWEN holds the chair in Mennonite Studies, Department of History, University of Winnipeg, Canada.

FREDERICK C. LUEBKE is Charles J. Mach Professor Emeritus of History at the University of Nebraska–Lincoln.

DEAN L. MAY is a professor of history at the University of Utah, Salt Lake City.

ROBERT C. OSTERGREN is a professor of geography at the University of Wisconsin–Madison.

WILLIAM TOLL is a historian living in Eugene, Oregon. He holds a doctorate from the University of Oregon.

ANNA ZELLICK is a historian living in Lewiston, Montana.

PERMISSIONS

HENRY WARNER BOWDEN, "Southwestern Indians, Spanish Missions," reprinted from *American Indians and Christian Missions: Studies in Cultural Conflict* (Chicago: University of Chicago Press, 1981) by permission of the University of Chicago Press.

ROBERT C. OSTERGREN, "Prairie Bound: Migration Patterns to a Swedish Settlement on the Dakota Frontier," reprinted from Frederick Luebke, ed., *Ethnicity on the Great Plains* (Lincoln: University of Nebraksa Press 1980) by permission of the University of Nebraska Press. © by the University of Nebraska Press.

DEAN L. MAY, "Fleeing Babylon: The Mormon English Migration to Alpine, Utah," adapted from *Three Frontiers: Family, Land and Society in the American West, 1850–1900* (New York: Cambridge University Press, 1994) by permission of Cambridge University Press.

DAVID M. EMMONS, "Irish Miners: From the Emerald Isle to Copper Butte," adapted from *The Butte Irish: Class and Ethnicity in an American Mining Town, 1875–1925* (Champaign: University of Illinois Press, 1989) by permission of the University of Illinois Press.

DINO CINEL, "Italians in San Francisco: Patterns of Settlement," adapted from *From Italy to San Francisco: The Immigrant Experience* by Dino Cinel by permission of the publishers, Stanford University Press. © 1982 by the Board of Trustees of the Leland Stanford Junior University.

WILLIAM TOLL, "The Origins of an Ethnic Middle Class: The Jews of Portland in the Nineteenth Century," reprinted from *The Making of an Ethnic Middle Class: Portland Jewry over Four Generations* (Albany: State University of New York Press, 1982) by permission of State University of New York Press.

198   Permissions

DAVID M. EMMONS, "Safe and Steady Work: The Irish and the Hazards of Butte," adapted from *The Butte Irish: Class and Ethnicity in an American Mining Town, 1875–1925* (Champaign: University of Illinois Press, 1989) by permission of the University of Illinois Press.

ANNA ZELLICK, "Childhood Memories of South Slavic Immigrants in Red Lodge and Bearcreek, Montana, 1904–1943," reprinted from *Montana: The Magazine of History* (Summer 1994), 34–45.

DINO CINEL, "Italians in San Francisco: The Second Generation," adapted from *From Italy to San Francisco: The Immigrant Experience* by Dino Cinel by permission of the publishers, Stanford University Press. © 1982 by the Board of Trustees of the Leland Stanford Junior University.

CAROL K. COBURN, "Ethnicity, Religion, and Gender: The Women of Block, Kansas, 1868–1940," reprinted from *Great Plains Quarterly* 8, no. 4 (1988), 22–32. The *Great Plains Quarterly* is published by the Center for Great Plains Studies, University of Nebraska, Lincoln.

JOSEF J. BARTON, "Land, Labor, and Community in Nueces: Czech Farmers and Mexican laborers in South Texas, 1880–1930," reprinted from Frederick Luebke, ed., *Ethnicity on the Great Plains* (Lincoln: University of Nebraksa Press 1980) by permission of the University of Nebraska Press. © 1980 by the University of Nebraska Press.

ROYDEN K. LOWEN, "STEINBACH AND JANSEN: A TALE OF TWO MENNONITE TOWNS, 1880–1900," REPRINTED FROM *Family, Church, and Market: A Mennonite Community in the Old and the New Worlds, 1850–1930* (Urbana: University of Illinois Press, 1993) by permission of the University of Illinois Press.